Richard Garnett

Edward Gibbon Wakefield

The colonization of South Australia and New Zealand

Richard Garnett

Edward Gibbon Wakefield
The colonization of South Australia and New Zealand

ISBN/EAN: 9783337153144

Printed in Europe, USA, Canada, Australia, Japan

Cover: Foto ©ninafisch / pixelio.de

More available books at **www.hansebooks.com**

EDWARD GIBBON WAKEFIELD

THE COLONIZATION OF SOUTH AUSTRALIA AND NEW ZEALAND

BY

R. GARNETT, C.B., LL.D.

With Photogravure Frontispiece and Maps

NEW YORK
LONGMANS, GREEN & CO.
91 AND 93 FIFTH AVENUE
1898

PREFACE

AMONG all the men celebrated in this series of biographies as 'Builders of Greater Britain,' Edward Gibbon Wakefield, inferior to none in genius and achievement, is perhaps the only one whose inclusion could excite inquiry or surprise. Not that his claims have at any time been weighed and found wanting, but that their existence is unknown to the multitude. By the mass of his countrymen at home he is chiefly remembered by the one incident in his career which he would have wished to be forgotten. The historians of the colonies he founded in general pass him over with slight notice, some omitting his very name.

If, however, judged merely by this popular

neglect, the name of Wakefield might seem one of those which the world is content to let die, it is far otherwise with students of the subject of colonization, to whose judgment popular opinion must ultimately conform.

A complete view of Wakefield's activity as an Empire-builder has not, indeed, existed until the publication of this little biography. But it is impossible to read even the casual notices of such an authority as Mr Egerton, in his *History of British Colonial Policy*, without perceiving the high place accorded to Wakefield as a practical statesman, not merely a founder of colonies, but a reformer and transformer of the entire British colonial system. Indications of a similar feeling in authoritative quarters are continually transpiring—as, for instance, in a recent article in the *Quarterly Review*—and the biographer's problem is how to permeate the oblivious and indifferent general public with the knowledge and appreciation of the better informed.

This is not a problem easy of solution, for, although Wakefield's biography is one of fascinating interest, it is a difficult one to write. Special obstacles will be brought to light by the story itself, but two capital ones may be mentioned here by way of preliminary apology for inevitable deficiencies. Most extenders of the British Empire have been emphatically men of action. They have plunged into the thick of war, pestilence and famine; have explored great unknown rivers, or defended beleaguered forts with handfuls of men. They have, at all events, planted the British flag where it never waved before, occasionally displacing some other to make room for it. Wakefield's work was not performed in this fashion. Though capable of vigorous action in emergencies, he wrought principally by the pen and by the tongue. His activity with both was prodigious; yet the former implement has left but inadequate traces of its employment, the latter none. Though living and breathing in an atmosphere of colony-making, he never saw a colony until his last days; he headed no exploring expeditions, overthrew no antagonists, except upon paper, and his battles were chiefly with the Colonial Office. Once, in Canada, he seemed to have a chance of letting his light shine before men, but the authorities promptly snuffed it out. That he should have brought this exclusion from conspicuous public life upon himself deepens the tragedy of his romantic career, and so far enhances its interest, but in no respect diminishes the biographer's difficulty in rendering this mainly subterranean activity visible and tangible.

Where the public life is thus sequestered, and mainly traceable in its effects, it is doubly important that the details of private life should be copious and interesting. The mere thinker or writer, however illustrious, must remain much of an abstraction. No real biography of some of the world's greatest benefactors will ever be written, simply because *il n'y a pas de quoi*. It is otherwise with Wakefield, a rich specimen of human nature, commonly admirable, sometimes condemnable, but ever potent, impassioned and dramatic. This much is clear even from the imperfect records of his political activity, but these greatly needed to be supplemented by traits derived from private life, and it might well have been that such would not have been procurable. Relying on the friendship and confidence of members of Mr Wakefield's family, the present writer ventured upon a task of which more competent executors might conceivably have been found. His expectations have not been disappointed, and his obligations cannot be sufficiently expressed. Everything available has been placed at his disposal; he has written free from constraint or suggestion of any kind; and, though conscious of having done his utmost, he knows well that the best pages in his book are from the pens of Nina Wakefield and Alice Freeman. Yet, by no fault of Mr Wakefield's present representatives, there are imperfections in the record which demand apology, and this rather as they might otherwise be liable to misinterpretation. The reader, observing that long periods of Wakefield's life are devoid of any illustration from private letters, which afterwards on the sudden begin to be comparatively numerous, and as suddenly cease, might reasonably conclude that a rule of selection had been exercised, and that much had been omitted which it was deemed inexpedient to publish. It is not so. The preservation or destruction of Wakefield's letters appears to have been a matter of mere accident. Many ought to exist in the hands of the representatives of Sir William Molesworth, Charles Buller, and others of his allies on colonial questions; but it has, for the present, appeared useless to search out documents which there was neither time to collect nor space to employ.

The reader on a subject so much passed out of notice as the colonizing career of Edward Gibbon Wakefield, may not unreasonably ask for some assurance, beyond the word of the biographer, that his study will be repaid. Abundant evidence of the high position accorded to Wakefield by his contemporaries might be collected from the books and journals of his own day, but it is less troublesome to produce two unpublished testimonies, one referring chiefly to the theoretical side of his work, the other to the practical. In reply, as would appear, to a letter from Wakefield, acknowledging the gift of his *Political Economy* (published in 1848), Stuart Mill writes:—

'INDIA HOUSE, *Thursday*.

'MY DEAR WAKEFIELD,—I am very glad

that you think the public statement in my book of what is so justly due to you, both as a colonizer and a political economist, likely to be of use at this particular time. I am still more glad to hear that you are writing the book you speak of. I have long regretted that there does not exist a systematic treatise in a permanent form, from your hand and in your name, in which the whole subject of colonization is treated as the express subject of the book, so as to become at once the authoritative book on the subject. At present, people have to *pick up* your doctrines, both theoretical and practical. I cannot help urging you to complete the book with as much expedition as is consistent with the care due to your health, which your life is too valuable to permit any relaxation of.—Ever truly yours, J. S. MILL.'

For Mill, doubtless, the chief interest lay in the Wakefield system of land sales and emigration funds, the system which regulated emigration and made it defray its cost, prevented it from running to waste over vast and indefinite areas, and provided that the flower and not the refuse of the old country should be transplanted to the new. Another and not less important aspect of his activity, the restoration of Imperial ideas and right relations between the mother country and the colonies through the agency of responsible government, is thus set forth in a letter to the author from almost the last survivor of Wakefield's associates, the venerable Lord Norton, who, at eighty-four, sets an example to younger men by a lively interest in whatever concerns the common weal :—

'Wakefield was a man of genius, and, circumstances having shut him out of Parliament, where he would have risen to the top of the tree, he devoted himself to make ministers dance in his leading-strings. Under his auspices I, in company with others, founded "The Colonial Reform Society," by which our colonial policy was restored to its original unrivalled success in the hiving out of English citizens. The disuniting from us of great colonies, owing to our infringement of the essential principles of their freedom, had led us to treat new colonies as dependencies, and misgovern them from London by way of keeping them tight. To Wakefield is due the chief merit in restoring our colonial policy—to let colonies be extensions of England, with the same constitution as at home—only not represented in the House of Commons, because of the thousands of miles of sea to cross— with their own Parliaments on the spot and Governments responsible to them under the Queen's Viceroys, who connect them with her supremacy.'

The man who has done this is assuredly a builder of the Empire, even a master-builder. Respecting Wakefield's personal character, the most profitable remark to be made seems to be that he is a conspicuous instance of the happy effect of public causes and wide views in ennobling man's nature. So long as he is intent upon private ends, a harsh critic might be warranted in terming him selfish and unprincipled, although even then displaying traits inconsistent with a low type of character. From the moment that he finds his work, and undertakes his mission, he becomes a memorable example of enthusiastic and mainly disinterested devotion to an idea, not indeed devoid of advantage to himself, since, though producing no brilliant pecuniary results, it took away the stain from his name, yet evidently followed for no such subsidiary end, but in the spirit of the creator, who must see of the travail of his soul that he may be satisfied.

Another principal figure in this history being, according to the popular belief, unprovided with a soul, can view posthumous censure and vindication with indifference. Even a corporation, however, has a claim to justice, and it is the writer's decided opinion that few persons and few institutions have been more unjustly treated than the New Zealand Company. That its precipitate proceedings occasioned much mischief and misfortune is certain, but it is equally certain that this precipitancy was forced upon it by the perverse malevolence of the Government. The part played by Government in the early history of New Zealand colonization is indeed a melancholy chapter in English history; save for Lord John Russell's magnanimous admission of error, and his good intentions frustrated by a charge of administration. The main cause of the unpopularity of the New Zealand Company, however, seems to have been not so much the errors they were driven to commit as the imputation of designs remote from their intentions. They were looked upon as land-sharks, bent on depriving the natives of their land, and some countenance was given to the charge by the extensive purchases by which their agent sought to protect New Zealand from a shoal of sharks from Australia. It is curious that their accusers are usually the persons who object most vehemently to property in land at all, or at least to the uncontrolled exercise of private rights over it, but who seem unable to perceive that if a white landowner has no moral right to reserve a barren moor for the pursuit of game, a brown landowner has still less to lock up a fertile territory for the pursuit of rats. Neither one nor the other, in fact, has a right to more land than he can use for the general good; within these limits his title is impregnable; but in Maori New Zealand these limits were exceedingly narrow. The New Zealand Company would have solved the problem by a plan for native reserves, conceived in a spirit of fairness and philanthropy, but which they were not permitted to carry into effect. Not all their proceedings were equally laudable, but the only one which appears open to very serious animadversion occurred after Wakefield had ceased to be concerned in their affairs.

The list of the author's obligations is long. He is, above all, indebted to members of Mr Wakefield's family, and among these principally to three of his nieces—Miss Frances Torlesse, of Christchurch, N.Z., daughter of his favourite sister Catherine; Mrs Harold Freeman, daughter of his brother Daniel; and Mrs D'Arblay Burney, daughter of his brother Felix. But for Miss Torlesse, in particular, this work would never have been undertaken. The countenance of Mr Charles Marcus Wakefield, of Belmont, Uxbridge; and of Mr Edward Wakefield, author of *New Zealand after Fifty Years*, also demand acknowledgment. Two ladies more remotely connected with the family—Mrs Chapman, wife of Lieutenant-General Chapman, C.B., the officer commanding the Scottish division of the home forces; and Miss A. M. Wakefield, of the Westmoreland branch, as great an organiser of music as her relative of colonization—have also been of material service to the author. He is, further, deeply indebted to Mr Albert Allom, of Parnell, N.Z., and his sister Mrs Storr, the children of Wakefield's old and faithful friends, Mr and Mrs Allom. The value of Sir Frederick Young's written contribution speaks for itself, while he has courteously provided the daguerreotype from which the frontispiece is taken. The writer must cordially thank Mr Stuart J. Reid, now engaged in a biography of Lord Durham, for the communication of documents illustrating Wakefield's connection with that nobleman. Lord Norton has been good enough to permit reference to be made to him respecting the New Zealand Constitution of 1852; and it has been a sincere gratification to the writer to find his account of John Robert Godley, Wakefield's coadjutor in the foundation of the Canterbury Settlement, approved by his son, Sir Arthur Godley, K.C.B., and his venerable widow, one of the original 'Canterbury pilgrims.' Mr Atchley, librarian of the Colonial Office, and Mr Boosé, librarian of the Royal Colonial Institute, have kindly furnished documents from their respective libraries. The lamented illness of Sir George Grey has deprived the author of assistance from him, but he has found a sympathetic, as well as judicious, counsellor in the Hon. W. Pember Reeves, Agent-General for New Zealand; although he must not be considered responsible for anything in the book.

R. GARNETT.

LONDON, *August 2d*, 1898.

CONTENTS

CHAPTER I

WAKEFIELD'S ANCESTRY AND EARLY YEARS—WESTMINSTER AND EDINBURGH SCHOOLS—EMPLOYMENT UNDER FOREIGN OFFICE—FIRST MARRIAGE—DEATH OF HIS WIFE—DIPLOMATIC POST AT PARIS—EARLY WRITINGS,   1

CHAPTER II

THE TURNER ABDUCTION—WAKEFIELD'S TRIAL—HIS IMPRISONMENT AND ITS RESULTS—LETTERS FROM GAOL, .   29

CHAPTER III

WAKEFIELD'S EARLY WRITINGS—'THE PUNISHMENT OF DEATH'—'LETTER FROM SYDNEY'—THE WAKEFIELD SYSTEM—'ENGLAND AND AMERICA'—WAKEFIELD ON THE AGRICULTURAL LABOURER, .   .   50

CHAPTER IV

THE COLONIZATION SOCIETY—THE SWAN RIVER SETTLEMENT—THE FOUNDATION OF SOUTH AUSTRALIA—THE SOUTH AUSTRALIAN COMMISSIONERS—MR G. F. ANGAS—NINA WAKEFIELD—HER DEATH—EARLY STRUGGLES OF THE COLONY—TESTIMONY TO THE WAKEFIELD SYSTEM, .   .   84

CHAPTER V

Project for Colonization of New Zealand—Condition of the Islands in 1837—The New Zealand Association—The Church Missionary Society—Lord Durham—Lord Howick—The New Zealand Company—Obstruction from the Government—First Expedition, . . 125

CHAPTER VI

Wakefield in Canada with Lord Durham in 1838—Recall of the Mission—The Durham Report—Wakefield's Subsequent Visits to Canada, . . . 158

CHAPTER VII

The Planting of New Zealand—The Company's Instructions to Its Agents—Colonel William Wakefield—His Land Purchases—Native Reserves—Treaty of Waitangi—Frustration of French Designs upon the Colony, . . . 192

CHAPTER VIII

Settlement of Wellington—Ill-judged Proclamation of Governor Hobson—Auckland made the Seat of Government—The Company and the Colonial Office—Massacre of Wairau—Governors Fitzroy and Grey—Wakefield's Illness, ... 216

CHAPTER IX

The Transportation Committee—The Colonial Lands Committee—The New Zealand Committees of 1840 and 1844—The New Zealand Company and Lord Stanley—Debates in the Commons—Wakefield and Adam Smith—Politics for the People, ... 234

CONTENTS

CHAPTER X

THE LAST DAYS OF THE NEW ZEALAND COMPANY—JOHN ROBERT GODLEY—SIR GEORGE GREY'S ADMINISTRATION—DEATH OF COLONEL WAKEFIELD—'THE ART OF COLONIZATION'—CRITICISM OF M. LEROY-BEAULIEU—DEATH OF CHARLES BULLER, ... 267

CHAPTER XI

CHURCH COLONIZATION—THE FREE CHURCH COLONY AT OTAGO—THE CANTERBURY SETTLEMENT—LORD LYTTELTON—GODLEY AS SUPERINTENDENT—FELIX WAKEFIELD ON THE COLONY—THE NEW ZEALAND CONSTITUTION—LIFE AT REDHILL AND REIGATE—WAKEFIELD LEAVES ENGLAND FOR NEW ZEALAND, ... 297

CHAPTER XII

WAKEFIELD IN NEW ZEALAND—SIR GEORGE GREY—THE FIRST NEW ZEALAND PARLIAMENT—ILLNESS AND RETIREMENT FROM PUBLIC LIFE—THE CLOSING SCENE—ESTIMATE OF HIS WORK AND CHARACTER, ... 336

LIST OF ILLUSTRATIONS

Portrait of Edward Gibbon Wakefield, from a Daguerreotype in the possession of Sir Frederick Young, K.C.M.G., . *Frontispiece*

Map of South Australia in 1837, *To face page* 92

Map of New Zealand, 1837 (showing Progress of Settlement up to 1850), *To face page* 200

Edward Gibbon Wakefield

CHAPTER I

WAKEFIELD'S ANCESTRY AND EARLY YEARS—WESTMINSTER AND EDINBURGH SCHOOLS— EMPLOYMENT UNDER FOREIGN OFFICE—FIRST MARRIAGE—DEATH OF HIS WIFE—DIPLOMATIC POST AT PARIS—EARLY WRITINGS

THE family of Wakefield belongs to the North country, and may well be supposed to have originated at the ancient Yorkshire town from which it derives its name. Those of the name who have achieved distinction, with the exception of Gilbert Wakefield, whose ancestors dwelt in Staffordshire, have nevertheless been connected with the branch of the family established near Kendal, in Westmoreland, whose representatives embraced Quakerism soon after its promulgation in the middle of the seventeenth century. The profession and consistent maintenance of unpopular opinions, when not absolutely perverse or fanatical, is usually a token of moral strength, evincing independence of mind in the first instance, and tenacity of conviction in the second. Hence the influence of small nonconforming sects surviving through several generations, a choice remnant sifted by a slow, selective process from age to age, is out of all proportion to their numbers; and much of this power and worth continue even with the families which have eventually relapsed into the general current, as has been the case with the majority of the Westmoreland Wakefields.

Six miles west of Kendal, on the road to Bowness, stands or has stood a hamlet called Quakers' Meeting, whose sequestered situation seems to hint at concealment necessitated by persecution. Six miles south of Kendal is the village of Preston Patrick, the home of Roger Wakefield, descended from another Roger Wakefield living at Challon Hall in 1592, but the earliest member of the family from whom the diligence of Mr Joseph Foster[1] can deduce a regular pedigree. In 1665 he married Hannah Preston of Farleton.

We do not know whether the constancy of Roger and his wife was tested by a twenty-four miles' journey, going and returning, to a possibly silent meeting; but the mere fact of his Quakerism in those days of

[1] *The Royal Lineage of our Noble and Gentle Families*, p. 846. It should be observed that royal descent is not claimed for Roger Wakefield, but for such of his posterity as can establish descent in the female line from Robert Barclay of Urie, whose mother, Catherine Gordon, was descended from Edward the First. It is remarkable that this descent could not have existed if one of the Gordons, Alexander, Roman Catholic Bishop of Galloway, had not become a Protestant and married.

intolerance reveals him as a man of resolute conviction. His rank of life was that of 'statesman,' or farmer holding and farming his own land. He lived to see better times, dying in 1724. His son Roger also lived and died at Preston Patrick, but the second Roger's second son, Edward, migrated to London, where he became a prosperous merchant, and by his second marriage (1748) with Isabella Gibbon, a distant relation of the historian, was the father of another Edward Wakefield, who conferred distinction on his family by his marriage (1771) with Priscilla Bell, great grand-daughter of Robert Barclay of Urie, author of the famous Apology, described by Mr Leslie Stephen as 'one of the most impressive theological writings of the century.'

Though inheriting a fortune from his father, this Edward Wakefield failed in business, and his descendants are unanimous in attributing their intellectual distinction and especial bent towards public questions to inheritance from his wife. He is depicted with her and his sister-in-law, Catherine (afterwards Gurney), in a picture by Gainsborough, still in the possession of a descendant, painted in 1775, engraved as the frontispiece to Mr Augustus Hare's *Gurneys of Earlham*. He appears a handsome man, attired in a costume equally remote from foppishness and Quakerism, and presenting some resemblance to the portrait of Edward Gibbon Wakefield as a young man, engraved in 1826, and reproduced in Mr Edward Wakefield's *New Zealand after Fifty Years*. The animated features seem to bespeak ardour and resolution; but if these qualities were ever exerted, no record of them remains. It is otherwise with his wife Priscilla, from 1794 to 1817 one of the most popular and useful contemporary writers for the young, but far more celebrated as one of the first to introduce the savings bank into England, under the name of the Frugality Bank. Some uncertainty exists respecting priority in the introduction of this great national boon; certain it is from the *Reports of the Society for bettering the Condition of the Poor*, vol. i., that her Friendly Society was established on 22d October 1798, though it is not quite clear whether the Savings Bank was a feature of it from the first. Amiable, sensible, industrious, placid, affectionate, she was a model of Quaker virtues, and a consistent Friend in religious practice, although she conformed to Quaker peculiarities neither in dress nor in abstinence from amusements. 'I suppose,' says her son, 'no one can relate having seen her in a passion or out of humour.' During her long widowhood she resided successively at Tottenham and Ipswich, where she died in September 1832.

Her two sons, Edward, born 1774, and Daniel, born 1776, displayed the interest in public questions, and the disposition to occupy themselves with industrial and philanthropic projects, which she appears to have introduced into the family, as well as other traits for which she probably was not responsible. It will abundantly appear in the course of this history that the Wakefield family possessed a fine irregular genius for marriage, and one characteristic of their unions was precocity. The first and second Edward had each married at twenty-one; the third broke the record by espousing Susanna Crash, daughter of a farmer at Felsted, Essex, at seventeen, the marriage taking place on 3d October 1791. Susanna's personal attractions were no doubt the motive. 'The most beautiful woman I have ever known,' says her husband. 'A soft, angelic beauty, but she was a model for a sculptor.' The younger brother made amends for deficiency in impetuosity by excess in imprudence, contracting a union which soon obliged him to seek, though he failed to obtain, a divorce. Edward's wife, on the contrary, appears to have been a simple-minded woman, who gave her husband little trouble except by the wretched state of health into which she fell about 1812. She died in February 1816: 'her death,' says her husband, 'full of charity and love, her last breath lisping blessings on me and on her children.'

The earliest notice of Edward Wakefield's vocation represents him as farming near Romford, in Essex, and afterwards at Burnham; he was subsequently employed under the Naval Arsenal. In 1808, when placing Edward Gibbon Wakefield at Westminster, he is described as of Ipswich; and his letters to Francis Place in 1813 and 1814 are dated from Bury St [illegible]. In [illegible] he established himself as a land agent [illegible]. [illegible] his agricultural employment seems to have [illegible] given place to land agency and surveying, in which he acquired the experience which qualified him to consider the [illegible] condition of Ireland which has [illegible]. The clearest view of him, apart from his own private letters, is afforded by the MSS. preserved in the British Museum, of his [illegible] Francis Place, the [illegible], [illegible] of Charing Cross, a man [illegible] of [illegible], who possessed the rare and [illegible] of a [illegible], [illegible] to bring the good qualities even of his adversaries to light.

"My acquaintance with Mr Wakefield" he says "must have commenced towards the close of [illegible] or in the beginning of [illegible]. We were soon well acquainted. [illegible] himself so [illegible] his [illegible] were then [illegible] upon him and [illegible]. His and [illegible] about the year [illegible]. When we first

[illegible] as in the first employment [illegible] George [illegible] servant to many persons of great property [illegible] intelligent [illegible] a memorial [illegible] the power of his judgment and integrity [illegible]. [illegible] mentions a visit from him in [illegible], with [illegible] from the [illegible].

became friends. Mr Wakefield's circumstances were by no means prosperous; he was, however, an active zealous advocate for anything likely, in his opinion, to be useful to mankind, and especially to the working people of Great Britain and Ireland. He was publishing his book on Ireland which contains abundance of information, and has been made use of in a multitude of ways. Mr Wakefield was at this time remarkably anxious to promote education amongst the poor, and I found in him an excellent co-operator for many useful purposes.

'Mr Wakefield's parents were Quakers, and he was well acquainted with a large portion of the most respectable persons of that sect, amongst the rest with William Allen, whom he always reverenced. He was also acquainted with Joseph Lancaster and Joseph Fox, and was a strong advocate for the Joseph Lancaster method of teaching, and very desirous to see it extended.'

'Soon after we became intimately acquainted, Mr Wakefield introduced Mr James Mill to me.'

Wakefield then knew Mill before Place himself did, and the acquaintance may have indicated its own's persevering attention, when soon after he converted Stuart Mill to his theory of education. It does not appear when Mill first became the in-

* As to Lancaster, says Wakefield at a later, 'I was once so prominent man in himself, and I am unable to think him to do to a great an instrument in enlightening the public mind as any, there is great a change, as ever Luther —

surdity on Edward Wakefield's part or the impropriety on that of his sons which obliged Place, in his own opinion, to renounce their acquaintance in 1822. Possibly Place, writing in 1833, represents the original misunderstanding in the light of more recent transactions: in 1825 he had thought it neither absurd nor improper to solicit Edward Wakefield for a subscription towards the Mechanics' Institute he was then promoting, and had received ten pounds. The formality of the letter accompanying the donation, nevertheless, sufficiently attests the estrangement of the two old allies.

Although, however, the ostensible cause of the estrangement of Place and Wakefield remains unknown, the germs of it are easily discoverable while their friendship was yet warm and active. Wakefield clearly had many failings, but of an amiable kind; Place comparatively few, but those unamiable. Wakefield was unquestionably extravagant and lax in money matters, and the influence of the example he thus set his sons was pernicious in many ways. He aroused his friend's scorn by a deference to rank and title certainly reprehensible even in an ex-Quaker, and even more so by what Place thought his culpable weakness in the concerns of his own family—his reluctance to place his invalid wife under guardianship, his indulgence to his sons' wildness, and what seemed to Place his great over-estimate of their abilities. These errors, for such no doubt they were, sprang from a sensitiveness and tenderness incomprehensible to Place, a worthy man, but arid as the 'dry places' of the parable, and who eventually deals so faithfully with his friend as to write him down an ass. Even the austere James Mill judged him more favourably. As a practical philanthropist he had done excellent work. So early as September 1801, his mother records: 'Edward dined with us; he is warm in a new chase. Prisons and workhouses are his game. May he be inspired to enlarge the sphere of human happiness and virtue!' He says in a letter from Leicester, 1823: 'There seems a fine county gaol. There has been a day when I should have gone and examined it, and conversed with the prisoners, but so many have taken up the cause that I recede.' His report on the educational and social condition of the Drury Lane district (1813) was printed in 1816 by Brougham's Committee. 'He had the idea,' says Place's biographer, Mr Graham Wallas, 'of which Mr Charles Booth has made such brilliant use, that if permanent educational visitors were appointed for all London, a thorough collection of social statistics might be made.' He also gave much thought to the improvement of lunatic asylums.

Edward Wakefield is still remembered by some as a beautiful old man of lofty stature, and energetic to a very late period of his life. He retained to the last his interest in public affairs and in his two principal pursuits, agriculture and education, and strove to make his experience of both available for the colony created by his son. The articles on New Zealand affairs in the *Colonial Magazine*, signed W., are in all probability by him. He was indefatigable in making communications to the press respecting natural products which could be derived from New Zealand or introduced there. These were usually addressed from Blois, where he and his second wife occupied a chateau, and where he endeavoured to establish an industry in silk. His latter years were principally spent near Macclesfield and in London, where he died in May 1854. As an educator, he lived again in some of his posterity, and especially in Edward Gibbon, whom we shall find always educating somebody; equally ready to admonish a minister when to change a policy, or a little girl when to lay aside a doll.

The work by which Edward Wakefield will be remembered is his *Account of Ireland, Statistical and Political*, 2 vols., 1812. It originated in the author's examination before a Parliamentary Committee in 1808, which produced a proposal from the Right Hon. John Foster, who had been Irish Chancellor of the Exchequer before the Union, that he should undertake a regular survey of the country, with a view to the ascertainment of its condition and resources. Provided with introductions to the chief landowners and leading personages on both sides of politics, he devoted nearly two years to the perlustration of Ireland, and two years more to carrying his book through the press, thus producing a work of great practical value in his own day and of great historical interest in this. 'This very able work,' says Arthur Young. 'Lively, dogmatical, disorderly,' pronounces Sir James Mackintosh. Not confining himself to his ostensible object, Wakefield added chapters on the political and religious condition of the country, distinguished by strong good sense and a genuine zeal for humanity and improvement. Had these been published separately, they would have been regarded as a highly entertaining book, but even the economical portion of the two bulky volumes is continually irradiated by humour, not so much from the author's own powers in this direction as from the nature of the circumstances which he describes. What a picture of the condition of a population is here presented by a single fact!

'Notwithstanding the population of Castle Pollard, which amounts to three thousand, a butcher will not run the risk of killing a bullock until the neighbouring gentlemen have bespoken the whole of it, which they generally do in quarters.'

Why the poor cannot keep pigeons. 'Because their habitations are so low that the pigeons would soon fall a sacrifice to the cats.'

It has appeared worth while to dwell at some length upon the character and performances of the elder Wakefield, as these serve to explain the particular direction taken by the activity of his son. Edward Gibbon Wakefield was brought up in an atmosphere of aggressive philanthropy, and what would now be termed altruism. His grandmother was a philanthropist by profession, and an educator by instinct, and such was even more conspicuously the case with her niece and Wakefield's own cousin, Elizabeth Fry, daughter of the sister of Priscilla Wakefield, who had married into the Gurney family. Edward Wakefield himself manifested his own ideal by naming one of his sons after John Howard, to whom he was in no way related (the youth thus named after a man of peace naturally became a colonel in the East India Company's army).[1] It was an era when zeal for human improvement was fruitfully rife, the era of Wilberforce and Clarkson, and Bentham and James Mill, and Elizabeth Fry and Robert Owen, the era of Bible societies and Lancastrian schools, and savings banks and mechanics' institutes, and the diffusion of useful knowledge. All the serious influences which surrounded Wakefield's youth were of a humanitarian nature, and when at last the wild young man, admonished by sharp discipline

---

[1] Howard Wakefield, nevertheless, was a real philanthropist, and died upon a temperance mission. He was an intimate friend of Havelock's, and a good Sanscrit scholar. *More Wakefieldiano*, he eloped with a native princess, whose affections he had gained in the disguise of a Mussulman. This royal descent made up for the absence of the otherwise indispensable sixteen quarterings when his daughter married Count Radolinski. The wedding took place at Kensington, attended by a motley assemblage of Poles, Quakers and ordinary mortals.

and craving to rehabilitate himself with society, turned his thoughts to practical usefulness, the spirit though not the form of his labours was already determined for him. The concentration of his powers on colonial questions was accidental, but that his project should rather be one for the relief of depression at home than a scheme of conquest was entirely in harmony with the influences which had really moulded his mind, indocile to them as he had appeared at first.

Edward Gibbon Wakefield, the eldest son and second child of a family of nine, was born in London on 20th March 1796. Of his early life little is known, but, as his grandmother speaks of sending him to school on her own responsibility, his education probably owed more to her than to either his father or mother. Some surviving fragments from her diary illustrate her anxious tenderness.

'May 1802. Walked to see my sweet Edward, who gives me great pleasure by the sweetness of his temper and behaviour.

'Feb. 4, 1807. An early summons to Haigh's on account of a great delinquency of dear Edward's almost rendered me incapable of application.

'Feb. 5. My mind most painfully engaged in the perverseness of my dear little Edward—his obstinacy if he inclines to evil terrifies me; turned to good, it would be a noble firmness.

'Feb. 7 . My thoughts much engaged with dear little

Edward, whom I tenderly love, but whose inflexible pertinacious temper makes me fear for his own happiness, and that of those connected with him.

'Feb. 13. My dear little Edward still in disgrace; my heart yearns to forgive him; he has some fine qualities, but he is a character that requires delicate handling.'

Wakefield's father can scarcely have designed him for his own profession when, in January 1808, he placed him at Westminster School, where he remained until 1810. The step was apparently quite inoperative in so far as it may have aimed at imbuing his mind with classical culture; his sinewy Saxon owes nothing to Greek or Roman models; although late in life he betrays an intelligent study of Gibbon. One observation, made at Westminster, evinces his shrewdness of perception. He says (*Punishment of Death*, p. 146) that the Newgate boys who are to be formally let off from sentences of capital punishment, 'have just the same air of agreeable excitement and self-importance, for days before the scene takes place, as marks a Westminster boy when he is about to be distinguished by acting in public.' The traditions yet linger of a series of fights by which, though always beaten, he eventually wore out the bully of his class; and of a Homeric battle, result unrecorded, between him and Erskine, Earl of Mar, who afterwards fought Napoleon. Westminster, however, did not suit the boy, who, in September 1810, positively refused to return to it. His good grandmother at first mourns over his perversity, but when at length the lad has gained his point, acknowledges her satisfaction at his removal to Edinburgh High School, 'where I trust he will be instructed in religion and morality as well as in Greek and Latin.' There are traces of considerable disturbances even at this excellent school, which Wakefield finally left in January 1812. Spoiled for business and unqualified for a profession, his destination in life gave his father much anxiety. 'Edward Gibbon,' observes his grandmother, 'is at home without sufficient employment to occupy the talents and activity of his mind; consequently his present situation is disadvantageous to himself, and troublesome to others.' He seems to have found no regular occupation until 1814, when he appears in the employment of the Hon. William Hill, afterwards Lord Berwick, at that time envoy to the court of Turin, but apparently much in England. Perhaps his specific duty was that of King's messenger, for the elder Wakefield writes to Place in October : 'Edward's letter is very short, and amounts to nothing except the probability of his going to Vienna. It was dated the 15th of September, by this time no doubt he has left Paris, and is either at Genoa or on his way to Vienna. His fate in life depends upon his conduct during the next six months. Should he settle down to business as he ought, he will make a man, but he is very likely to go off at a tangent, and then I cannot tell what may happen to him.'

Whether Edward Gibbon Wakefield proceeded to Vienna is uncertain, but this appears to have been the winter he mainly spent at Turin, as stated in a passage of his *Letter from Sydney*, to be afterwards quoted. On 20th July 1815, Place writes to James Mill : 'Wakefield's son returned from Turin soon after you left London, much improved in appearance, and somewhat softened, though not much, in manners ;[1] this has been produced by the contrasts his journeys have presented him ; and the visible superiority of the English over all the nations of the continent has made him like them better than he did ; his conduct has, however, been very ambiguous, and his tales have contradicted one another, so that his father, who has more of feeling than of solid judgment in his composition, has been distressed beyond anything you will be able to imagine. I have not allowed him to trifle, but have plainly and fully told him of his follies, and, as I think, with some effect. He has left Mr Hill, but not with disgrace.'

Genius commonly has its *Sturm und Drang* period, during which it is a nuisance to itself and everybody near it : contracts imprudent marriages pregnant with future misery like Shelley ; or takes poison to bed

---

[1] The fond grandmother thought more favourably. 'July 19, 1815.—My dear Edward Gibbon arrived, greatly improved in body and mind. His aspect and manner pleased me, but what most delighted me was his noble, independent spirit.'

with it like Goethe; or sends academic youth out to rob on the highways like Schiller; or confides its money to hopeless speculations like Tennyson. In the light of Wakefield's subsequent history it is easy to discern that he was then traversing such a period, but it must be admitted that he had not up to this time given any indubitable token of genius. The worthy Place, so little a discerner of spirits that he thought the word itself might be advantageously omitted from the writings of Bishop Berkeley, was so far from any notion of the kind that he shortly afterwards writes to Mill: 'I can tell you very little respecting Edward Wakefield; his conduct is wholly inexplicable. He despises his father's advice, and laughs at his opinions; he talks largely of being on his own hands, and independent of his father. I hope, and expect too, that he will obtain some employment at the Foreign Office. He is best adapted for that line, and it is well adapted to him. I wish his father could make up his mind to see only a common man in him.' Appearances spoke in Place's favour, but the elder Wakefield's parental instinct was sounder than his friend's judgment.

Place's opinion that the Foreign Office under Castlereagh offered a career highly suitable to young Wakefield was by no means designed as a compliment to the latter, who, probably by the interest of Mr Hill, his connection with whom was resumed, actually obtained some minor appointment which took him to Paris. From thence, 29th August, he wrote a spirited letter describing the popular resentment and indignation produced by the execution of General Labedoyère. There is nothing to show that it was addressed to Place, though it is now among his papers in the British Museum, but it fell in some manner into his hands, and through him became the first composition of Wakefield's to attain the distinction of print, appearing in the *Statesman* newspaper. Not only was the letter printed without Place's authority, but the authorship was divulged in conversation, and on 9th September, Place writes a dismayed remonstrance. 'I would have paid £100 rather than that that letter should have been printed. Should it ever be known at the Foreign Office, all his prospects in the line of life he has chosen, and the only one he is fit for, would be blasted in an instant, and all the shame and reproach would fall upon me.' Nothing can have come of the indiscretion, for on 9th December Place writes to Mill: 'Edward is with Mr Hill in London. Wakefield is in raptures with him, ridiculously so. Edward is, however, provided for, and that too in the line in which he is most likely to continue; and Wakefield, who expected him home without a shilling and without employment, has much to rejoice at. It is a rascally employment, but the world does not treat it as disreputable, and Edward cannot be spoiled by it. Edward's manners are far more agreeable than they were; his knowledge of diplomacy has shown him the necessity of this.' The 'rascally employment,' then, was not devoid of redeeming features, and Edward's employer must have found him serviceable, for Place continues : 'Mr Hill will not allow him to be away from him for an hour even, and endeavours to detach him from his family, telling him his father has eight other children, and can spare him ; he laughs at him for writing to any of them, and hints that he will be good for little until he divests himself of all affection and feeling for any of them. Mr Hill is right ; to become an accomplished man in his employment, one must stifle humanity and destroy all the kinder emotions of the heart.' Curious that the art of negotiating with men, in which Place himself was no mean proficient, should be innocent and respectable as long as it stays at home, but becomes fit only for such good-for-nothing young men as Place thought Wakefield so soon as it goes abroad and calls itself diplomacy! In truth Mr Hill's exhortations were wasted upon Wakefield, who, after the first extravagances of youth had subsided, made an excellent son, and was beyond most men *notus in fratres animi paterni.*

Several months now elapse without any mention of Wakefield in Place's correspondence until on 9th August 1816 comes the startling announcement, 'He is to be married to-morrow!' From other sources of information it appears that the bride's name was Eliza Susan Pattle, that she was the orphan daughter of a merchant in the East Indies, living under her mother's care, and that it was a runaway match. Tradition, now getting dim, alleges that Wakefield, deeply enamoured of the beautiful girl, and naturally regarded by her family as a 'detrimental,' followed her down to Tunbridge Wells, where she stayed with her mother and two elderly uncles addicted to cock-fighting. Love is depicted on ancient gems enjoying a combat between quails; and so mighty was his power on this occasion that Wakefield, who in a private letter calls cruelty to animals 'disgusting,' became to all appearance devoted to the sport, and the uncles began to deem him quite an exemplary young man. He profited by his opportunities, and one July day two carriages simultaneously left Tunbridge Wells, driving in opposite directions, one containing Edward Gibbon Wakefield and Eliza Pattle, the other, two persons dressed to represent them. The uncles followed the wrong one. Shortly afterwards cousin Head at Ipswich was awakened by Edward Gibbon entering his room at dead of night with the observation, 'I want your boat.' They descended into the garden. Eliza came forth from under the bushes, and the pair entered the boat, and rowed up the Orwell to a place of safety, news of their movements interrupting the good grandmother in the perusal of Bishop Watson's *Sermons*.

The young lady being a ward in Chancery, the Lord Chancellor was invoked against Wakefield, but his address prevailed not only to persuade the Chancellor of the propriety of the marriage, but even to conciliate the mother, with whom he kept house for a time, and who remained his friend until her daughter's premature death and her own marriage to a second husband. 'Edward,' writes Place to Mill on 30th August, 'his wife, and her mother will soon depart the land. I have not given and will not give your "congratulations to the young Benedict;" he does not deserve them.' Here again Place was to be confuted by events. Wakefield's private letters, as well as family recollections, attest that he was affectionately devoted to his wife, and that the too brief union was a very happy one. 'Mr Hill,' the elder Wakefield writes in 1823, 'has been delighting me by talking in the highest terms of Edward's wife. She lived with him for four years as a daughter, and he thinks of her just as I do, describes her excellent acute sense, and yet the kind, reserved way; she never forced it on you, but left it to you to find it out; he talks of her gentleness, relates the impression which she made upon all his friends, and how they speak of her now; he says that he could relate the most amiable stories that he heard of her at Genoa since she left.'[1]

It is well for Wakefield's credit that unequivocal testimonies of his tender devotion to his young wife

[1] 'Lord Byron,' Wakefield adds, 'has lived a great deal with Mr Hill lately. He says he is a most delightful, pleasant person, but most vindictive when he takes dislikes.'

exist. Miss Pattle was not only a beauty but a fortune, and a penniless young man who carries off an opulent damsel in defiance of her family cannot complain if he is supposed to have hunted the ducats rather than the daughter. In the light of subsequent events, it is no breach of charity to attribute a share in determining his conduct to interested reasons, while, at the same time, the genuineness of his attachment is unquestionable. He probably thought with Tennyson's Northern Farmer :—

> 'Thou can love thy lass and her money too :
> Making them go together as they've good right to do.'

The immediate result of the marriage was an improvement in his official, no less than in his pecuniary, position. He returned to Turin as Secretary to the Under Secretary of the Legation, the Hon. Algernon Percy, who became an intimate friend. It would seem from Mr Hill's statement that he chiefly lived at Genoa, where his daughter Susan Priscilla, known by her mother's pet name of Nina, was born on 4th December 1817. On 25th June 1820, his son, Edward Jerningham, was born in London, an event followed on 5th July by the death of the mother. This tragic event not merely occasioned him the deepest agony, but raised up a barrier he could never quite displace between him and his infant son, and prepared his estrangement from his wife's family. It seemed an unmitigated disaster ; without it, nevertheless, the world might never have heard of him. He appears to have been for some years following connected with the Paris Embassy as 'secretary general and attaché ad libitum.' At Paris, in 1822, the elder Wakefield, who continued to carry on his business in Pall Mall, and whose private address was in Charles Street, St James's Square, contracted, at the British Embassy, an eventful marriage, long kept secret, with Frances, daughter of the Rev. David Davies, headmaster of Macclesfield Grammar School; and at Paris also, in September 1823, Edward Gibbon acted as second in a duel. We must think of him at this time as a young man of fashion, a buck in his attire, of wild and almost insolent spirits, ready for any frolic, and not discriminating too nicely between frolic and mischief.

That Wakefield, nevertheless, was not entirely devoted to fashionable society, appears not only from his father's statement, ' Parliament and office are his first objects; he will go in to support Mr Canning with the full expectation of holding a considerable official situation :' but from two highly interesting documents not until now connected with his name. His authorship is proved by copies in his handwriting, with marginal directions showing that they were to be printed in some journal which apparently had not existed very long, and doubtless contained other examples of his composition. The longer and more elaborate of the two may be described as a general review of the state of public feeling, in the form of a letter to the Marquis of Titchfield, heir-apparent to the Dukedom of Portland. This young nobleman died in March 1824. The letter, therefore, is prior to that date, and internal evidence shows it to have been written after Canning had become Foreign Secretary in August 1822. It is remarkable not so much for any extraordinary force of diction, as from the affinity and the contrast it simultaneously presents to the ideal of another youthful genius then equally eager to open the oyster of the world. Although the stuff of Disraeli's *Vivian Grey* is neither more nor less than the negotiation for the establishment of the *Representative* newspaper, transferred with sublime audacity to the world of statesmanship, the novel undoubtedly expresses Disraeli's intimate conviction ; and this is precisely the same as that of Wakefield's essay—the great opportunity for a new departure in politics afforded by the exhaustion of both the old parties. Each proposes to effect this object under the ægis of a man of rank, the Marquis of Titchfield, Wakefield's selection, being probably recommended by the character he had acquired as a steady and at the same time independent member since his entrance into the House of Commons in 1818, and still more by his relationship to Canning. Both Disraeli and Wakefield lived to make their dreams realities, Durham being to the one what Bentinck and Derby were to the other. But the future

Colonial statesman approves himself as superior to the future Prime Minister in penetration as he is inferior in brilliancy and humour. In *Vivian Grey* there is not a word about the people. The only forces recognised as operative are a few noble families and conspicuous politicians whose ability to dispose of the country at their pleasure is taken for granted. With Wakefield, on the contrary, the third estate is everything. The one test of the possibility of the new political party is, Can such a party obtain the confidence of the nation? and, even though the Reform Bill was not yet, the passage of political power from the few to the many is assumed throughout as self-evident. The second and much briefer essay, *Political Creed*, is chiefly remarkable for an outbreak of the ardent patriotism and sanguine optimism which made Wakefield a vital force in politics, a man whose bent was ever to create, not merely to preserve or to destroy.

'But we are enthusiasts. To be sure we are! We commenced writing on politics because we are political enthusiasts; because we are sick of the dull, calculating, measured trash of one set of newspapers and the prejudiced, senseless, savage violence of others; because we would give to such hearts as our own the pleasure of reading, whilst we have the pleasure of writing, warm and enthusiastic praise of all that tends to the good of our country, and censure, bold, unqualified and uncompromising, of every word and deed that appears inimical to the honour, the interests and the glory of dear old England. Enthusiasts indeed! And is it not high time that enthusiasts should appear in the only cause that is worthy of enthusiasm? We spurn the mawkish affectation which supposes that England has seen her brightest day of civilisation, prosperity and glory. We defy history to show us a country like England where all classes of people have been advancing together in knowledge, prosperity, virtue and happiness. If it be true that our nobles are luxurious, is it not also true that our peasants and mechanics have learned to read? If it be true that we take more pains than formerly about what is ornamental, is it not also true that every day produces some new useful invention? Have not our merchants, manufacturers, farmers and tradesmen made as great a progress in knowledge and virtue as any other class of people in the arts of luxury? Is there not more sterling sense and virtue amongst the people at large than at any period of our history? The attainment of knowledge, virtue and happiness are so many arts, and they have been practised in England, for the first time in the history of the world, by all classes of the people with equal success. History can furnish us with no materials for the discovery of what may happen to the English people. They may (and, if those who conduct their public affairs do but assist them, they will) reach that point of perfection which shall enable a good patriot to say without extravagance, "See England and die." Perish then the miserable despondency of those who contend that the decline and fall of England have commenced, and that her bright day of prosperity, virtue, happiness and glory has passed away for ever!'

This passage reveals half the secret of Wakefield's strength. Though his faculty of interesting himself in public questions came from his grandmother, he had inherited from the paternal side an adventurous spirit which did not belong to the house of Bell. He was eager, impetuous, enthusiastic. When he had an object before him he made as light of obstacles as though to overlook them had been to overleap them. This is the temperament for a successful projector. But obstacles cannot be 'wished away' like the wassailers in the *Eve of St Agnes*, and his undertakings, both public and private, suffered from his refusal to recognise difficulties patent to any ordinary man. Yet, as his view of the greatness of his country, and the general progress of the age, extravagantly roseate as it was, was still very much nearer the truth than the contrary notion, so his schemes were in general essentially reasonable. Their defects could frequently be remedied or mitigated by the fertility of resource so commonly an attribute of the genial prolific temperament. When united with self-reliance, ambition and shrewdness, such qualities should carry a man far; in Wakefield's case this constellation of remarkable endowments nearly bewitched him to his ruin. The success of his first hymeneal adventure was a snare to him; he should have rested his reputation upon that.

CHAPTER II

THE TURNER ABDUCTION — WAKEFIELD'S TRIAL—
HIS IMPRISONMENT AND ITS RESULTS—LETTERS
FROM GAOL

On 7th March 1826, a carriage appeared at the door of Miss Daulby, a schoolmistress near Liverpool, and a servant presented a letter to that lady purporting to come from a Dr Ainsworth, stating that the mother of one of her pupils, Miss Ellen Turner, daughter of Mr William Turner of Shrigley, a wealthy manufacturer in the county of Cheshire, and at the time sheriff for the county, had been suddenly attacked with paralysis, and desired her daughter to come to her immediately. Miss Turner was not to be told of the cause of the summons, a crafty precaution which prevented the discovery that no Dr Ainsworth existed. The schoolmistress, completely deceived, allowed the young lady to depart. She was met on the road by Edward Gibbon Wakefield and his brother William, who on various pretexts allured her to Carlisle, where she was informed that her father's affairs were in a desperate condition, and that the only way to retrieve them was to consent to marry Edward Gibbon Wakefield.

Gretna Green was handy, the proposed bridegroom was 'gay and fashionable,' and the form of a matrimonial ceremony was gone through, but the marriage was never consummated, Wakefield promising that the union should be nominal until he had taught her to love him, as with time he assuredly would. They then proceeded to London and thence to Calais, Ellen Turner, it must be said, evincing throughout a docility and complacency only explicable on the supposition that she considered herself to have got a very good husband. Wakefield was equally satisfied. 'My dear little wife,' he wrote while they were still together, 'is an excellent creature, and promises to be the delight of my life.' 'I would have made her love me,' he said afterwards. The residence of the parties becoming known, they were followed to Calais by Mr Turner's son and friends. Ellen, confronted with them, elected to renounce her abductor, who on his part offered no opposition to her departure, subscribed 'a solemn declaration that she and I have been as brother and sister,' and passed the severest condemnation on his own conduct by acknowledging that if any man had thus behaved to his own daughter, he would have shot him.[1] His friends advised him to take refuge in America, but he returned to England to share the fate of his brother William, who was already in custody. Frances Wakefield, the young

---

[1] 'They took off her ring,' he says, 'and gave it to me. I shall preserve it carefully. They should have thrown it away.'

men's youthful stepmother, whose clandestine marriage with the elder Wakefield was now acknowledged, Edward Wakefield saying, 'I must stand by my wife,' was made a party to the indictment. She was in fact innocent of criminal complicity, yet her social ambition had lain at the root of the whole adventure.

After tedious preliminary proceedings, beginning with Wakefield's committal to Lancaster Castle in May, and frequently interrupted and resumed, the case was tried at Lancaster Assizes on 23d March 1827. Serjeant Cross and Brougham were counsel for the prosecution, the conduct of the case chiefly falling upon the latter. The Wakefields had secured Scarlett, the ablest advocate of the day, but there could be no defence upon the merits of the case. The legal questions involved were a different matter, and the problem whether, under the law of Scotland, Miss Turner was or was not Mrs Wakefield, was so obscure that it was found necessary to set it at rest by a special Act of Parliament annulling the marriage. The evidence abundantly established that no force or intimidation had been resorted to; it was equally clear that fraud had been employed, and there could be no doubt of the verdict as concerned the principal defendants. The judge summed up favourably for Frances Wakefield, and the jury deliberated over her case for an hour, but eventually found her guilty. She was not, however, called up for judgment, and ought to have been acquitted, for, suspicions as her conduct had been,

Wakefield's subsequent declaration established her innocence. Many yet remember her in her old age as a lady of charming manners, and remarkable for her beneficence. Wakefield appeared to receive sentence on 14th May. In his plea for mitigation, he stated that the legal proceedings had cost him £6000, and that half this amount had been raised by the sale of a reversionary interest of £1500 a year. Further he could not go without sacrificing the interests of his children under their mother's settlement. This he was resolved never to do; a fine, therefore, would be equivalent to a sentence of perpetual imprisonment, and he prayed that this might not be imposed upon him. The court took him at his word, and awarded three years' confinement in Newgate, a sentence unanimously ratified by public opinion. William Wakefield, although the lesser offender, received a similar term in Lancaster Castle, probably because the costs of the trial had fallen entirely upon Edward. The latter was heard once more when pleading against the dissolution of his marriage before the House of Lords; he spoke ably, said all he could, but what could he say?[1]

It must have occurred to everyone that—moral considerations apart—such a wild adventure was the very last that one would have expected a man of Wakefield's astuteness to engage himself in, and that the love of adventure must have entered into it in a

[1] Ellen Turner married in 1829 Mr Legh, representative of one of the first Cheshire families, and died in childbirth in 1831.

considerable degree. 'Every age does not produce such a Quixote as Mr Wakefield,' said *Blackwood's Magazine*. It came out upon the trial that the scheme had been concocted amid the idle and fashionable circle of Paris, where the Wakefields were enjoying what they were pleased to consider 'the first society in the world.' Prominent in this set was Miss Bathurst, the stepdaughter of the Bishop of Norwich, who had set herself to work most disinterestedly to find rich wives both for Edward and William.[1] Wakefield found himself entangled by a promise to his set that he would carry off 'the weaver's daughter,' but he must have got entirely out of touch with his own country ere he could look upon such an exploit as practicable. In addition to the levity and recklessness engendered by a course of fashionable dissipation in one of sanguine temperament and overflowing animal spirits, there was a potent motive in the background which for the time perverted his feeling of right and his generally vigorous common sense. This was not cupidity, but ambition. As we trace his subsequent career we shall frequently find him resorting to strong irregular steps, but not from

[1] Miss Bathurst, it should be said, had reason for her regard for Wakefield. Her deceased sister had been attached to his intimate friend, Percy. 'Percy's mare,' Wakefield wrote to his father in 1824, 'must be kept without work of any sort. It is a point which Percy has at heart, and he depends upon me in preference to other friends to secure the comfortable existence of the animal which was the favourite pet of Miss Bathurst.'

C

motives of mere self-interest. When, in the course of the legal proceedings, he accounted for his presence in Macclesfield by a desire to investigate the case of the distressed silk weavers with a view to advocating it in Parliament, the public, aware that this was not the only motive, naturally thought that it was no motive at all. They did not know what strong pressure, from a quarter most difficult to resist, had been put upon the elder Wakefield to induce him to stand for Parliament. He actually did become a candidate for Reading in 1826, without the smallest chance of success; and in 1823 he had promised that he and his son should both sit in the next Parliament. Frances Wakefield was no less urgent with the son than with the father, and, though no party to the abduction, sowed the seed of it by urging Wakefield to obtain Miss Turner's hand as a preliminary to representing Macclesfield. Lack of means disabled the younger Wakefield from obtaining a seat by his own resources; and there is no doubt that when, in a privately circulated paper which got into the *John Bull*, he spoke of offering himself for Parliament at the general election then actually impending at the time of the Turner affair, he fully meant what he said, and expected to be returned for Macclesfield, where his stepmother's father already held an important position, by the influence of his reconciled father-in-law. He felt himself made for public life, and was resolved to enter upon it. This does not excuse his outrage upon family peace, or the deception by which he accomplished it, but it does relieve him from the imputation of the merely sordid motive to which his conduct was then inevitably ascribed, but which is out of keeping with the tenor of his after life. It was a just punishment that the very means to which he resorted to obtain a seat should seal his perpetual exclusion from Parliament, while at the same time indirectly opening to him a career more important than he can well have anticipated when he first thought of entering the House of Commons under the auspices of Canning.

The change from the society of Paris to the society of Newgate, however mitigated by transition through intermediate regions peopled by judges and lawyers, can be no slight test of the virtue of fortitude. Persons of Wakefield's sanguine temper and effervescent spirits are frequently liable to extreme dejection in adversity. It was not so with him. Hope, he says in the *Letter from Sydney*, if you know how to indulge it, is more grateful than reality. In Newgate, as will be seen, he found consolation not merely in the studies and observations which were to make him a power in the English world, but in the exercise of the domestic affections which he cherished with such singular intensity. The following letters, dating from an earlier period of his tribulation, are perhaps even more conclusive proofs of the buoyancy and intrepidity of his spirit, written while he was still agitated by hope and fear, and oppressed by the galling consciousness that the dexterity and astuteness on which he valued himself had proved downright folly. All are addressed to his stepmother, Frances Wakefield :—

'LANCASTER CASTLE, *May* 26.

'I think it more than probable that I shall remain here till the Assizes. I have many reasons for preferring a sojourn here to the doubtful attempt to procure admittance to bail. I do not say doubtful as to the fact of my being admitted to bail, for that I take for granted, but doubtful as to the wisdom of injuring my defence in making the application. I am very well lodged and treated in this castle. You ought to know how little I care for personal luxuries. Air, exercise, water, privacy and books are all-sufficient for any man of common sense and courage. I have all these, so I give you my word that, could I forget what others feel for me, I should at this time be as much at my ease as I ever was in my life.'

'*May* 30.

'I have got to myself a room twenty-four feet square and a yard fifty feet long. I have a fire, a table, two chairs, plenty of water, which to me is the same as plenty of air, plenty of books, pens and paper. I am locked into my cell at seven, but have candles, and I am obliged to attend chapel every day; when, however, at my own request, I sit alone, unseen, in the *condemned pew*. [Ominous!] My confinement is solitary at my own request, but I and myself could always make company. At present we walk, talk and laugh together, without a moment's lassitude during the day.'

'*June* 5.

'I am pretty fully occupied in preparing my defence, and corresponding with lawyers with a view to it. Half an hour a day to read letters from named and nameless correspondents, one of which, by the way, has produced me the most important article of evidence that I shall have to produce. Some of my unknown correspondents write law to me, some consolation, some love, and one an offer of marriage! Without something to love I should be very unhappy, so I have a cat, with one woolly draggle of a kitten, and a root of grass which grows in a hole in a wall, and which I watch and nurse as if it were a cutting from the Tree of Life. My fellow prisoners are a stout Wigan engineer, confined for three years unjustly, a Manchester thief, and a miserable Irishman, one Patrick Blake, who, " Plase your honour and long life to your honour," expects to be hanged for a violent highway robbery. The magistrates come to stare at me, so I compel them, by standing and staring formally with my hat on, to be regularly introduced by the turnkey.'

Newgate must have been a less tolerable house of detention than Lancaster Castle, but on the other hand a brighter sunbeam visited the shady place. No trace remains to show at what period of his imprisonment Wakefield began to study the question of criminal reform, but it probably must have been as soon as he had become in any measure accustomed to his new and repulsive society. Colonial subjects, it is almost certain, did not occupy him until a later period of his incarceration. For a while a nearer and deeper interest absorbed him—his children. With him, on a superficial view, the intellectual and animal souls seemed incongruously mated. By so much as the former was crafty and aggressive, by so much was the latter affectionate and self-denying. Tender solicitude was no new thing with him. A letter of 1822 has escaped the wreck of his correspondence, encyclopædic in its directions for the weal of his little Nina, in whom he beheld the image of her mother, and to whom he felt himself father and mother too. 'Let her have a sufficiency of strong and thin shoes, and let some of the latter be of silk or jane, with sandal-like strings to tie crosswise round her ankles —teach the nurse how to tie them and how to put on and adjust all her clothes neatly and prettily. This may be done in half a dozen dressings and undressings, and they will be a good trial of my soul's patience, a virtue which she must practise against her will very often before it becomes habitual.' Then follow directions about pomatum, calomel, knitting needles and similar matters, expressed with as minute care as if he were freighting a ship to found a colony. It may be imagined how one who could write thus while leading a life of amusement would feel when his child seemed all that was left to him.

'*Feb.* 27, 1828.

'My dear Grandmother,—I received yesterday your kind letter with the inclosures for my children; and to-day arrived the books from Darton's. My boy, upon reading your letter, became very red, sprang towards me and exclaimed, "Why, great-grandmamma wants me to be a *sloth*, and I want to be a general or a prime minister or something of that kind!" So, you see, he is of an aspiring nature, considering that he is only seven years old. Nina, on the contrary, quite approved your peaceable sentiments, but then she is a little old woman in good sense; and, to speak quite seriously, she has the tenderest heart in the world. They will write to you immediately.

' My confinement is in some respects very advantageous to them, as I have nothing to do but to attend to their education, which is proceeding to my heart's content. Their progress during the last six months surprises even me, who am bound to think my own children prodigies.

'Your list of Catherine's children is enough to brighten one; but I know you think a numerous family a great advantage; that is, I believe, the only opinion of yours in which I cannot agree with you. What should I do, for instance, with six? Why, they must eat each other, for I could not keep them. But, to show you that I do not altogether disagree with you, I will add that I should like to have forty daughters with as many thousands a year to divide amongst them at my death, or their marriages. I know you would quote the bundle of sticks, but if all the sticks are rotten, that is, poor, what becomes of the argument?

'Both my children are learning to draw, and are as fond of it as I used to be when I scrawled upon everything in your Tottenham house. What a number of recollections that word brings to my mind! among which your incessant care and kindness hold the highest place. Mrs Fry came to see me the other day, and made me think of you and the old house, and that pond which you used to dread so much. You do not remember, I daresay, so I will tell you that she and her husband being on a visit to you, he gave me half a crown and told me to throw it into that same pond. I, being six years old, thought him a very honest man, and concluded that the money was bad, and that he wished it to be thrown away. Away I threw it, therefore, and came back from the pond, quite proud of my share in so honest an action. What I had done coming out, Mr Fry gave me another half-crown, which I kept. And at night, as if there could be no good without evil in this world, I went to sleep chuckling over the idea that I had got five shillings out of my father's enemies, as from something I heard during the day I imagined our cousins Fry to be. What do you think of that for a recollection?

'I hope you heard of Torlesse's visit to me for the sole purpose of advising me to send my daughter abroad, upon which subject he didn't open his mouth. His silence did him honour; and I hope he was not blamed for the fruitlessness of his journey. If he were, it was unfairly, for had he talked till now he must still have gone back to report no progress. If anyone were to ask me for my teeth or half my limbs, I might perhaps part with them, but my daughter! What could have put it into their heads?

'I have never told you of what I am sure you will be glad to hear, that I have learned to regard my uncle [1] with affection, to say nothing of gratitude. His disinterested, generous, and most friendly, I may say more than paternal, conduct in all my late troubles is far above my praise. I shall be grateful to him as long as I live, and afterwards, if we remember this

[1] The Daniel Wakefield already mentioned, who, after a course of pamphleteering and private secretaryships, became an eminent Chancery barrister and Q.C. He shared the sanguine, enterprising temper of his brother and nephew. He must have possessed one professional quality—assurance—if there be truth in an anecdote told by his nephew that, being pressed by Pitt to write a pamphlet : 'No,' he said, 'I can't write myself, but if *you* will sit down and write, I will dictate to you !' He died in 1846, in embarrassed circumstances,' says the *Morning Post*, ' owing to his benevolence, having often been known to refuse fees from needy clients.'

world in the next. I never, I am sorry to say, gave him any cause to wish me well. Yet when I was in need he chose to become my friend; he risked much for himself, and nothing could check his generous ardour, not even the earnest persuasion of some who, whilst I flourished, thought they could never do enough for me. I rejoice to add that he has not suffered by his kindness to me. On the contrary, having lost nothing, he has gained the good opinion of many who before regarded him with indifference. This is a fact, whatever you may have heard to the contrary. I need not apologise for thus singing his praises to so partial an audience as yourself.

'You will please my children very much by writing to them. They are taught to be proud of a letter from you, and to look forward with pleasure to going to see you when I can take them. Of course you will see Arthur. He will give you a pleasing account of Sierra Leone.

'I am ashamed quite to fill this monstrous sheet, and therefore wish you good night.—Ever yours affectionately, E. G. W.'

An enormously long letter to his sister, Catherine Torlesse, commenced on 1st September 1828, begins with the most particular details of the health and disposition of his son, and continues :—

'Tuesday Night.

'I have been in a fever all day with the anxiety of

expecting and the joy of receiving dear Nina. She reached me at five, and has been with me till just now (nine). Edward and she met in tears, and were both speechless for some time. He, to my surprise, was pale and almost faint with emotion. I took no notice of them, and after a time Edward left us. She then talked at a great rate ; but I observed that her spirits were artificial. At length, about seven o'clock, in the midst of an indifferent conversation, she burst into tears and threw herself into my arms, saying, or rather sobbing, " I didn't half take leave of aunt, we parted in such a hurry ! " I consoled her as well as I could. She said that she very nearly cried at getting into the coach, but that, fearing the strangers, she conquered herself till she got to Nayland, where she put her face into the corner of the coach and cried heartily. She said that she liked Stoke much better than she expected, and that she loved aunt more than she expected, and that she could not believe in the pain she suffered in coming away. After that, every mention of you or your children set her off again, and I was obliged to cut the subject. But nothing would make her cheerful again, though she became calm enough to thank me for having her here alone this evening, in order to have her cry out in comfort. Were I an ass I should say you have stolen her heart ; but I rejoice at the feelings of affection for you which have been renewed and strengthened by this visit ; and I well know that she does not love me a bit the less for loving you so much. In fact, I know her tears and sobs were caused by a double excitement, that of losing you and finding me. What a beautiful, yet what a dangerous character! I have sent her home with directions that she may go to bed immediately, and now I am Tom Fool enough to cry myself.'

Such excessive sensitiveness might well excite Wakefield's fear for his child, and justify the minute directions he gives his sister to communicate to the lady then in charge of Nina — themselves only a portion of an infinity of similar directions most touching in their thoughtful tenderness, but far too voluminous for our pages.

'I would mention' [in writing to Mrs A.], 'having been struck by Nina's great sensitiveness, which amounts almost to a disease, and say that it requires the utmost care and judgment in those who surround her, but more especially in Mrs A. and her father, from either of whom a word or a frown is as bad as a blow to most other children. That Nina's disposition is so affectionate, even to excess, as to cause her a great deal of pain, and that though for the world you would not destroy so beautiful an attribute, you think that her father (this has been the case) excites it too much, that you think all questions of feeling should be avoided, and that reason only should be employed in the management of her. 'That you are satisfied she is injured every time she feels strongly, either joyfully or sorrowfully;

that every tear she sheds, be the occasion glad or melancholy, is a mischief done; that occasions which excite in her tears of joy have just the same tendency to increase her too great sensibility as occasions which excite tears of sorrow. That in order to aid Mrs A.'s endeavours you wish to mention the subjects or points which most readily excite Nina's feelings. 1. Anything like a doubt of her affection for those whom she likes. 2. Any reproach which conveys a reflection on her truth or honour. 3. The belief that she has hurt the feelings of those whom she likes. 4. Seeing anyone whom she likes offended with her. 5. And most particularly, any lasting but silent (if you can otherwise express "sulky" without being offensive, do so) displeasure in her father or Mrs A., or indeed anyone to whom she is much attached.'

The letter concludes :—

'I feel very, very much obliged to you for your great attention to Nina, more than I can well express. Her visit has been as a short time of sunshine coming in the midst of a dreary season. Your basket was very acceptable to some of the liquorish mouths that surround me, and as its contents were distributed in Nina's name, they have raised her in the esteem of some of her fellow-creatures. My cook, slut and butler, who is an Irishwoman, said on receiving some cake and fruit, "Sure she's a sweet cratur, sir, and it does my heart good to see her in this black place." There's an affecting mixture of bitter and sweet in that remark.'

Strange that he who could feel so exquisitely for his own daughter should have had so little regard for the daughter of another! Perhaps there are inconsistencies as startling in every heart.

Little could the public, when it chanced to think of Newgate, surmise what treasures of affection were hidden in one breast within its gloomy walls; nor is it likely that any voice from one end of the kingdom to the other was raised in Wakefield's favour. What, indeed, could be said? If any man had committed social *felo de se*, it seemed to be he. It would have appeared the wildest of prophecies had anyone told the crowds that watched him withdraw from the dock at Lancaster, or from before the bar of the House of Lords, that within eleven years the convicted offender would go forth as the confidential adviser of a British Proconsul, charged to reconcile a great disaffected dependency to the Empire; that in aiding to accomplish this end he would lay down principles which would all but extinguish colonial disaffection for the future; that his ideas would create one colony, and his daring action preserve another; that senators and statesmen would honour him as a superior, or contend with him as an equal; that almost his last exertions would be devoted to co-operation with philanthropists and ecclesiastics in the establishment of a model colony. There were, in fact, two Wakefields, one of whom was suddenly obliterated by a catastrophe which destroyed the careless man of fashion, ready out of pure idleness and irrepressible spirits for any mischief, and left the powerful will and the unequalled gift of personal fascination concentrated on the intense purpose of rehabilitating the fallen man in the opinion of society. By itself, however, this would have taken Wakefield but a little way. The services to criminal reform which his longing to regain his place in society induced him to undertake might have atoned for his transgression, but he could not have ranked among the builders of Greater Britain if he had not been very much more than a practical philanthropist. To the surprise of all who had known him, he revealed himself as a man of ideas, not merely capable of conceiving them, but of surrendering himself to them with absolute devotion. From the moment that his colonial system occurred to him, he became its ardent votary on its own merits, and not merely as an instrument of social rehabilitation. How his convictions came to him the next chapter must describe, and the remainder will show how ideas became incarnate in colonies. The lesson of his career is the same that is to be derived from every human life that has risen above the common level, that so long as man's action is merely egoistic, he is a poor, and it may be a perverse creature; but give him an object transcending the sphere of his personal interests, and inspire him with devotion to follow it out, and the height to which he may rise will be only limited by the quality of his own powers. In Wakefield's case these were of the highest order, and when the sharp lesson of adversity had once for all cured him of the pursuit of private ends by unlawful means, and decisively severed his connection with the frivolous, fashionable society which had so long kept him idle and useless, the hereditary but latent element in his character of a passion for public usefulness asserted itself, and he became an almost unparalleled instance of redemption from an apparently hopeless position in virtue of his devotion to a single illuminating idea— the regeneration of the British colonial system by the principles which came to be connected with his name. There was still not a little indirectness to lament, his powers were still frequently impaired by that adventurous and paradoxical bent of mind which alone could render such an escapade as the Turner affair possible—but in the main, after his ideas had once become matured in the salutary solitude of his prison, he is our best example of a type of heroism uncatalogued by Carlyle, the Hero as Colony Maker. No one can read his writings and correspondence intelligently without admitting that personal advantage, and even the recovery of his social standing, weighed far less with him than the realisation of the idea of which he had become enamoured, and for which he fought with the chivalry of Cœur de Lion, if with the weapons of Capel Court. It was this felicitous linking of his own fortunes to a great public cause in which he sincerely believed that, even more than his abilities, lifted him from the well-nigh desperate plight in which this chapter leaves him to the position of influence and honour in which he will shortly be found. 'Hitch,' says Emerson, 'your waggon to a star.'

It is very extraordinary that the Turner escapade should have indirectly produced the regeneration of the British Museum, but such appears to have actually been the case. The Museum, at a low ebb of public usefulness in 1827, owes, as all know, its reform to Antonio Panizzi, who was introduced into it by the patronage of Lord Brougham in 1831. According to his biographer, Mr Fagan, Panizzi, who in 1827 resided in Liverpool, and had himself given Italian lessons to Ellen Turner, deserved Brougham's gratitude by the assistance he rendered him at the Wakefield trial, where Brougham would hardly have displayed 'the extraordinary knowledge of the principles and practice of the jurisprudence of different countries' with which the reporter credits him, if he had not had an Italian Doctor of Laws at his elbow. The obligation was handsomely requited; and it really seems that but for Miss Turner's abduction, both the British Museum and the British colonies would have wanted their providential man.

CHAPTER III

WAKEFIELD'S EARLY WRITINGS—'THE PUNISHMENT OF DEATH'—'LETTER FROM SYDNEY'—THE WAKEFIELD SYSTEM—'ENGLAND AND AMERICA' —WAKEFIELD ON THE AGRICULTURAL LABOURER

EDWARD GIBBON WAKEFIELD's antecedents and hereditary connections have been treated with some minuteness, as, without acquaintance with them, it is impossible either to appreciate his character or to understand his surprising ascent from a prison cell to a position of influence in the national councils rarely indeed accorded to one unknown or disadvantageously known to the public and irrevocably excluded from Parliament. Like many other men, as has been already implied, Wakefield had two characters—one natural, the other superimposed. But whereas with most the engrafted character is the prop and ballast of the man, fortifying weak points and tempering congenital failings by the discipline of routine and public opinion, with Wakefield it was the reverse. He came, as we have seen, of Quaker stock, and all hereditary influences were of utilitarian, philanthropic and altruistic tendency. From this circle of ideas he had been projected into quite a different sphere, partly by his father's ambition and weakness for the countenance of the nobility, so deeply deplored by the Cato of Charing Cross, partly by the extraordinary revolution in his circumstances effected by the brilliant marriage which had introduced the youth of twenty to a fashionable and frivolous society. All this was now at an end. The crystal sphere lay in shivers on the floor, and Wakefield, Faust-like, must build it up again elsewhere ; the phantoms of pleasure and gaiety fled, wailing, never to return ; blue books and statistics were to be his companions henceforth. We hear no more of the best society in Europe and the stepdaughter of the Bishop of Norwich. The unworthy aims and trivial pursuits of his engrafted character were for Wakefield absolutely annihilated, save for the considerable—and, indeed, for his future mission, indispensable—acquisitions of the ease and charm of manner obtained by association with the great world, and of the tact in dealing with men which he had gained in the pursuits of diplomacy. The original nature—the instinct to mend the world and work for public ends—recurred in full force, and with so much the more energy the more clearly Wakefield discerned that only by giving it full play could he retrieve himself from the unenviable position into which the reckless pursuit of adventure, rather than deliberate ill-intent, had precipitated him.

It was the maxim of a wise man, the late eminent

solicitor, Edwin Field, 'Always have one horse and one hobby.' Sometimes the hobby is the better horse. And so it was with Wakefield; the more obvious mission yielded in importance and interest to one apparently more remote. Labouring at once to benefit the public and to redeem himself, it was natural that he should think first of the phenomena presented by the criminal society around him. His first idea was to write the history of Newgate, preparation for which so engrossed him that he had, he implicitly informs us, spent a year in prison before turning his attention to colonial subjects. 'Nearly seven years ago,' he says, writing to the South Australian Commissioners in June 1835, 'I was induced to inquire into the cause of the disasters which,' etc.[1] His cousin Elizabeth Fry, it might well occur to him, had gained great fame and done much valuable work by her errands of mercy to prisoners, including himself, upon whom she had doubtless bestowed a piece of her mind. It remained for him, whose opportunities for observation were so much greater than hers, to lay bare the causes which peopled Newgate, and the effects of Newgate discipline for good or evil. With less air and fire in

[1] An article in the *Colonial Gazette* for 29th July 1840, evidently written or inspired by Wakefield, says that 'it has been stated' that the first idea of his system occurred to him while studying the land regulations promulgated for the Swan River settlement. These appeared in January 1829, but his study of them implies that his mind was already occupied with colonial subjects.

his composition, Wakefield might have become a sort of minor Howard. Happily, however, his sanguine, active temper was not one that could long attach itself to the repulsive details of the ripening of the hangman's harvest, and ere he quitted prison the problem of colonial regeneration, at first taken up as a theme of somewhat remote speculation, had become the controlling influence of his life. This theme was treated by him in a work memorable in the catalogue of books composed in prison, even though their roll includes the *Consolation* of Boethius, Grotius's *De Veritate*, Ralegh's *History of the World*, and, above all, *Pilgrim's Progress*.

Wakefield's other literary production of this period, *The Punishment of Death*, does not concern his activity as a colonial statesman, but it is too remarkable for its riveting power, and too essential to the appreciation of the author's genius, at once so imaginative and so realistic, to be passed over without some notice. Though not actually written, it virtually took shape in his mind during his imprisonment, which lasted from May 1827 to May 1830. During that period he witnessed the scenes and held the conversations which so deeply impressed him, and it was easy to reproduce them upon his release. The book appeared in 1831, and a second edition was called for before the end of the year. It contributed largely to its immediate purpose of greatly restricting the denunciation of the death penalty, even when merely employed as a threat *in terrorem;* it laid the foundation of the agitation against transportation, to which much of the writer's best energy was subsequently given; and it served his own interests by displaying him in the light of one rising on the stepping-stone of a dead self to higher things, and pressing his own errors and chastisement into the service of the State. *Melius sic poenituisse quam non errasse.* In a literary point of view the book is most powerful; but like all Wakefield's more comprehensive books, it fails of being a complete whole, and rather resembles a series of essays akin in subject and spirit, but which might very well have stood apart.

The frequency of the punishment of death in Wakefield's time was undoubtedly a scandal; Wakefield shows that it was also a danger. Though evidently opposed to its infliction under any circumstances, he abstains from entering into the question, and contents himself with proving that its indiscriminate enactment, rather than execution—for in many instances it was known to be merely an empty threat—fostered corruption in prosecutors, weakness in witnesses, judges and juries, and reckless defiance or by no means unreasonable hopes among criminals, and thus injured society by striking at the root of the deterring influence of punishment, the conviction of its certainty. His remedies are by no means limited to the mitigation of the penal code, but include valuable suggestions not yet sufficiently carried out, the establishment of a public prosecutor, and the organisation of a preventive police. He is particularly earnest on the importance of rooting out the agencies by which youth was systematically decoyed into crime. His description of one of these recalls a study by a contemporary observer no less shrewd and graphic, George Borrow's delineation of the old apple woman on London Bridge. The repulsive subject is not unfrequently illuminated with humour, as in the description of the mock trials got up by criminals among themselves, with parodies of the peculiarities of learned judges and eminent counsel; and the character of thieves as practical philosophers, Epicuruses in their conviction of the omnipotence of chance, Babbages in their acute estimate of its probabilities. The manner in which a man's life might be muddled away is set forth in the story of a military officer named Montgomery, who, although the Bank of England, against which he had offended, was quite willing that the penalty should be mitigated, only escaped the halter by the phial. Wakefield had been kind to him, and the doomed man left a letter behind him which, being read at the inquest, appeared in the newspapers of the day. 'And so even you I dared not confide in—how dreadful have been my fears! how torturing my hopes! The bitterness of reflection, that even my inestimable, most devoted friends, who would have done anything to save my life, I dared not trust with my hopes of death! How little have I been known! But for your note, but for the pressure of your hand, last Saturday evening would have ended the dreadful tragedy. God bless you! May you find such a friend as your heart deserves!'

Another letter, addressed to an unnamed young lady, is not less affecting, and the sentiment they irresistibly excite illustrates the truth of Wakefield's own impressive words:—

'Everyone who comes in contact with a man whose death by the hangman is probable, treats him not as a criminal, but as an unfortunate. In the treatment of other prisoners, even before trial, when they are presumed to be innocent, I never observed anything like commiseration from persons in authority over them. At the best they are treated with neglect, except for their safe custody, and all convicts not capital are treated as criminals. The same men, once capitally convicted, are treated as brothers or children in distress. Why is the capital convict—he whose crime is most grave and is proven—so favourably distinguished? Because the punishment of death shocks every mind to which it is vividly presented, and overturns the most settled notions of right and wrong.'

The most remarkable pages in *The Punishment of Death*, however, are the chapters on the religious observances connected with it, too long and too remotely connected with the main subject of this volume to quote here, but one of the most powerful pieces of writing in the language. What a picture of the wretched quartette in the condemned pew—the bright, prepossessing youth, whose theft, unhappily for him, has been just over instead of just under five pounds; the savage, hardened burglar, a returned convict; the crazy sheepstealer, to be hung in spite of much intercession because many sheep have lately been stolen by others; 'the miserable old man in a tattered suit of black, a clergyman of the Church of England, convicted of forgery'! What traits, pure records from actual observation, but which the imagination of Dante could not have surpassed, as where the Ordinary, perceiving that the youth cannot find the place in his prayer-book, says quite simply, *The Service for the Dead!* 'The youth's hands tremble as they hold the book upside-down.' And so it goes on until, the service over, the condemned return to their cells; 'the forger carried by turnkeys; the youth sobbing aloud convulsively, as a passionate child; the burglar muttering curses and savage expressions of defiance; whilst the poor sheepstealer shakes hands with the turnkeys, whistles merrily, and points upward with madness in his look.' Such writing was more potent to effect the writer's object than his able arguments and unimpeachable statistics, and could have been produced by no one whose destiny had not led him to combine theory with experience. The *Athenæum* well said, 'Out of evil comes good, for to Mr Wakefield's three years' imprisonment in Newgate we are indebted for this judicious, sensible and serviceable publication. Mr

Wakefield has laboured wisely and diligently to atone for the wrongs he committed, and every good man will be content to forget that he ever erred.'

The *Punishment of Death* was indeed a remarkable book, but neither in its literary merit nor the momentous and durable character of its effects could it be compared to the other product of Wakefield's imprisonment, the *Letter from Sydney*. Vigorous as the former was, it still related to matters within the writer's own cognisance; the literary gift displayed was that of a consummate reporter. In the *Letter from Sydney*, Wakefield undertook to describe things not seen, and only known from reading, or from oral information, and to draw lessons from them which had escaped the attention of intelligent observers on the spot. Success as a depicter of the unseen demanded creative imagination, or at least a gift of vivid realisation hardly less exceptional; conclusive reasoning from such premises required a most unusual share of shrewdness and penetration. The problem was the elucidation of the causes which had rendered Australia well nigh useless to the mother country, and these the inmate of Newgate undertook to point out from the other side of the world. The time, however, was in the writer's favour, however vexatiously he might be enthralled by too strict unity of place. The public mind had in a measure wakened up on the subject of the colonies. During the years of war, systematic emigration could not of course be thought of, but the lean kine which had followed in the train of Peace forced statesmen to consider seriously how to provide for a redundant and destitute population. America continued to take the mass of exiles, but men naturally felt indisposed to see our emigrants' blood and sinew entirely absorbed by a foreign country. Emigration to Canada increased; much was really done towards colonising the Cape with Scotch agriculturists; a new colony was actually founded in Western Australia, whose disasters afterwards supplied Wakefield with his most telling arguments. The idea of studying the principles of colonization as the outlet of his energies may well, as has been stated, have been suggested to him by the habit of brooding over maps or calling up pictures of foreign lands as a relief from the actual circumstances of his lot; even more probably, perhaps, by the natural contemplation of the colonies as the best asylum for what must have then seemed broken fortunes and an irretrievably damaged character. The quotations in the *Letter from Sydney*, which appeared in 1829, show that he must have occupied himself for some time with the study of literature relating to the colonies. 'I had occasion,' he says himself in *The Punishment of Death*, 'to read with care every book concerning New South Wales and Van Diemen's Land, as well as long series of newspapers published in those colonies.'

Had Wakefield, however, written under his own name, he could have promised himself no such success as was to attend *The Punishment of Death*. He had qualified as an authority upon prisons; on colonial subjects he could then produce no special credentials. His personality was accordingly suppressed, and the book was cast in an imaginative form. It appeared under the name of Robert Gouger, an actual ex-colonist and writer on colonial subjects (who, after a brief interlude of combat on the July barricades, became colonial secretary in South Australia), and purported to detail in the form of 'a letter from Sydney' the experiences of a settler with a magnificent grant of land, which, owing to the dearth of labour, was hardly of more use to him than a castle in the air. So thoroughly had Wakefield thought himself into the situation and realised the sufferings of his Australian Tantalus, so natural was his composition and so unaffected his style, that no one doubted the genuineness of the letter, which could hardly have been more graphic had it indeed been written upon the spot. Always racy, often eloquent, its argumentative cogency is continually irradiated by flashes of humour which indicate how exuberant under normal circumstances must have been the animal spirits which could thus struggle through the gloom of a prison. The main contention is that the admittedly undeveloped state of the colony is owing to a want of labour, and that this arises from indiscriminate land grants. Enormous tracts had been given away to wealthy colonists, or sometimes stay-at-home landlords, whose means, it was supposed, would enable them to clear them and bring them under cultivation. But capital without labour was even more impotent than labour without capital. You could not hew down a tree with a bank note, or cleave the soil with a sovereign. The sturdy arms which bank notes and sovereigns ought to have set in motion were not to be had, being all too few, and engaged in cultivating the small plots which their owners had obtained on terms equally easy, and which supported families sinking into barbarism. The little cultivated properties and the great uncultivated properties alike remained stationary; want of labour enchained the one, and want of capital the other. There was indeed a resource in the employment of convict labour; but this was more suitable for the execution of public works under Government supervision than for the cultivation of the estates of private men, who had money to be stolen, and throats to be cut; it was, moreover, a mere temporary palliative. 'If,' the imaginary colonist remarks with sarcastic humour, 'for every acre that may be appropriated here, there should be a conviction for felony in England, our prosperity would rest on a solid basis; but, however earnestly we may desire it, we cannot expect that the increase of crime will keep pace with the spread of colonization.' Wakefield's answer to the problem he had stated consisted in the promulgation of the famous theory known as the 'Wakefield System.'

Before entering into any discussion of this much debated subject, it will be desirable to show clearly what the system was by the citation of its leading principles as embodied in the *Outline of a System of Colonization*, annexed to *A Letter from Sydney*, it being premised that some of them were slightly supplemented and modified in the author's more mature *Art of Colonization* (1849).[1]

'It is suggested:—

'I. That a payment in money of — per acre be required for all future grants of land, without exception.

'II. That all land now granted, and to be granted, throughout the colony, be declared liable to a tax of — per cent. upon the actual rent.

'III. That the proceeds of the tax upon rent, and of sales, form an *Emigration Fund*, to be employed in the conveyance of British labourers to the Colony free of cost.

'IV. That those to whom the administration of the fund shall be entrusted be empowered to raise money on that security, as money is raised on the security of parish and county rates in England.

'V. That the supply of labourers be as nearly as possible proportioned to the demand for labour at each settlement; so that capitalists shall never suffer

---

[1] Stuart Mill points out in his *Political Economy* that some of Wakefield's views had been in some measure anticipated in an article in the *Westminster Review* for January 1826, by William Ellis, which it is not likely that Wakefield ever saw.

from an urgent want of labourers, and that labourers shall never want well-paid employment.

'VI. That in the selection of emigrants an absolute preference be given to young persons; and that no excess of males be conveyed to the Colony free of cost.

'VII. That colonists providing a passage for emigrant labourers, being young persons and equal numbers of both sexes, be entitled to a payment in money from the Emigration Fund equal to the actual contract price of a passage for so many labouring persons.

'VIII. That grants be absolute in fee, without any condition whatsoever, and obtainable by deputy.

'IX. That any surplus of the proceeds of the tax upon rent and of sales, over what is required for emigration, be employed in relief of other taxes, and for the general purposes of colonial government.'

Such were the regulations as originally proposed. The following vigorous statement of the evils they were intended to combat, and the benefit they were expected to effect, is taken from Wakefield's remarkable letter to the South Australian Commissioners, June 1835, printed in the appendix to the South Australian Report of 1841 :—

'When each member of a society employs no more capital than his own hands will use, the labour of the whole society is necessarily cut up into separate fractions as numerous as the families ; each family, necessarily, in order to live, cultivates the ground, and does scarcely anything else. As each family is occupied in the same mode of production, there is no motive for exchange between the different families; and as, in such a society, there is no co-operation, so there can be no division of employments; capital and labour are so weak, so unproductive, that surplus produce, either for foreign exchange or for accumulation at home, cannot be raised. This is the primitive or barbarous state of things, under which famine is the necessary consequence of one bad season; it is a state of things which all nations have suffered, and which, during the earlier stages of the world's progress, was in every nation succeeded by a state of slavery. As the goodness of God and the progressive nature of man are unquestionable, and as God has permitted every nation to undergo the state of slavery, so we may be sure that slavery has not been an evil unmixed with good. Slavery appears to have been the step by which nations have emerged out of poverty and barbarism, and moved onwards towards wealth and civilisation. <u>While in any country land was so abundant in proportion to people that everyone could and did obtain a piece for himself, free labour presented no way of escape from that primitive and barbarous condition under which poverty is the lot of all; but along with slavery came combination of labour, division of employments,</u>

surplus produce of different sorts, the power of exchanging, a great increase of capital, all the means, in short, to that better state of things in which slavery becomes an unmixed evil, and when, accordingly, it has been abolished. But what is the conclusion bearing on the present question that we are to draw from this review of one of the steps by which Providence has ordered that nations should advance from barbarism to civilisation? <u>That conclusion is that the only means by which labour may be comibned and employments divided, so as to prevent a state of miserable poverty, are either slavery or the existence of labour for hire.</u>

'The process by which a colony goes to utter ruin, or is reduced to misery, and then gradually recovers, has been witnessed over and over again. The colonists, proceeding from a civilised country, possessing capital, divided into classes, skilful, accustomed to law and order, bent on exertion, and full of high hopes; such a body of people reach their destination, and then what happens? The society which at the moment of its landing consists of two ranks, bearing towards each other the relation of master to servant, becomes instantly a dead level, without ranks, without either servants or masters. Everyone obtains land of his own. From that moment no one can employ more capital than his own hands will use. The greater part, therefore, of the capital which has been taken out necessarily wastes away. In a few months nothing in the shape of capital remains beyond such small stocks as one isolated person can manage. But those of the society who have not been used to labour cannot, with their own hands, manage even that small stock so as to increase or even preserve it; while those who have been accustomed to nothing but labour, and to labour in combination with others, finding themselves each one alone in a vast wilderness, are unable to use with advantage such small stocks as they begin with; and thus both classes (or rather the whole body, for there are now no classes) soon fall into a state of want. In these cases when the colony was preserved by some sort or assistance from without, a state of want has continued until some sort of slavery was established. Such unfortunate results were the necessary results of placing civilised men in a situation where they could not but sink into that state of weakness and poverty which is but one step above the condition of the naked savage. An extensive and uninhabited country is a field where, unless something be done to counteract the influence of too much land, a small body of civilised people must inevitably fall back into what is called a primitive state. Hitherto, in young colonies, the influence of too much land has been counteracted no otherwise than by means of slavery. In this case [of South Australia] slave labour of every sort, whether that of slaves, bondsmen, redemptioners or convicts, is wholly out of the question. What we have to consider, therefore, is the other means by which to preserve civilisation. The history of modern colonization exhibits a great number of expedients, not one of which, I venture to say, ever effected its object. Hence the project of an undertaking of which the object is to try whether, in countries where land is superabundant, free or hired labour may be secured by rendering land dear enough for that purpose. The projectors of the undertaking have concluded that, by putting a certain price upon public land, labourers may be induced to work for wages during a certain term. The South Australian Act excludes all other than this one means of securing hired labour; it is based upon the assumption that no other expedient for that object is likely to succeed, or ought, after so many failures, to be tried again; and that a price may be put upon all public land, which will have constantly the same effect as if land were never superabundant.

'Such are the grounds on which it has been decided to employ, for an object never yet accomplished, means never used before.'

It will be seen that the essence of the plan consisted in directing labour to land, and retaining it there. The system may be compared to a system of irrigation, by which water is guided in artificial channels to the fertilisation of the soil, instead of being allowed to spread indiscriminately over it and ultimately run away. Theoretically, it followed the lines of Adam Smith, who ever insisted on the indispensable alliance of land, labour and capital; practical effect was to be given to this by the observation of two cardinal maxims. Land was to be sold in moderate quantities at a sufficient price, *i.e.*, a price representative of its actual value in its unimproved condition, instead of being given away in enormous grants, as in Western Australia, where it had been distributed at an average of 2000 acres to every man in the colony. In the second place, the amount received by the sale of land was to be expended in bringing out labourers to cultivate it, and the high price set upon it would prevent the poorer emigrants from becoming landowners until they should have accumulated property by labour, in pursuit of which end they must necessarily have done much to develop their employer's estates. As democratic ideas came to prevail in the colonies, Wakefield was attacked as though he had contemplated the creation of a servile caste, and the perpetuation of the social anomalies of the Old World. But he had no such object, or he would never have obtained the support of the great advocate of small landed properties, Stuart Mill; nor has any such consequence followed the adoption of his system where it has been applied. Four years, he thought, would suffice to convert the exported labourer into a small landowner, and when civilisation had once obtained a hold upon the country, additional land sales would provide funds for further importations of emigrants, to be elevated into ownership in their turn.[1] Nor was there more foundation for the idea that sales of land to limited amounts would interfere with pasturage; lands best adapted for pasturage were expressly excluded. 'It is the extreme cheapness, not of natural pasturage, but of land for cultivation, which occasions scarcity of labour for hire. Labourers could not become landowners by using natural pasturage.' It was no doubt the fact that the comparatively high price of land would encourage the settlement of persons of affluence, and thus not only bring a much needed stream of capital into the colony, but tend to impart aristocratic polish and culture to its society, which Wakefield deemed no disadvantage. The sufficient price he always refused to define; it depended upon the peculiar circumstances of the colony, and required the nicest computation. In the early days of the Otago settlement, for example, it was found necessary to stimulate sales by reducing, sorely against the will of the colonists, the price of land from forty to ten shillings to obtain funds for needful public improvements. The gold discoveries made a few years later would have altered the situation. In any

[1] 'Les Portugais des Açores y prospèrent [at Hawaii] admirablement, et sont devenu en grande partie petits propriétaires après avoir travaillé aux plantations des Américains. Leroy-Beaulieu (*Les nouvelles sociétés Anglo-Saxonnes*, ch. 1). Why should an English labourer fare worse than a Portuguese?

case, the price was to be absolutely fixed by responsible authorities, and not determined by the conflict of an auction. Practically it may be said to have averaged a pound an acre, the amount at which it was originally fixed in South Australia, and which was re-established after a trial at twelve shillings. Wakefield would have preferred two pounds.

The soundness or unsoundness of the Wakefield theory will be best discussed after the history of South Australia and New Zealand has afforded us the means of viewing it in actual operation; and also after considering the form finally given to it in its author's *Art of Colonization*. But one quality it had which alone went far to render it a boon to the Empire, it was a scientific theory. 'The subject,' Wakefield forcibly remarks, 'presented before 1830 one very remarkable feature, namely, an immense amount of practice without any theory. There were long experience without a system; immense results without a plan; vast doings, but no principles.' Colonial questions, involving serious problems in statesmanship and political economy, had hitherto been treated in the roughest fashion. For most people the Colonial question was the Convict question, or at most a contribution to the more urgent problem how to rid the mother country of idle and useless incumbrances. In Disraeli's *Popanilla*, a speck upon the sea, originally mistaken for a porpoise, proves to be a rock, and is immediately provided with a governor, a deputy-governor and storekeepers, 'more plentiful than stores,' not to mention clergy, lawyers, engineers, and an agent for the indemnity claims of the aborigines. 'Upon what system,' asks Popanilla, 'does your Government surround a small rock in the middle of the sea with fortifications, and cram it full of clerks, soldiers, lawyers and priests?' 'Well, your Excellency, I believe we call it the colonial system!'

Wakefield's pamphlet was the first great literary blow to this hap-hazard and this pampered officialism, and its exposition of the great opportunities which awaited the colonist with capital, provided only that this capital was placed in a position to command labour, gradually enlisted the sympathies of the most valuable section of the community, those not ill off nor yet so well off as to be indifferent to the prospect of bettering themselves. It came, too, at a most auspicious moment, just on the eve of that development of the means of communication which was to afford such an impulse to emigration and commerce. Ere this had quite arrived, the public mind was fully awake on the subject of colonization, and the man who had chiefly aroused it was Edward Gibbon Wakefield. 'Never,' says Herman Merivale (*Lectures on Colonization*, vol. ii., p. 56), ' was there a more remarkable instance of the success of a principle against all manner of misapprehension, against the fear of innovation, against corrupt interests, against the inert resistance which all novelty is sure to encounter.' Yet it has been recently asserted that 'the proposal took London by storm.' 'Pictures,' it is added, 'of fruitful land, lovely scenery, mineral wealth, and all that could excite the cupidity of small capitalists, were deftly drawn in this publication, and fortunes that were to be made in creative land values were dangled before the eyes of the public in the most seductive literary style.' There is nothing of the sort in the *Letter from Sydney*, beyond the incontestable observation that in Australia 'Nature fully performs her part in bestowing upon man the necessaries, comforts and luxuries of life.'

In the consideration of the Wakefield theory, it must not be forgotten that colonization was at the time much more an affair of the home Government than is now the case. There were no ocean going steamers to bear emigrants swiftly and cheaply across the water, and no free communities on the other side to whose enactments and regulations they could be subjected upon their arrival. There was no possibility of despatching them in any considerable numbers except by the agency of the Government or of a private company, and no authority to prescribe the conditions of settlement except the former of these, or an association to which its authority should have been delegated. No such wholesome principle as that of the numerical equality of the sexes, a valuable feature in the Wakefield plan, could have been realised without such control. It was therefore of the last importance that sound principles of colonization should be impressed upon a Government whose main object in colonizing was the relief of the mother country by the exportation of convicts, a system against which Wakefield always set his face, and which, as will be seen, he did more than any other man to destroy. At the present day emigrants can in general remove themselves to their new country, and the colonies themselves are in a position to stimulate the stream of emigration if necessary. In Wakefield's time the movement had to be guided and fostered, nay, to some extent artificially originated. The almost untrodden regions of Australasia teemed indeed with unsuspected riches, which would in time be a sufficient impulse to emigration, but the first steps needed support, only to be obtained from Government or from the powerful co-operation which it required a Wakefield theory to call into being. Whatever the abstract merits or demerits of his system, it was invaluable as providing a standard and a rallying point for colonial reformers.

One article of the Wakefield faith to which, taught by miscarriages in South Australia, he afterwards attached the highest importance, is not much insisted upon in the *Letter from Sydney* the necessity of an accurate preliminary survey. 'The survey! the survey! the survey!' he reiterates when writing to Godley at Canterbury, and Godley repeats to the colonists, 'Nothing that Mr Wakefield has said upon this point is too strong.'

The *Letter from Sydney*, indeed, was too brief and occasional a production to constitute a systematic exposition of Wakefield's views; this must be sought in *England and America*, and in *The Art of Colonization*, more recent by twenty years. The main idea, however, was there: 'I constantly ask myself whether it be possible to devise any means by which to establish in a new country such a proportion between labour and land as would render labour plentiful and not extravagantly dear.' The whole may be described as a variation on this text. One digressive passage, a little idyll worthy of Goethe, may be cited as establishing once for all the rank which Wakefield might have attained in pure literature if his mind had not been so completely engrossed by the practical side of life :—

'You remember that Genoese girl before whom you trembled, and I became faint, though she only handed us some grapes? Do you remember that, having recovered ourselves, we measured her eyelashes? Do you remember how long they were, and how she laughed? Do you remember that bright laugh, and how I patted her cheek, and told her that it was softer than her country's velvets? And how she blushed—do you remember that?—to the tips of her fingers and the roots of her hair? And then how—do you remember how?—peasant as she was, and but just fifteen, she tossed her head and stamped her little foot with the air of a queen? And then how, on a sudden, her large eyes were filled with tears; and the grace with which she folded her arms across that charming bosom; and the tone—I hear it now—the deep, grave, penetrating tone in which, half angry, half afraid, she at once threatened us with her "Berto," and implored our respect? We did not care much for Mr Berto, certainly, but did we not swear, both together, that not a hair of her head should be hurt? And when, flattered by our involuntary devotion, she departed with a healthy, lively step, showing her small, smooth ankles, and now and then turning her profile to us and laughing as before, did we not, dashing blades as we thought ourselves, snuffle and blow our noses and shake hands without the least motive, like two fools? And afterwards, notwithstanding that gratuitous fit of friendship, did we not feel jealous of each other for three days, though neither of us could hope to see the little angel again? Yes, you remember it all. Well, just such another girl as that brings fruit to my door every morning.'

Wakefield's next book of importance, *England and America* (1833), is an undesigned proof that the advice of the *Athenæum* had been largely taken by the British public, and that the author knew it. It betrays the satisfaction of a man who feels that he has liquidated his accounts with society, and that past errors will not deprive him of the privilege of speaking his mind with the freedom of Figaro, and with a more extensive choice of topics. Like the *Letter from Sydney*, it is anonymous, but the writer's identity can have been no great mystery. It was published by Bentley, whom Wakefield accuses in a subsequent work of having taken advantage of his absence on the Continent to disfigure it with 'a puffing title.' This title certainly misleads; the book does not offer that close and accurate parallel between the two countries which the reader is naturally led to expect; but in truth the entire work somewhat disappoints from its desultoriness; it has not the unity and directness of purpose of its predecessors, but rather offers the miscellaneous reflections of an acute and powerful mind. The first chapter presents a brilliant description of the wealth of England, explained as the result of the combination of labour and capital, and of the minute subdivision of the former. The second chapter is devoted to an equally powerful, and unhappily equally accurate, description of the misery of the lower, and the harassed anxiety of the middle classes, followed by a retrospect of recent political occurrences, and an inquiry into the most likely means of averting the menaced revolution. These are, free trade in corn, the extension of trade with the East, and scientific colonization. The writer argues with great power for the total and immediate, rather than gradual, abolition of the corn laws. This view was held by so many of the scientific political economists of the day that it is very remarkable that their reasoning should have virtually produced no impression until taken up by a body of men little enamoured of abstract truth—the Lancashire manufacturers. The demonstration that the admission of foreign corn must produce a greatly extended demand for British manufactures had been perfect, but remained merely academical until the pocket gave it access to the head. The other side of the question—the danger of exclusive dependence upon foreign countries for the necessaries of life—is no more considered by Wakefield than by the Manchester School. He predicts, indeed, that America would grow grain cheaper than any other country, but the fabulous cheapness of transport by the power of steam could not then be anticipated, nor the consequent injury to British agriculture foreseen. The remarks on the China trade may be read with interest now that the question of opening up China has become of such importance. It is strange that nothing should be said about India; and none could then foresee that the Eastern countries, with their fabulous cheapness of labour, and the material at their doors, would manufacture on their own account, or on the account of foreign capitalists, with an energy and success which may yet convert Manchester to protection.

The most important part of the book, however, is Wakefield's re-statement of his theory of colonization, which he had been unable to exhibit scientifically in the *Letter from Sydney* on account of the lively and dramatic form in which that book is cast. As concerned the interests of the colonies, he had little to do but to set forth the case of the mischief caused by enormous land-holdings and the consequent scarcity and inefficiency of labour from its dispersal over too wide an area; but having now a foot at home as well as abroad, he is able to enter more fully into the case of the mother country, whose requisites in this point of view he sums up under three heads—extension of markets, relief from excessive numbers, enlargement of the field for employing capital—all of them objects which the system or no-system of colonization practised up to his time tended in but the slightest degree to promote. Whether his own theory was sound or unsound, he compelled men to think, and an era dates from him. This luminous chapter, being entitled 'The Art of Colonization,' has been frequently mistaken for the elaborate work on the subject published under the same title sixteen years afterwards, which is dated in many bibliographies 1833.

The style of *England and America* is less finished than that of most of Wakefield's writings, and the chapters wear less the appearance of literary essays than of imperfect reports or of memoranda for speeches. Effective as they are, they would have been more powerful still as oral deliverances. But this could never be. Ample as had been his atonement for the offence he had committed against society, he could not be safely brought forward for any open borough, and the nomination boroughs which might have procured him admission to Parliament disappeared contemporaneously with his entrance upon public life. He did, indeed, offer himself to the electors of Birmingham in 1836, but the appeal met with no response; the party managers were little likely to entrust their cause to one so obviously vulnerable. Could he have entered the Commons, he must sooner or later have fought his way to the Cabinet, and it may have been the bitterest part of his penalty to contemplate the success of inferior men in the career from which he had irrevocably excluded himself. Yet it was best as it was. But for his disaster it is extremely doubtful whether he would have been specially attracted to the colonial department of affairs. As a Member of Parliament he would have been obliged to apply his mind to a variety of subjects, and his energies might have been frittered away among them. Circumstances compelled the concentration of the discursive activities of his mind upon a single subject, and gave him the mission without which he might have gone down to posterity as a useful M.P. and a successful administrator, but not as a builder of Greater Britain. The cause of the colonies was at this time better served by wire-pulling than by oratory. Our colonial heroes were no longer great voyagers and discoverers, nor even great administrators of distant dependencies, but the thinkers who worked out principles of colonization at home, and the organisers who impressed them upon public opinion.

Both these characters were united in Wakefield in a surprising degree. What he was as a thinker we have seen, but his insight into the abstract science of colonization was no greater than his gift of controlling and managing men. No man knew better how to play upon the various human passions, from the loftiest philanthropy down to the most sordid self-seeking, capable of being enlisted in the support of a colonizing venture. None could make himself so readily all things to all men, none could so dexterously guide the inquiries of a Parliamentary committee to the desired point, or attract a patron, or inspire a newspaper. But the greater part of these subterranean activities never came to light, and cannot now be retrieved. Their really gigantic sum can only be inferred from comparatively scanty vestiges—enough, however, to show that the labours of colony-making would have excluded all possibility of attending to other subjects, or even of sharing in the ordinary committee work of the House of Commons.

Before becoming entirely engrossed with colonial subjects, Wakefield produced some pamphlets on social questions at home, only one of which is worthy of especial attention. The title, *Swing Unmasked*, happily conveys no idea to the present generation, who have not seen the systematic burnings of farm produce attributed in the slang of the perpetrators to 'Captain Swing,' and for which bad poor laws, bad corn laws, and the absence of all educational legislation were mainly responsible. It did not need Wakefield's sagacity to discover causes so near the surface, but few could have equalled the vividness of his picture of the prowling serf hugging the tinder-box that makes him terrible, and the ensuing reflections are as just as they are striking :—

'A Swing fire has taken place ; what a commotion ensues in the parish ! Is it credible that the pauper should not view with satisfaction the flurried steps and pale face of the rector, the assumed air of indifference, not half concealing the uneasiness of my lord who owns the soil on which the stacks were burnt, and the violent rage of a neighbouring squire, mixed with nervous indications ? The powerful of his neighbourhood, before whom he used to tremble, now shake in their turn. He is anxiously noticed by well-dressed passers-by, who before treated him as a beast of the field, but now make anxious inquiries after his wants, and take pains to become acquainted with his peasant's nature. What is yet more to the purpose, a new scale of wages becomes the topic of his parish, and is probably adopted, after an understanding between the landlords, clergymen and tenants that rent and tithes shall be reduced in proportion as wages are raised. When his family ask for bread, they receive it, and at noon there is an unusual smell of bacon about the cottage. He has now firing enough to dry his clothes, which, before the stack was burnt, he used to put on of a morning as wet as when he had taken them off at night. Moreover, his rustic vanity is gratified by reading in the county paper a minute account of the deed that he has done. Lastly, when he returns home, thinking of what he has also read in that paper, as coming from the lips of a Parliament man, about "the urgent necessity of some permanent improvement in the condition of the poor," he becomes fonder than usual of his wife, and kinder to his children; and when they ask him why, he is prevented from speaking by what he would call a lump in the throat, but he answers, aside, with one great rude tear of joy. He has burnt a stack, and his heart (it has just been discovered that paupers have hearts), lately so poor and pinched, is now swelling with the strange pleasure of hope.'

Such observations, probably made at his brother-in-law's Suffolk parsonage, were calculated to nourish Wakefield's enthusiasm for colonization. He might well deem it a good deed to place the degraded serf where he might become a man; and if he did not think him fit to become a landed proprietor until he had done something to discharge his obligation to the benefactors who had planted him in a new soil with new hopes and new opportunities, such a view appears in no respect inconsistent with equity, humanity or common sense.

Wakefield was released in May 1830. He had throughout had to congratulate himself upon the loyal support of his family, who continued to recognise him as their natural chief notwithstanding the discredit he had brought upon them. His principal comforter during his captivity, however, appears to have been his cousin, John Head, who upon his liberation took him to his house at Ipswich, where his aged grandmother was verging towards the close of her long and useful life. Her admonitions and benediction, we may be sure, were not wanting to Wakefield, who after no long interval returned to London, to gather around him the more thoughtful of the readers of *A Letter from Sydney*, and to commence his career as a founder by founding the Colonization Society—the little leaven destined to leaven the whole lump.

CHAPTER IV

THE COLONIZATION SOCIETY — THE SWAN RIVER SETTLEMENT—THE FOUNDATION OF SOUTH AUSTRALIA—THE SOUTH AUSTRALIAN COMMISSIONERS —MR G. F. ANGAS—NINA WAKEFIELD — HER DEATH—EARLY STRUGGLES OF THE COLONY— TESTIMONY TO THE WAKEFIELD SYSTEM

THE year 1830, memorable as the date of the overthrow of the Tory party, which, with scarcely an interruption, had governed England for forty-six years, of the Revolution of July in France, and of the outbreak of the struggle between creationist and evolutionary theories which Goethe thought so infinitely more important than the last-named event, also witnessed the inauguration of a reform of the colonial system of the British Empire.[1] 'When,' asked Roebuck with a sneer before the Colonial Lands Committee of 1836, 'when was it that your peculiar doctrines on colonization were first broached?' 'In 1830,' Wakefield replied; and he

---

[1] It should be superfluous to remark that, whenever 'Britain' is mentioned in these pages, Ireland is included as one of the British Islands, the *Britanniæ* of the ancients.

frequently repeats this date in his *Art of Colonization*, and describes himself and his associates as 'the theorists of 1830.' 'When,' he observes, 'Englishmen or Americans have a public object, they meet, appoint a chairman and secretary, pass resolutions and subscribe money ; in other words, they set to work for themselves, instead of waiting to see what their government may do for them. This self-relying course was adopted by a few people in London in 1830, who formed an association which they called the Colonization Society.' The views promulgated in *A Letter from Sydney* had attracted attention, and the author's ability to take an active personal part in their propagation fortunately coincided with an event which demonstrated that, whether or no Wakefield was very right, our colonial administrators were very wrong. 'The ideas of the founders of the Colonization Society of 1830,' he says, 'grew out of the first proceedings of the British Government in settling the Swan River in West Australia.' Prevision of the lamentable failure of this undertaking had, it will be remembered, inspired his first work on colonization. The cause and the nature of the disaster are described in his *England and America*, but were even more graphically narrated *viva voce* to the Colonial Lands Committee of 1836 :—

'That colony, which was founded with a very general hope in this country that it would prove a most prosperous colony, has all but perished. It has not quite perished, but the population is a great deal less than the number of emigrants; it has been a diminishing population since its foundation. The greater part of the capital which was taken out (and that was very large) has disappeared altogether, and a great portion of the labourers taken out (and they were a very considerable number) have emigrated a second time to Van Diemen's Land and New South Wales. The many disasters which befell this colony appear to me to be accounted for at once by the manner in which land was granted. The first grant consisted of 500,000 acres to an individual—Mr Peel. That grant was marked out upon the map in England—500,000 acres were taken round about the port or landing-place. It was quite impossible for Mr Peel to cultivate 500,000 acres, or a hundredth part of the grant; but others were of course necessitated to go beyond his grant in order to take their land, so that the first operation in that colony was to create a great desert. The Governor took another 100,000 acres; another person took 80,000 acres; and the dispersion was so great that at last the settlers did not know where they were; that is, each settler knew where he was, but he could not tell where anyone else was, and therefore he did not know his own position. That was why some people died of hunger, for although there was an ample supply of food at the Governor's house, the settlers did not know where the Governor was, and the Governor did not know where the settlers were. Then, besides the evils resulting from dispersion, there occurred what I consider almost a greater one, the separation of the people and the want of combinable labour. On finding that land could be obtained with the greatest facility, the labourers, taken out under contracts which assured them of very high wages if they would labour a certain time for wages, laughed at their masters. Mr Peel carried out altogether about 300 persons. In six months after his arrival he was obliged to make his own bed, and fetch water for himself and light his own fire. All his labourers had left him. The capital, therefore, which he took out—implements, seeds and stock—immediately perished; without shepherds to take care of the sheep, the sheep wandered and were lost, eaten by the native dogs and killed by the natives and some of the other colonists, very likely his own workmen; his seeds perished on the beach; his wooden houses were there in frame, in pieces, but could not be put together, and were therefore quite useless, and rotted on the beach. This was the case with the capitalists generally. The labourers, obtaining land very readily, and running about to fix upon locations for themselves, very soon separated themselves into isolated families, like the Irish cottiers, but having, instead of a small piece of land, a large extent of land. Everyone was separated, and very soon fell into the greatest distress. Falling into the greatest distress, they returned to their masters, and insisted upon the fulfilment of the agreements upon which they had gone out; but Mr Peel said, "All my capital is gone, you have ruined me by deserting me, by breaking your engagements; and now you insist upon my observing the engagements when you yourselves have deprived me of the means of doing so." They wanted to hang him, and he ran away to a distance, where he secreted himself for a time till they were carried off to Van Diemen's Land, where they obtained food.'

'The kingdom of heaven cometh not with observation.' Who the original members of the Colonization Society were we have not been able to ascertain. Wakefield says that the number of founders did not pass a dozen, and describes them as 'an unknown and feeble body, composed chiefly of very young men, some of whose names, however, have long ceased to be obscure, while others are amongst the most celebrated of our day.' Grote, Molesworth and Stuart Mill were probably among them; the last-named, at all events, says that he became convinced of the substantial soundness of the Wakefield theory from the discussions which he heard about this time. Mill's interests, however, were too numerous and various to allow him to devote his main attention to colonial matters; and more practical service was rendered by one who seldom wrote a line, but in whose journal the reformers entrenched themselves as in a fortress. This was Robert Stephen Rintoul, the clear-headed, practical, and at the same time tenacious and loyal Scotchman who had come from Dundee to edit the *Atlas*, and seceded from it to the *Spectator*. Whether by the fascination of his personal magnetism, or by cogency of reasoning, Wakefield established a complete ascendancy over Rintoul, and, until his departure for New Zealand in 1852, could look upon the *Spectator* as his organ in all matters relating to the colonies. Warm-hearted and grateful as he ever was to friends, he was forward to acknowledge the obligation. 'By far the heaviest of my debts of gratitude is due to the proprietor and editor of the *Spectator* newspaper' (*Art of Colonization*, p. 59). And addressing Rintoul personally in December 1841, he describes him as 'the person to whom I am especially indebted for having been able to propose with effect recent improvements in the art of colonization. You patiently examined my proposals and manfully upheld them when they were treated with disdain or ridicule. For whatever share of credit may be due to me, I am chiefly indebted to you. I should have done nothing at all if you had not constantly helped me, during the years when the pursuit of systematic colonization was a continual struggle with difficulties.'[1]

[1] Rintoul annotates with no less magnanimity : 'With the generosity of most high intellects, Mr Wakefield attributes to the aid of others

Another very distinguished person, who afterwards contributed much to give practical shape to Wakefield's ideas, Colonel Torrens, was not altogether friendly at first. 'But,' he told the Colonial Lands Committee, 'I very soon, in discussing the question with the gentlemen of the Colonization Society, found that they defined their terms or modified their principles so as to obviate the objections raised by Mr Malthus and myself. As soon as I found the system so explained or modified as to permit population and capital to spread freely over the most fertile and best situated lands, my objection was removed and my opposition ceased.' The more I consider, the more entirely I approve. I have a strong and growing conviction that at no distant period the country will have to acknowledge a large debt of gratitude to the author of this plan'—that is, to Wakefield. Wakefield, however, was much more than the author of the plan; he was also its chief executant. 'It would be affectation to pretend,' he says, 'that in the labours of the theorists of 1830 I have had any but the principal share.' The justice of this claim has never been contested. There have been greater thinkers and there have

successes commanded by his own great powers; it was these ever that compelled the aid which he acknowledges. The kind of merit which the *Spectator* seeks not to disclaim, is simply that of not being frightened by the novelty of a scientific proposition; and of having, when examination had assured us of its solidity, held by it until others have become as convinced of its utility and of its practical nature as we are.'

been greater workers, but there have been few in whom the gifts of the thinker and the worker have been so harmoniously combined. Cobden was an unanswerable debater, but a cipher on a committee. George Wilson could neither convince by argument nor move by eloquence, but he was unsurpassed as a political organiser. Wakefield was Cobden and Wilson in one, only marred by the sallies of passion which he could never quite suppress, and the propensity to paradox almost inseparable from a vivid imagination.

The Colonization Society in its first phase appears to have never been influential or numerous; it approached Ministers unsuccessfully and circulated pamphlets not now easy to trace. A controversy with Mr Wilmot Horton and Colonel Torrens, Wakefield says, put an end to it, but it revived in 1837, when it had three hundred members, and traces of its activity are found down to 1844. Long ere this period, Wakefield's principles had passed from the domain of theory into that of practice. The first step had been taken in 1831, when, at the instance of the Society, Government determined to abolish the system of free grants of land in New South Wales, and to exact the price of five shillings per acre, a measure which, although in Wakefield's view very inadequate, nevertheless conceded his principle. The employment of the purchase money as a fund for defraying the cost of transporting emigrants was also recognised. But the promoters could neither be satisfied with the hesitating application here nor with any application of their ideas to a community where transportation was still maintained. They determined to found a new colony.

'At that time,' says Wakefield, 'the country now known by the name of South Australia was a nameless desert about which nothing was known by the public or the Government.' The shore line had been merely coasted, though French adventurers had landed on Kangaroo Island. The interior had been discovered and very slightly explored by Captain Sturt, who in 1829 had followed the River Murray down to its mouth, and ascertained that it was practically inaccessible from the sea owing to the shallowness of the lake into which it debouches. But Sturt had never stood where Adelaide now stands. In the handbook to the colony which Wakefield wrote and published anonymously in 1834, when, by the incorporation of the Company, South Australia had become something more than a mere geographical expression,[1] he can only say, after having adduced all procurable testimony in favour of its capabilities, 'Everyone must be left to draw conclusions for himself as to the fitness of the place for the purposes of colonization.' The boundaries of the 'place,' as traced by Wakefield

---

[1] *The New British Province of South Australia.* Charles Knight, 1835. The author's name nowhere occurs in this handbook, but there are frequent quotations from his writings.

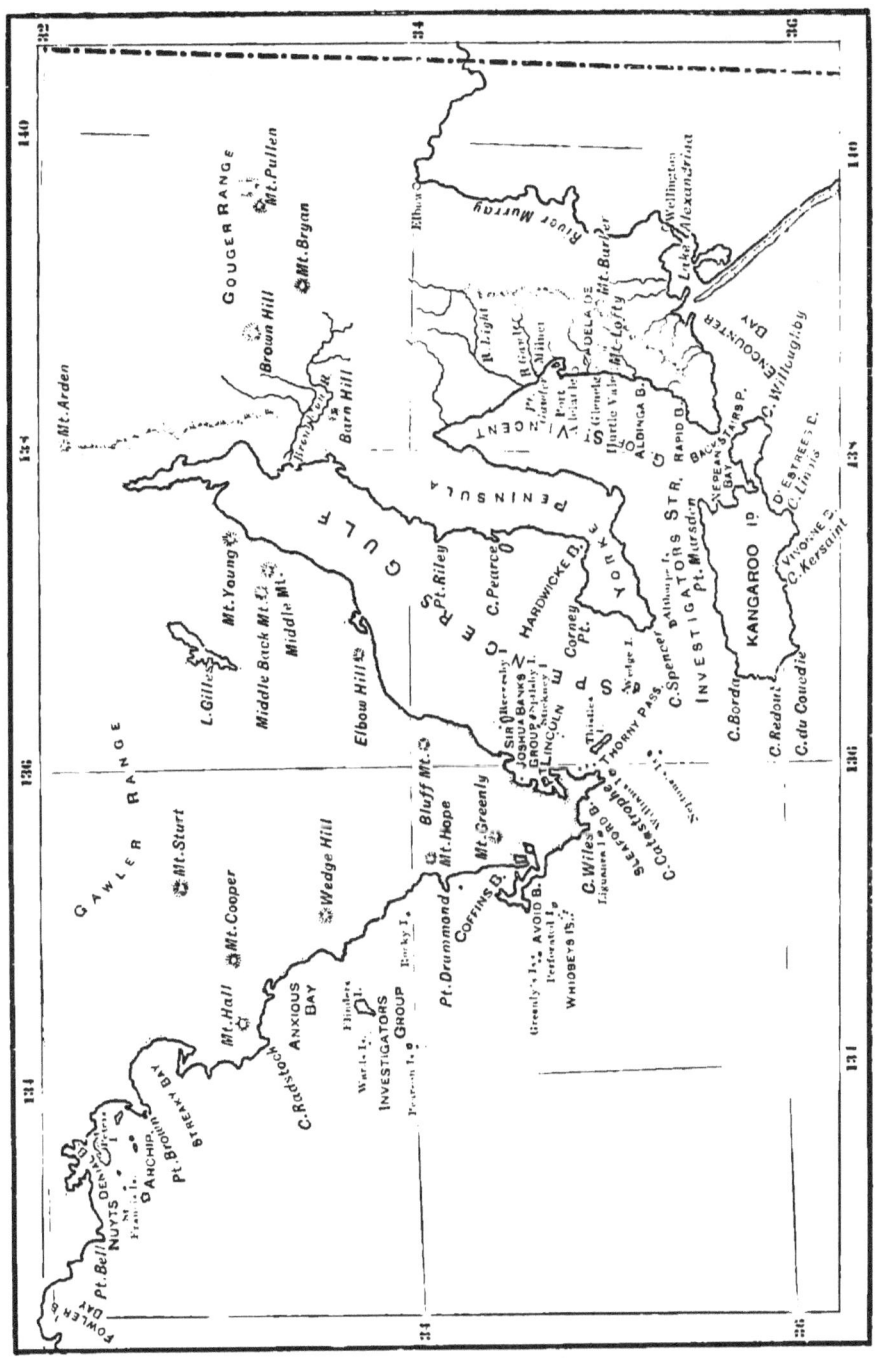

SOUTH AUSTRALIA IN 1837.

and Charles Buller jointly with a pencil upon a map of Australia, and subsequently defined by Act of Parliament, were 'all that part of Australia which lies between the 132nd and the 141st degrees of east longitude, and between the southern ocean and the tropic of Capricorn, together with the islands adjacent thereto'—about a third of the extent of the colony as it exists to-day. It was necessary to keep clear of Port Phillip, now Victoria, then comprehended within the limits of New South Wales. The new colony, it was especially provided, was to be for ever exempt from convicts, and this sufficed to make New South Wales and Van Diemen's Land inimical. The courage of the adventurers will not be duly appreciated without consideration of the risk they ran of total failure in a region so little known, and where it was but common prudence to expect many unforeseen obstacles. Yet Wakefield could argue powerfully from analogy that South Australia must, like New South Wales, be capable of producing oil, wine, silk and tobacco; the exports of meat and fruit which we now see could not be dreamed of in the absence of steam and ice, nor was it surmised that South Australia was a country 'out of whose hills thou mayest dig brass.'[1] But there was the certainty of valuable timber and

[1] The French explorers of Kangaroo Island mention a curious source of profit, the silk of the mussel, or *pinna marina*, which, Wakefield says, is highly valued in Italy for its convertibility into a fine and durable stuff. We do not know whether it has been utilised in Australia.

the promise of coal and slate ; while it was clear that, if the new colony was fit for anything at all, it must be productive of wool. In fact, the prejudice that it might be eminently but solely fit for pasturage required to be combated. The narratives of voyagers were ransacked for facts, but Wakefield was greater still in the application of his theory. His residence in Italy had familiarised him with the practice of irrigation, and he showed that neither the reclamation of morasses nor the clearing away of the heavy timber would be practicable with the dispersion of labour which the no-system of older colonies encouraged, and which his system had been devised to cure. 'If existing colonies had been prosperous and attractive, there might have been no sufficient motive for forming another settlement. The existing colonies are not very prosperous and attractive, only by reason of certain great defects of which the causes may be discovered by any diligent inquirer. The merits of the plan rest upon the errors of other plans, and become obvious only when contrasted with those errors.'[1] Hence Wakefield's South Australian handbook has inevitably a more polemical tone than might have been looked for in an exposition of the advantages of a new colony.

---

[1] Robert Gouger, probably under Wakefield's inspiration, had initiated a colonizing movement in 1829, but the scheme quickly fell to the ground, and Gouger's efforts to revive it proved fruitless until it was taken up by the Colonization Society.

When this handbook was published, the infant colony, though aground for want of money, had surmounted parliamentary and official impediments. The history of its difficulties with the Colonial Office and in the House of Commons has been often told. No one who has had any experience of official ways will wonder at the obstacles raised by the Colonial Office; and it must in fairness be owned that the repression of crude schemes and the probation of sound ones really are important official functions, the efficient discharge of which has saved the British tax-payer many a good penny. To rise to the height of a great occasion, to put aside plausible objections and even overlook serious irregularities, to feel warmly towards an individual or an association which seeks to promote great national objects, and to judge him or it by a higher standard than that of the code or the ledger, require quite a different order of gifts, which, though not absent from the Colonial Office of our own day, would have been vainly sought there in 1831, when the South Australian projectors approached the authorities with what officialism deemed an unseemly buoyancy. They consisted of two classes. The one comprised the theorists of the Colonization Society, including their new and illustrious convert, Colonel Torrens, who looked at the matter partly from a patriotic point of view, as a relief to a struggling country swamped with pauperism, partly from a scientific standpoint, as a beautiful experiment in economics.

The other was composed of capitalists and men of business, partly actuated by the hope of profit, but to a very great extent, and especially in the case of Mr George Fife Angas, the most prominent among them, by philanthropic motives, including antipathy to convictism and State churches. The first division had already approached the then Colonial Secretary (probably Sir George Murray) on the subject of systematic emigration. 'He told us that the Government rather wished to discourage emigration. When requested to observe that the scheme was not one of emigration, but of colonization, which itself would deal with the emigration, his reply showed that he had not conceived the distinction, nor ever paid any attention to any part of the subject.' But the hopes thus dashed had been revived by the action of Sir George Murray's successor, Viscount Goderich, who, at the instigation, as was thought, of the Under Secretary, Lord Howick, had given partial effect to Wakefield's ideas by stopping gratuitous grants of land in New South Wales, a step highly to the honour of these statesmen, and a remarkable instance of a reform accomplished without popular pressure. 'The colonies,' says Wakefield, 'if they had been consulted, would have earnestly objected to this resolution, as they afterwards protested against it; the colonial governments, and the members of the Colonial Office as a body, greatly disliked it, because it went to deprive them of patronage and power; the very few persons who at the time desired this change were obscure and feeble, and yet all of a sudden, without inquiry by Parliament or the Executive government, without a word of notice to those most concerned, and without observation from anybody, out came an Imperial decree, by which, in the principal colonies of England, the plan of selling waste lands was completely substituted for that of free grants.' The second great principle of the Wakefield system, the employment of the proceeds of the land sales in bringing out emigrants, was also adopted, and the promoters of the South Australian project felt sanguine ; but soon discovered that though their ideas might find favour, they themselves were objects of jealousy and suspicion. This was in some measure their own fault. Colonel Torrens and Wakefield, the authors of the draft of the charter for which, after an abortive attempt to start colonization in 1831 on the strength of a supposed verbal sanction, promptly disavowed by Lord Howick, application was made in 1832, wanted to regulate everything, from the boundaries of the colony to the prospective enrolment of a militia. This latitude of plan gave scope for innumerable objections on the part of the Colonial Secretary, the general drift of which may be condensed into one, 'that it was proposed to erect within the British monarchy a government purely republican.' When the plan was modified in deference to these objections, the unpropitiated Secretary retorted that, ' As the Committee were so ready to abandon essential

G

portions of their scheme, he had serious misgivings as to the maturity of their knowledge and counsel.' 'The error,' Mr Hodder justly observes, 'was in asking too much and then too little, the result being that they got nothing.' Yet the idea which lay at the root of their error was sound. 'We attached,' says Wakefield, 'the highest importance to the subject of government, believing that the best economical arrangements could not work well without provisions for a good political government for the colonists.' Here is the germ of the famous Durham Report, and of the struggle for responsible government which occupied Wakefield's last active years. 'As,' he continues, 'we could not move an inch without the sanction of the Office, we now resolved to abandon the political part of our scheme, in the hope of being able to realise the economical part.' So baseless is the assertion of late gravely made, that '*naturally enough*, the scheme was hailed with rapture by Government'!

In 1833, *England and America* was published, with an appendix containing some of the correspondence which had passed between the projectors and the Government. 'The publication,' says Wakefield, 'enabled us to get together another body of colonists, most of those who had previously wished to emigrate to Australia having gone to America.' The siege of the Colonial Office was resumed, but with little effect until 1834, when a powerful company was formed under the title of the South Australian Association, with Mr Whitmore, M.P., for chairman, and including among the directorate such names as Buller, Grote, Molesworth, Torrens, Warburton and H. G. Ward. Wakefield pulled every string, but his connection with the company was not ostensible. His name was never mentioned—and at the period it would have been inexpedient to have mentioned it —at the large and influential meeting held at Exeter Hall on 30th June (reported in the appendix to his book on South Australia), though all the speakers, except Robert Owen and other dubious allies, merely reiterated the ideas he had instilled into them. By this time a change had taken place at the Colonial Office, and the new Minister, Mr Spring Rice, afterwards Lord Monteagle, a former schoolfellow of Wakefield's at Westminster, was not unfriendly. On condition of the promoters giving up their ambition to be a chartered company, and consenting that their settlement should be established as a Crown Colony, he promised neutrality, though not active support. Not more than fifty members could be induced to vote upon the bill of the Association when, on 25th July 1834, the second reading was carried by thirty-three to seventeen. Four days afterwards a formidable opponent appeared in the representative of the great house of Baring, who thought that the promoters might have *sixty or a hundred square miles* to operate upon 'somewhere,' but objected to trust them any further. Spring Rice, stung into animation, answered warmly, and the bill triumphed by seventy-two to seven. It is marvellous how so novel and important a measure could have escaped further discussion in the Committee stage, which must have wrecked it at so late a period of the session. It was, in fact, read a third time on 2d August. Probably its opponents had calculated upon dealing it a fatal blow in the Lords, where its prospects were indeed most gloomy. 'Opposition,' says Wakefield, 'threatened to prove fatal, because, though it was confined to a few peers, not a single one except the proposer of the bill' [the Marquis of Normanby] 'had any active good will towards our measure. The Ministers, however bound by their colleague's promise of neutrality, would give no assistance in either House, and for a time the loss of the bill in the House of Lords seemed inevitable. In this extremity one of us' [Wakefield himself, with assistance from Mr R. D. Hanson and Matthew Davenport Hill] 'thought of endeavouring to interest the Duke of Wellington in our favour. He assiduously examined our plan, came to the opinion that "the experiment ought to be tried," and then, with a straightforward earnestness that belongs to his nature, and with a prompt facility for which his great personal influence accounts, lifted our poor measure over all obstacles. In order to mark our gratitude to him, we intended, and told him so, that the metropolis of the new colony should bear his name, but this intention was shabbily frustrated by some whom I abstain from mentioning.'[1]

Thus the famous soldier, who won no territories for his country by his sword except in the East Indies, added to her by his parliamentary influence a domain then of 300,000 square miles, now of 900,000. Nothing was then certainly known of its capabilities, except that the banks of a great river seemed promising for settlement. Now, although vast tracts in the interior must remain for ever barren, and the northern portion is only fit for Coolie labour, the mere fringe along the southern coast has two millions and a half acres under cultivation; there are six millions and a half of sheep, exporting forty-seven millions of pounds of wool; and nearly fifty million pounds worth of gold, silver and copper have been raised since the settlement of the colony. There are 350,000 inhabitants, raising two millions and a half of revenue, and annually exporting products to the value of eight millions. There are nearly 2000 miles of railway, and half a million has been spent in bridging the whole Australian continent with a telegraph wire. When the railway shall have followed the telegraph, its northern and southern termini (the latter possibly Port Lincoln, on account of its splendid harbour) will become the two great *entrepôts* of the Australian waters.

[1] 'They' (the Commissioners) 'sought profit by pleasing the King rather than honour by paying an honest debt.'—*New Zealand Gazette*, 28th November 1840. Hence the courtly appellation, Adelaide.

The great problems now before the colony seem to be to effect this junction, and to fill the northern regions with permanent Chinese or Indian settlers who will not seek to return to their own land. Much prejudice will have to be surmounted first, but prejudice cannot for ever obstruct the development of the colony, any more than it could its foundation.

The act under which South Australia was constituted will be found in the appendix to Wakefield's handbook to the colony. It embodied his two chief articles of faith — the sale of land at a fixed price, which in this instance was not to be less than twelve shillings an acre, and might be more (Wakefield thought it ought to be a good deal more), and the application of the proceeds to an immigration fund. The introduction of convicts was entirely forbidden, and self-government was secured for the colony as soon as the population should amount to 50,000. It was a great blot in Wakefield's eyes that no provision was made for popular control over local expenditure in the interim; and in other respects the act as originally proposed was grievously mutilated, while Wakefield was still less satisfied with the machinery appointed to carry it out. 'The South Australian Act confided the business of colonization apart from Government to a commission, the members of which were to be appointed by the Crown—that is, by the Colonial Office. The commissioners were not to be paid. It was a grand point, therefore, to find three or four persons, masters of the theory, willing to undertake the task, and likely from their personal character to perform it under a strong sense of honourable responsibility. Such persons were found, but were not appointed.' It may be plausibly and not quite untruthfully suggested that Wakefield would have liked the commission to have been composed of his friends and disciples, whom he could guide at his will, instead of the new set that excluded him, and *hinc illæ lacrimæ*. The innuendo of Mr Angas's biographer that Wakefield turned his attention to New Zealand from having failed in his efforts to obtain a foremost place in colonizing South Australia, is supported by a remark of Wakefield's own. But on the other hand, the ten commissioners, with the exception of Torrens, Angas and Hutt, with their able secretary, Rowland Hill, seem to have been what Wakefield called them—amateurs; and Mr Angas was driven, by his impatience at their slowness in procuring the requisite funds, to establish a supplementary company to buy land at the temporarily reduced price of twelve shillings an acre, with the prospect of reselling it for twenty. The introduction of a speculative element was much to be deplored, but it at all events floated the commissioners into deep—into very deep—waters. It necessitated Angas's resignation of his seat on the commission. At this time (September 1835) Wakefield had been effectually ostracised, an experience destined to be repeated in the case of the New Zealand Company twelve years afterwards. The remarkable letter he wrote to the commissioners of 2d June 1835, from which a long extract has been made, reveals wide divergences of opinion, especially on the question of a sufficient price for land. Meanwhile, the colony had at least been set going, and, under Angas's direction, a ship, admitted by Wakefield himself to have served as a model for all subsequent enterprises of the kind, sailed in February 1836. A landing was effected in July, and the colony was formally constituted in December of the same year.

Not only was the colony of South Australia the visible incarnation of Wakefield's idea, but its establishment had cost him an enormous amount of literary and other labour.

'The plan,' he tells the South Australian Commissioners in 1835, 'has been defended in so large a number of pamphlets and books that a list of them would surprise you.' Now, all those books were written by me or by friends of mine; while I also composed nearly the whole of the advertisements, resolutions, prospectuses and proposals, and of the applications, memorials, letters and replies to the Government, and other documents of any importance adopted by those three associations' [the Colonization

---

* Besides the one already mentioned, two of the most important were, *Plan of a Company to be established for the purpose of founding a Colony in South Australia*, 1831. *South Australia. Outline of the Plan of a Proposed Colony*, 1834.

Society and the South Australian Companies of 1831 and 1834]. 'The draft of a charter submitted to the South Australian Association, and the Act of Parliament which was substituted for that proposed charter, were drawn by a near relative of mine' [his brother Daniel] 'under my immediate superintendence. As I was concerned in the formation of those three societies, so with each of them I held constant communication, partly by means of frequent interviews with some leading members of their committees, partly by almost daily conversation or correspondence with some person or other who represented my opinions, informed me of whatever was done or proposed, conveyed suggestions which I wished to make, and resisted, with arguments agreed on beforehand, all sorts of endeavours to alter the plan of colonization which I had formed. By entering more into detail I could readily satisfy you that in the steps which led to the passing of the South Australian Act I have had even a more constant and active participation than appears by this general statement.'

Tantæ molis erat Romanam condere gentem! Can there after this be any doubt as to the identity of the founder of South Australia? The services of Mr George Fife Angas were such as to justify much enthusiasm on the part of a biographer, but the limits of truth and soberness are preposterously exceeded when he is styled on the title-page of the record of his life 'father and founder of South Australia.' To be the father of anything one must have begotten it ; and a founder must at least have laid the first stone. For anything that appears in Mr Hodder's biography, Mr Angas took little interest in South Australia until the receipt, on 31st March 1832, of the prospectus of the South Australian Land Company, drafted by Wakefield. In fact, his biographer does him injustice, for his name appears on the committee of 1831. He does not reappear upon the committee of the association of 1834, and, although appointed one of the commissioners under the Act, beyond lending his advocacy to principles which Wakefield had enunciated years before, he does not seem to have taken any prominent part until, in the autumn of 1835, and consequently a year after the passing of the Act, the threatened stagnation of the enterprise for want of the circulating medium led him to pledge his credit to the association he established to provide the lacking funds. A spirited act, but the act of a founder not of a colony, but of a company. Curtius highly distinguished himself by plunging into the gulf, but he did not thereby become Romulus. Happily, in a work where he may be supposed to have written with greater freedom,[1] Mr Hodder, recognising, like the Yorkshireman who got credit for killing the bear, that 'mother helped a bit,' calls up three other founders to share the honours formerly monopolised by Mr

---

[1] *History of South Australia*, vol. 1, p. 46. The date of Mr Hodder's biography of Angas is 1891, that of his History 1893.

Angas ;—Wakefield, Gouger and Colonel Torrens. Gouger, according to Mr John Stephens, a contemporary authority, had worked with indefatigable perseverance to launch the colony ; and Torrens, the first ostensible head of the undertaking, and long chairman of the commissioners, was fully entitled to claim, as he did, the honour of having 'planted' it. His name should not have been excluded from the just—except as it ignores Wakefield's superhuman activity as scribe and wirepuller—estimate of the respective services of Wakefield and Angas in Garran's *Australian Atlas*. 'Two names are conspicuous above all others in the history of the early settlement. They are those of Edward Gibbon Wakefield and George Fife Angas. To the former belongs the honour of devising a new method of successful colonization, and to the latter that of being chiefly instrumental in bringing it to the test of actual experiment. Mr Wakefield was a political economist and a reformer in the best sense of the term, and Mr Angas a colonist of exactly the right stamp.'

How Wakefield's circle looked upon South Australian affairs is vividly shown by the most lovable and after him the most interesting of its members. His affection and tender care for his child had not been unrequited. It was his brief and frail happiness to possess one of the greatest blessings granted to man, a charming, gifted and devoted daughter who saw everything through his eyes, entered with enthusiasm into his every project, and to whom her father's colony was at the time incomparably the most interesting spot on the face of the earth. She was in her seventeenth year, ardent, animated, impressionable, and endowed with the elevation of sentiment and precocity of intelligence which at so early an age often indicate that the root of life has not struck deep. In August 1834 Nina Wakefield writes to her aunt, Catherine Torlesse, wife of the Vicar of Stoke-by-Nayland, Suffolk, Wakefield's favourite sister, a striking beauty and a woman of most solid worth :—[1]

'In common with papa and Dodo' [Daniel], 'my mind has been so completely engrossed for the last six months with the old subject of a new colony that I have never been able to think of anything besides. You remember how hot we were about it when we last enjoyed the pleasure of seeing you (which is now two years and a half ago), and you must have heard how, shortly afterwards, our sanguine hopes of success were upset by His Majesty's Government, to the great damage of our loyalty. Well, then, you can easily imagine our joy, mingled with eagerness and anxiety, when, after another trial and another failure, the plan has at last met with the approbation of the new Colonial Minister, has been made law by the Parliament, and is certain of being carried into effect immediately. In the spring of 1832 I wrote you a

---

[1] I shall hardly find anybody whose example I should so much wish her to follow as yours,' he had written in 1822.

letter telling you that the colonists were soon coming to the practical part of their scheme, and expressing the warmest wish of us all emigrating to Spencer's Gulph. I was wrong in thinking the termination of our toil was at hand; we had to go through two more years of tedious expectation, harassing procrastination, uphill labours and chilling disappointments, the very thoughts of which make me feel sick; but at length we have triumphed over all our open and hidden foes, we are within an ace of the goal, nothing but a miracle can wrest the prize from us, and again, I hope more truly, I say the colonists are at the practical part of their work. In the meantime I have not changed my mind as to emigration; I still wish very much to go out, especially if you were going, and even more than when I saw you. I have to tell you, as I suppose you have no means of knowing it before, that Dodo expects to obtain the appointment of judge-in-chief in South Australia,[1] in which case he turns colonist immediately. William also, who, now peace is restored in Portugal, has got nothing to do, and finds it a hard matter indeed to get paid for his former services, talks of leaving the Queen's [Donna Maria's] service; in which case, as Felix is already there, and Howard is sure to join them from

---

[1] Daniel did not come to judgment until twenty years afterwards, when he was appointed a judge in New Zealand. He had previously been Attorney-General of Wellington and the Middle Island under Sir George Grey, but resigned in consequence of his brother's opposition to the Governor's policy.

India presently, there will be a nice party of our family at our antipodes. The more I think of it, the more I wish that Uncle Charles would give up his poor living and turn South Australian with you and all yours, including dear Priscilla; for then I think papa might be persuaded to go too, and then what a nice party we should make!—flying from straitened means and anxiety for your children in future, to plenty, large profits for yourself, and easy, happy prospects for all your family! Have you read papa's *England and America*, the third chapter especially? If not, get it, read that part carefully, and then reflect on the happy opening formed by a new colony for a man of small fortune and large family. Then get a little book called *South Australia*, compiled and edited by papa. In it you will find full information on every point connected with the colony, and all I pray is that it may make some impression upon you. Tell Uncle Charles from me to read the chapter in the little book called "Inducements to Emigration." I wish I were at Stoke, for I am sure I could persuade him, and then if I succeeded we should have nearly the whole family of us joined together in South Australia; for I take it for granted that if you went papa would go too, with both his chickens.'

Girlish as this epistle is, it expresses the feelings then rife in many an English middle-class circle for which the mother country's bosom had become too dry, and her arms too narrow. Writing a month afterwards under less restraint, Nina thus pours out her feelings to her friend Rosabel Attwood,[1] in a strain that proves her indeed her father's daughter. In truth, there is nothing in the *Letter from Sydney* to rival this vivid realisation of scenes beheld only by the gaze of imagination through the glass of description.

'HARE HATCH,'[2] 4*th Sept.* 1834.

'MY DEAR ROSABEL,— ... When we took leave of you ten days ago, I was afraid that we should not meet again for many months, but I hear there is a possibility of your family all turning South Australians at once, in which case, as I am trying hard to persuade my father to the same thing, and feel pretty sure of success, we may calculate on the chance of meeting again very soon, and probably of going all in one party. If so (of which, as I am naturally sanguine, I feel certain already), we shall have a second set of happy days on shipboard and in South Australia. If "Victoria" is built on the shores of Port Lincoln, we can have regattas in the large harbour and donkey excursions to Sleaford Mere on the Louth Hills, and if Lake Alexandrina be fixed upon as the site of the new

[1] Daughter of Thomas Attwood, M.P., founder of the Birmingham Political Union, whose daughter Angela married Edward Gibbon Wakefield's brother Daniel. His life has been written in a privately printed volume by his grandson, Charles Marcus Wakefield.

[2] Near Reading, the seat of Edward Gibbon's uncle Daniel, who was engaged at the time on Mr Attwood's side in the celebrated case of *Small* v. *Attwood*, which he gained.

city, the large lake itself and the beautiful glens and valleys of the promontory of Cape Jones seem made on purpose for our parties of pleasure. But that which above all would please you, who are of an imaginative turn of mind, is an exploring expedition into the interior of the country. I have heard you talk of the pleasure of stepping on a shore on which no one had been before yourself, but unfortunately for that idea, there have been so many navigators, sealers, runaway convicts, etc., on that coast that you cannot feel sure of treading an unbeaten track, and the only way of standing where white man never stood before is to be one of the exploring party which will be sent, immediately after the landing of the people, up the country to discover and survey it. The explorers travel through forests, across rivers, and over vast plains, which have never been seen before; making maps and taking sketches as they go along; amused at every mile with some new feature in the country they pass through, and every now and then enlivened by petty accidents or the jokes of the excited young people of the party. An exploring expedition is like a donkey excursion on a large scale, but you have the extra satisfaction of knowing that you run the risk of some little danger, and that you are enjoying a pleasure which cannot be enjoyed by anybody in England. Think of standing on a high hill and looking for leagues in every direction without seeing

EDWARD GIBBON WAKEFIELD

a human being, or any animal except a few quiet kangaroos and emus, and hearing no noise but the rustling of the trees and the bubbling water of the little cascade at the foot of the hill, or the bustle of your party pitching their tents for the night on the hillside, and preparing for supper a fat Wallabee kangaroo which one of the sportsmen of the party shot that morning as they were traversing some beautiful grass plains. To pursue this picture. Having looked on till the sun has set, and the moon (aided by a set of stars totally different to those to which you have been accustomed in this hemisphere) has risen to light you to bed, you hear a voice from the tent, "Supper is ready." You run back, having had your appetite sharpened by a long ride on a rough-haired pony, or perhaps a gallop after a long-legged emu, and the whole party sit down on the grass under the tent, and, making their laps serve as tables, make an excellent supper on the haunch of poor Wallabee. After supper someone asks you for a song; you give one in your best style, making your shrill voice echo through the adjoining forests, and frightening the poor variegated parrots who have gone to roost in the trees there. In token of the gratitude of the party for your condescension, the captain of the expedition proposes that the hill on which you are going to pass the night be called after you; all present instantly assent; a glass of wine is poured on the grass at the entrance of the tent, the party rise and give three hearty cheers, and the captain proclaims that henceforth the hill shall be called Mount Rosabel. We mark it so on the map; a short speech of thanks from you succeeds, and then all go to rest, undisturbed by the howling of the native dogs, who are kept off by the fear of your firearms, and sleep till you hear the captain's bugle next morning, when you jump up, breakfast, strike your tents and set off again, and so on till after a few weeks' absence you return to headquarters with all your zoological, botanical, geological and topographical discoveries. How do you like this idea of an exploring party?

'As for our occupations and amusements on board ship, they will be manifold, and as neither you nor I mean to be sea-sick, we shall make ourselves very comfortable. But I hope that you will make up your minds quickly to going out, for remember it is not safe or pleasant to leave England between the 20th of October and the beginning of January, so that, as I am almost sure of going with papa in October, we shall not have the pleasure of forming one party on the voyage unless you make very great haste in your preparations, which, by-the-bye, are different in their magnitude when you are going to the other side of the world to when you are taking a trip to a watering-place. But I hope and trust that you will be ready by the 20th of October, and we will all sail together, singing merrily, "The deep, deep sea!" I have been thinking that, as your eldest brother is a poet and you are a musician, you ought to consult with him on writing a national song for us South Australians, and setting it to some popular and spirited tune. Let the first verse be the invocation of "the future sons of Australia" to their mother to raise a future empire on the shores whither the blue waves of the Southern Ocean are bearing them along; then go on to describe, in the following verses, the landing of the colonists, the occupations to which they betake themselves, and the gradual rising of the city on the waste and barren coast, bringing in descriptions of the excitement and ambition of the settlers, and ending each verse with a spirited chorus on the model of "The Parisienne." Let the tune be grand, but simple and marked, so that every South Australian may easily learn it and sing it both on the voyage and on shore; for we must practise a great deal of music, as it keeps the people in good humour; so we will have concerts and private theatricals on board ship, balls and musical festivals on land, but no raffles or wheels of fortune.

'I have written you a long rambling letter, for which I should apologise, but that I know that the soberest spirits are apt to run wild on the exciting subject of the new colony, and moreover, that you also are much interested in the same subject. I have not written you any directions concerning Beau, as I had at first intended, in consequence of the length of this epistle, but I hope that you will not allow him to neglect his exercise, as he is a lazy fellow, and will take every advantage of your indulgence. Pray give my best love to your mother and sister, remember me kindly to your father and brother; give Beau two pats on the back and a kiss on the nose from me; present my best respects to Dash and the parrot; and give my kind regards to Miss Cecilia Clock.'

Alas! poor Nina was to take a longer journey. This letter, so full of brilliant youthful spirits, is dated 4th September. On 18th October, two days before the day on which she had pictured herself as embarking, her distracted father writes to Mrs Attwood :—

'Though I do not like to leave Rosabel's letter unanswered, I cannot write to her. She is too young to be told of my wretched feelings, and I cannot hide them. Besides, my dear Nina talks of her very often with a strong affection, which you will see is natural when I tell you that she was never intimate with any other girl at all near her own age; and thus I am unmanned only by thinking of her.

'My dear child is declared to have a mortal complaint of the lungs. Two or three months is all the time that I can expect to keep her in England; but a vague hope is held out to me that a warm climate may save her. Of course I am on the point of removing her; but of giving her even that poor chance I am not sure, so great is her weakness, and rapid the sinking of all her bodily powers. She is reduced to a skeleton, but is patient, cheerful, rational and fearless. Heartbroken myself, I am obliged to laugh and play with her as when she was quite well. You will see why I cannot write to Rosabel, and will excuse me for indulging, while writing to you, in these expressions of grief. It is a sort of comfort to me to imagine that you will feel with as well as for me. Yet what right have I to give you the pain of sympathising with me? None, nor can I tell why I inform you of my misery, unless it be that my only present consolation is the number of people who have shed tears at the thought of never seeing my darling again.

'I have but just left her at the seaside, and am hurrying to make arrangements for our departure—to what distance must depend on her state. If Mr Attwood be with you, pray give my kind regards to him, as well as to your children. Accept yourself my grateful thanks for your kind attentions to my poor child, believing me to remain very truly and faithfully yours, E. G. WAKEFIELD.'

They went to Lisbon. The following letter, which must have been written from that city, bears the London postmark of 3d February :—

'MY DEAR MRS ATTWOOD,—Yesterday my dear child, becoming aware of her danger, wished to write to several friends by dictating to me. A letter to her brother so much exhausted her that she could proceed no further, but she desired me to write in her name to those whom she could not but neglect, and amongst them to Rosabel. It is only to keep my promise to her that I send this scrawl, so that I may tell her when she wakes that I have done what she desired. She is sinking fast. All hope has been at an end for some weeks.'[1]

Nina died at Lisbon on 12th February 1835. On 14th April, Wakefield wrote to his sister :—

'More than once of late I have tried in vain to write to you, and I should not have got courage to do so now if I had not promised to convey to you the kindest expressions of regard which were uttered by dear Nina on the very last day of her life. It was only then that she became entirely conscious of her situation. She desired me to give you a lock of her hair, and to tell you that in her last moments she thought of you with the tenderest affection. Indeed, the prospect of dying seemed to strengthen the strong love which she bore to all whom she loved at all. She forgot nobody of those for whom she had ever felt a regard. Of you she spoke frequently, and made for

---

[1] 'I love her so much that I am sure almost that I shall be deprived of her,' he had written in Nina's infancy.

you with her poor starved hands a little packet of her hair, which I shall send to you when I am able to open the box that contains it. I have nothing more to say. As you did not know her when she was no longer a child, when she had become my friend and partner in every thought and object of interest, you cannot sympathise with me, you cannot estimate my loss. The vulgar notion of death has no terrors for me; but I feel half dead myself, having lost her for whom alone of late years I have lived. The world seems a blank. But probably, as usually happens in such cases, I shall find other objects of interest. To make a beginning, I intend that henceforth Edward shall live with me.'

A living memorial of his daughter accompanied Wakefield from Lisbon, a little Portuguese girl, whose playfulness had cheered the sufferer's last days, and whom he begged from her parents. He educated her and sent her out to New Zealand, where she married well.

This domestic tragedy, and the absence from England which it necessitated, doubtless weakened Wakefield's hold upon South Australian affairs, and perhaps accounts in some measure for the suppression of his friends and himself in their management. At the time he must have felt the slight bitterly, but it proved a most fortunate circumstance, allowing him to devote his attention to a new enterprise in New Zealand, where, as will be seen, his interposition was urgently necessary, not merely to introduce improved methods of colonization, but to preserve this Southern Britain for the English race. It was also most fortunate that he thus escaped responsibility for the initial difficulties and failures of South Australian colonization, which would have been attributed to him if he had taken any active part in it. Indeed, those were not wanting who charged them upon the Wakefield system, but the groundlessness of the accusation is apparent, not only from the unanimous testimony of South Australian historians, one personal adversary excepted, but from the proceedings of the Parliamentary Committee which sifted the matter in 1841. It is sufficiently plain that, on the other hand, the disasters arose from neglect of Wakefield's principles. The land surveys proceeded so slowly that the colonists could not get upon the soil; concentrated about Adelaide, they consumed without producing all the necessaries of life, sold at fabulous prices; and famine might have supervened but for the unexpected and welcome discovery that cattle could be driven a thousand miles through the bush from New South Wales. When the colonists got to work, South Australia immediately became a wheat exporting colony; and a further impulse was given by the public works undertaken by the new Governor, Colonel Gawler. Unfortunately Gawler's zeal far outran his means; the bills he drew on London were dishonoured, and general bankruptcy seemed to impend. The temporary revival, moreover, had generated a reckless land speculation, the character of which may be appreciated from the single circumstance that Mr Angas's agent drew upon him for £28,000, expended in buying an estate without any authority.¹ The very magnitude of the trouble saved the colony by compelling the Home Government to come to its assistance by advancing funds, and abolishing the unsatisfactory system of government by commissioners. Captain (afterwards Sir George) Grey, already renowned as an Australian explorer, was sent out to govern, and by harsh but salutary retrenchments, including a nobly self-sacrificing reduction of his own salary, kept the colony afloat until the discovery of the Kapunda and Burra Burra copper mines brought it the capital needed for a career of prosperity.

These incidents, it is manifest, had nothing to do with the Wakefield system, which obtained the most unqualified approval of the Parliamentary Committee,²

¹ Mr Angas was nearly ruined, but rode out the storm. The estate ultimately justified the anticipations of the sanguine purchaser, and Angas died upon it at an advanced age in wealth and honour.

² The proceedings of this Committee were reviewed in the *Edinburgh Review* for April 1842 by James Spedding, and, he being called away to the United States as private secretary to Lord Ashburton, the article was revised by Henry Taylor. Jeffrey says, in writing upon it to Napier the editor: 'To one who looks, as I do, to those regions as the destined seat of another and a greater Britain, from which the whole Eastern world is hereafter to be ruled in freedom and happiness, no subject can possibly be more interesting and important.' It is interesting to meet this anticipation of the title of Sir Charles Dilke's famous book twenty-six years before the publication of the latter. Sir Charles, however, did not derive it from Jeffrey, whose letter was not published until 1879.

and has given perfect satisfaction in the colony itself. After quoting a disparaging passage from Mr Samuel Sidney, author of a cheap colonial handbook published in 1852, Mr Anthony Foster remarks : 'That sentiments such as these might have been written by some prejudiced or splenetic historian in 1840, when South Australia was suffering from difficulties incident to the settlement of a new country, might easily be imagined ; but that they could be written at a period when the success of the principles upon which the colony was originally founded was apparent to everybody, is somewhat astonishing. There has never been, in South Australia, any doubt as to the wisdom of appropriating a large proportion of the proceeds received for the sale of waste lands to the importation of immigrants.'[1] Mr J. P. Stow, in his account of South Australia written for the Calcutta Exhibition of 1883 by direction of the South Australian Government, observes : ' For the first two or three years delays in the survey of the country lands, official mismanagement, the unwise policy which induced the settlers to remain in Adelaide instead of going into the wilderness to attend to the rich soil, only waiting for the plough to make it yield bounteous harvests, prevented the Wakefield system from having fair play ; but when there came a wise administration of public affairs, all that was propounded as the natural result

[1] *South Australia, its Progress and Prosperity.* By Anthony Foster, 1866, pp. 12, 13.

of the system came to pass.' Mr Stow adds, indeed, the important qualification, 'It worked well till the colony outgrew it.' We have already remarked on the enormous change created by the cheapening and acceleration of communication, which has superseded much that was admirable and necessary in 1834. Great rushes to a colony, moreover, such as those occasioned by gold discoveries, inevitably mar one of the most valuable features of the Wakefield system, the equal representation, by a judicious selection of immigrants, of all classes of the mother country, from the highest to the lowest.[1] But if it was rather for an age than for all time in its practical operation, the system preserves an undying importance in history as the first attempt since the days of the Greeks at organised colonization on scientific principles, and as the agent by which vast tracts were reclaimed from the mere squatter, the beachcomber, the convict, the savage, and devoted to the enterprise and capital of the mother country as fields for the employment of her wealth and outlets for the relief of her poverty.

In 1873 Lieutenant-Colonel Palmer, one of the original South Australian Commissioners, observing that by the extension of the colony across the Continent the name of South Australia had become

[1] South Australia, a Wakefield colony which has escaped inundation by rushes of adventurers, 'was,' says Mr Walker (*Australasian Democracy*, p. 33), 'fortunate in her original settlers, and has always attracted a good class of emigrants.' Cause and effect. Yet she has the most democratic constitution of any colony.

inappropriate, and that it possessed no memorial of its founder except the name of a harbour, memorialised the Colonial Secretary to alter its appellation to Central Australia, and to erect a monument to Edward Gibbon Wakefield. Two admirable proposals, which at the time, but not for ever, failed of their effect.

CHAPTER V

PROJECT FOR COLONIZATION OF NEW ZEALAND—CONDITION OF THE ISLANDS IN 1837—THE NEW ZEALAND ASSOCIATION—THE CHURCH MISSIONARY SOCIETY—LORD DURHAM—LORD HOWICK—THE NEW ZEALAND COMPANY—OBSTRUCTION FROM THE GOVERNMENT—FIRST EXPEDITION

'WHEN they persecute you in one city, flee to another.' The salutary ingratitude of the South Australian Commissioners had prevented Wakefield from wasting his energies upon an undertaking at the time presenting no adequate outlet for them, and urged him to a new enterprise which he might hope not only to shape but to control. So late as December 1835, indeed, he had not renounced all idea of active participation in the South Australian project. He tells his sister Catherine that the first ship is to sail next month, and adds: 'I have half a mind to go myself for a year to tell the tale of the beginnings.' But that ship sailed without him, and if he had any intention of following in another, this must have been diverted by the highly important Parliamentary inquiry into Colonial Lands, under the chairmanship of Mr (afterwards Sir) Henry George Ward, probably set on foot at his instigation, but before which, at all events, he was the most important witness. Its report, to which we shall have to recur, was a great victory for his ideas; at present we have only to cite <u>a passage from his evidence,</u> showing distinctly in what direction his thoughts were tending. In the course of an eloquent exposition of suitable fields for emigration, including the elevated interior of Ceylon, and what we now call British Columbia, he says :—

'<u>Very near to Australia there is a country which all testimony concurs in describing as the fittest country in the world for colonization; as the most beautiful country, with the finest climate and the most productive soil,</u> I mean New Zealand. It will be said that New Zealand does not belong to the British Crown, and that is true, but Englishmen are beginning to colonize New Zealand. New Zealand is coming under the dominion of the British Crown. Adventurers go from New South Wales and Van Diemen's Land, and make a treaty with a native chief, a tripartite[1] treaty, the poor chief

---

[1] So printed, but Wakefield must have said *triplicate*. He was evidently thinking of the remarkable deed, executed in triplicate, by which, on 6th June 1835, Mr John Batman conceived himself to have acquired, in consideration of certain blankets, knives, tomahawks, etc., the entire site of the future city of Melbourne from the chiefs Jagajaga, Cooloolock, Bungarie, Yanyan, Moowip and Mommarmalar, whose marks and seals are duly appended, and who must be supposed to have declared in the Australian language, 'I deliver this as my act and deed.' One of the

not understanding a single word about it; but they make a contract upon parchment, with a great seal: for a few trinkets and a little gunpowder they obtain land. After a time, after some persons have settled, the Government begins to receive hints that there is a regular settlement of English people formed in such a place; and then the Government at home generally has been actuated by a wish to appoint a governor, and says, "This spot belongs to England, we will send out a governor." The act of sending out a governor, according to British constitution, or law, or practice, constitutes the place to which a governor is sent a British province. We are, I think, going to colonize New Zealand, though we be doing so in a most slovenly, and scrambling, and disgraceful manner.'

This evidence was given in June 1836. The step from denouncing the actual irregular colonization of New Zealand as slovenly to proposing an orderly and systematic method was so short, that Wakefield must have taken it in his own mind ere he had left the committee room. The effect of his words upon others was equally immediate. 'In consequence of that statement,' he told the New Zealand Committee of 1840, 'a member of the committee' (Mr F. Baring) 'spoke to me upon the subject, and afterwards other persons, and we determined to form an association.'

three copies is exhibited in the Manuscript Room of the British Museum —the nearest modern representative of the bull's hide wherewith Dido encompassed the site of Carthage.

To enlist influential support and organise the means of carrying the project out would evidently be a work of time, and it is not until May 1837 that we obtain unequivocal evidence of its being actually on foot. On 12th May Wakefield writes from his then residence in Hans Place, Chelsea, to his brother-in-law, the Rev. Charles Torlesse :—

'I have set on foot a new measure of colonization on the principles which have worked so well for South Australia. The country is New Zealand—one of the finest countries in the world, if not the finest, for British settlement. A New Zealand Association is now in course of formation; it will comprise a more influential body than that which founded South Australia. The colony, that is, the body of capitalists who will first emigrate, is already considerable, and comprises persons qualified for every occupation but one. WE HAVE NO CLERGYMAN.' After dwelling on the grievousness of this deficiency, and exhorting Mr Torlesse to ferret out a suitable ecclesiastic, not 'unequally yoked'—'He must be a superior man, and if he have a wife she must be superior too'—Wakefield continues : 'Captain Arthur' [the third brother, born in 1799, and in Place's opinion 'the flower of the flock'[1]] 'thinks

---

[1] Arthur Wakefield, his nephew Jerningham says, 'first went to sea at ten years of age, with a pay of £20 a year, and never afterwards occasioned his family the expense of a shilling. He never owed anybody a farthing, and yet always seemed to have money in his pocket for a generous purpose.'

of commanding the first expedition, and my own thoughts are turned in that direction. For me, all will depend upon the manner in which the foundation shall be laid : if it be very good, superior to any other thing of the sort, then I become one of the builders of the superstructure.'

On the same day Arthur Wakefield, a lieutenant in the navy, who, after serving twenty-five years with high credit in various parts of the world, had just seen sixteen other lieutenants put over his head, writes from his brother's house to Catherine Torlesse :—

'You will recollect that I mentioned to you at Stoke that Edward had his eyes upon New Zealand. I am so far interested about it that I fancy I see an opening for useful and active employment. I have made up my mind to go, if not previously employed. I have been reading a great deal on the subject, and am delighted with the accounts of the country. I think anybody you could enlist with the qualifications stated by Edward would receive very powerful aid in the furtherance of his objects, although they would probably be advanced more from philanthropic motives than religious ones. The influence is great which will be brought to bear in establishing the settlement, and I fancy it may become a very grand undertaking.'

Arthur was right. The possibilities of New Zealand were unlimited, but it was a seed-field in great danger from its weeds. It will be convenient to take a brief survey of its actual condition when the New Zealand Association came to the rescue.

Colonization in New Zealand had one advantage over colonization in South Australia, that the capabilities of the country were well attested. None doubted or could doubt that the sombre, fern-covered land of silent evergreen forests, snowy peaks and boiling springs, inconspicuous for the floral growth of the soil, but brilliant with creepers and flowering trees, fulfilling in its strangeness and its charm the ideal of an antipodal country, was in the main fertile, pleasant and well-watered. Discovered by the Dutch in 1642, and afterwards more thoroughly examined by Cook, distance and the dread of its stalwart cannibal population had kept it from European intrusion until the settlement of New South Wales, when sealers and whalers began to frequent it, and by commercial intercourse paved the way for a drift of the worst and best elements of Australasian society; convicts and missionaries. The native population, according to their own tradition, arrived from the north-east, probably Tahiti, about the beginning of the fifteenth century,[1] and in the nineteenth was declining in numbers so seriously

---

[1] That they have been long separated from the other Polynesian tribes appears from the fact that although the *kawa* plant grows in New Zealand, and is called by the same name as elsewhere, they had not learned to use it as a stimulant. It may, perhaps, be conjectured that *kawa* (which literally means *bitter*) is cognate with the Arabic *kahwin*, *wine*, probably in some other Semitic form the origin of οἶνος and *vinum*, and undoubtedly of our *coffee*.

that, in the words of Mr Busby, the Resident, 'the population is but a remnant of what it was in the memory of some European residents. All the apparent causes in operation,' he adds, 'are quite inadequate to account for the rapid disappearance of the people.' Everything invited the advent of a more vigorous race. Already, in 1825, a company had been formed with the support of Mr Huskisson, President of the Board of Trade, to colonize a large land-purchase near Hokianga, on the coast opposite to the Bay of Islands, perhaps the sanest speculation of that crazy year. The land, though legitimately acquired, remained unused, the leader of the expedition being intimidated by what he took for a war-dance of the natives, which others interpreted as a welcome. In 1829, the Duke of Wellington received a deputation on the subject, but he who was virtually to add South Australia to the empire then thought that 'we had enough colonies.' The issue thus lay between the company which Wakefield had so nearly brought to maturity in May 1837, and the *vis inertiæ* of the British Government.

A mass of information respecting the condition of New Zealand when the New Zealand Association commenced its operations is to be found in the report of the House of Lords Committee, 1838, presided over by the Earl of Devon. Much of it is ably digested in Surgeon-Major Thomson's instructive and entertaining *Story of New Zealand* (1859). The Committee, contrary to the wish of their chairman, made no recommendation on the subject of the extension of British authority over the country, holding this to be a matter of public policy to be decided by the Government, but the evidence they collected spoke sufficiently for itself. Population, as already stated, was on the decline. The European element, settled and afloat, consisted of seven classes, only one of which could be considered an entirely satisfactory contingent—'beachcombers,' now familiar to the English reader in the pages of Stevenson and Louis Becke; runaway convicts; traders; whalers; sawers of kauri timber; 'Pakeha Maoris,' or tame whites maintained by the native chiefs, frequently loose characters, but pioneers of civilization in many ways; and missionaries. It had to be owned with shame that evil had in general followed in the track of the white man. Where, as was frequently the case, a fine harbour was rendered useless by a bar, and whites accordingly came but sparingly, things were far more satisfactory than at the magnificent haven of the Bay of Islands, where ships could work in and out with any wind. There a town had sprung up named Kororareka, which in 1838 contained a floating European population of a thousand persons, with 'a church, five hotels, numberless grog-shops, a theatre, several billiard tables, skittle-alleys, "finishes" and hells.' There was a British resident, 'a man-of-war without guns,' solely dependent upon his moral influence, and no other restraining force except the missionaries; although the Committee had scarcely ceased its sittings when this very community of Kororareka, finding itself in danger of dissolution, established a Vigilance Committee, made a sea-chest with gimlet holes do duty for a gaol, and arrayed minor malefactors in what Sydney Smith called 'the plumeo-picean robe of American democracy.' One point of much importance, not sufficiently attended to, came out in the course of the investigation. The natives could not flee from these demoralising influences, for they were a nation of fishermen. They could not, like the inhabitants of other parts of the world, subsist by hunting, for there was nothing to hunt except rats. They had not generally learned to cultivate useful vegetables, and but for fish would have had little to live upon but fern roots, a diet which produced the same effects upon them as Mr Perceval, according to Peter Plymley, expected the prohibition of the export of prunes and senna to produce upon Napoleon's grenadiers. Hence they were confined to the coast line, exposed to contamination from the lowest class of Europeans, who must continue what they were until some government should be established capable of encouraging the advent of decent people. Meanwhile, the cultivable lands in the interior remained waste, and the greater part of the Middle Island was almost uninhabited. Several courses lay before the Government. They might take the country over themselves as a Crown Colony; they might grant the New

Zealand Association a charter, like the East India Company; they might recognise the independence of the native chiefs and govern them through the missionaries; or they might wait until France annexed the islands, or the Vigilance Committee at Kororareka declared them an independent republic. This last course, the last which they could have wished to take, was the one to which their vacillation would have conducted but for the daring and determination of Edward Gibbon Wakefield.

Nervous shrinking from responsibility, and a disposition to let things drift until difficulties have become dangers, are common faults of the official mind in all departments of State, and, until counteracted by the recent development of Imperial sentiment, were especially characteristic of the Colonial Office. To this must be added that the then Colonial Secretary, Lord Glenelg, was probably the weakest man who had ever held the post. He thought that the jealousy of foreign powers might be excited by the extension of British colonies; that England had colonies enough; that they were expensive to govern and manage, and not of sufficient value to be worth developing. Other influences, moreover, weighed with him and his far stronger Secretary, Sir James Stephen, by no means improper or discreditable in themselves, but to which they allowed undue weight. Both were fervent Evangelicals, and actually officials of the Church Missionary

Society, of whose interests, as a consequence, they were exceedingly tender. Both were philanthropists, and, with very good reason, greatly dreaded the contact of Europeans with the natives. It was not in human nature that the missionaries should omit to take full advantage of the official bent of mind to protect what they had learned to regard as their special preserves in New Zealand. From their own point of view they had a strong case. They and they only had laboured to benefit the people. They had now been upwards of twenty years in the country, where they had originally gone at the risk of their lives, and the position they held in the esteem of the natives was entirely owing to their virtues and their beneficence. They had taught useful arts, introduced useful products, combated native diseases, too often derived from Europeans, with European medicines, laid the foundation of education, reduced the native speech to writing, translated the Scriptures into it, done much to abolish cannibalism and other barbarous practices, and made their own dwellings object-lessons of the beauty and advantage of a well-ordered home. Darwin writes on 30th December 1835: 'New Zealand is not a pleasant place. I look back to but one bright spot, and that is Waimate, with its Christian inhabitants.' At the same time they were open to criticism for having done so little to improve the domestic arrangements of the natives, and Captain Fitzroy could not but remark that they showed a comparative neglect of their white congregations. Doubtless they followed 'the line of least resistance,' and the fact explains their extreme repugnance to an extensive immigration of European settlers, who, even if moral and religious, might have little affection for a theocratic regime. The missionaries also had very good reason to fear that white colonists would soon get into land disputes with the natives, and that the latter when exasperated would make no nice distinctions between laymen and ecclesiastics of the obnoxious hue. The opposition, therefore, which found expression in the pamphlets (dated November 1837), one public, the other private and confidential, of Mr Dandeson Coates, lay secretary to the Church Missionary Society, was by no means unnatural, but must, nevertheless, be condemned as unpatriotic, ill-considered and short-sighted. It was unpatriotic, because it contested the sovereignty of Great Britain over a region of so much importance to her. It was ill-considered, because it failed to suggest any other remedy for admitted evils than the multiplication of consular agents as helpless as the existing Resident, and the stationing of a small coastguard ship off the coast to awe delinquents on dry land. It was doubly short-sighted, inasmuch as, by denying Great Britain's right of sovereignty, it denied her jurisdiction over any of her subjects domiciled in the country who might choose to set up a republic little likely to be conducted agreeably to missionary principles; and because it left the door open for French annexation, a real peril to which the missionaries themselves awoke shortly afterwards. They certainly had a case in the deplorable results which had so frequently attended the contact between Europeans and aborigines; but they ought to have seen that this contact was inevitable, and that the mischief could best be counteracted by a cordial understanding with the Association, whose interest in the well-being of the islands was not less than theirs; the pity was that while one party wanted none but the best class of settlers, the other wanted none at all. Mr Coates frankly told the deputation from the Association which sought to conciliate him that 'though he had no doubt of their respectability and the purity of their motives, he was opposed to the colonization of New Zealand in any shape, and was determined to thwart them by all the means in his power,' and 'exclude colonization,' or some equivalent phrase, continually occurs in his pamphlets. It may be guessed that other motives concurred which could not well be avowed. Mr Coates was obliged to acknowledge before the Committee that one effect of annexing New Zealand would be to open it to the evangelising efforts of the Propagation Society, whose charter restricted its operations to British possessions. No objection could decently be made to the introduction of another Christianising and civilising agency, but the Church Missionary officials were hardly likely to welcome a rival society with enthusiasm.

That the New Zealand Association might well have gone hand in hand with any religious society appears from the most important evidence given on its behalf before the Lords' Committee. The soul of the company and its official head were absent with Wakefield and Durham in Canada, and it was chiefly represented by Dr Samuel Hinds, chaplain to Archbishop Whately, and afterwards Bishop of Norwich ('almost the most agreeable and sensible man I have met,' says Arthur Wakefield in a letter to Catherine Torlesse), and by Dr G. S. Evans, a barrister versed in international law, not more of a Vattel than of a Stentor. Dr Hinds gave a luminous statement of the circumstances under which a civilised state is justified in extending its authority over barbarous countries, dwelt on the humane intentions of the Association towards the natives, and thus put the case against the Church Missionary Society from its own point of view: 'A missionary station will spread Christianity immediately about; but when you come to contemplate the civilisation of a whole country you must look for a stronger and more effective measure. What the savage wants is to have before his eyes the example of a civilised and Christian community.' Mr Dandeson Coates's panacea, on the other hand, was the recognition of Maori New Zealand as an independent power. He pointed out that the chiefs and heads of tribes in the Northern Island, probably under the influence of the British agent, had already, on 28th October 1835, declared themselves a nation under the title of 'the united tribes,' but he did not say, perhaps did not know, that this ridiculous farce had been denounced by the Governor of New South Wales as 'silly and unauthorised.' He could not deny that the missionaries themselves had petitioned for protection, to meet which necessity he recommended that the natives should be induced to adopt a code of laws, and that this New Zealand jurisprudence should be administered by a visiting judge from the Supreme Court at Sydney. Dr Evans, for the Association, easily showed that no respectable person could settle in the colony under such a system, unless he went with an armed party of squatters, without authority from the Crown. Still the Government deferred taking action, and it cannot be doubted that they were at heart hostile to all colonization. This jealous and unsympathetic attitude was the cause of all the early misfortunes of the colony, and of everything questionable in the proceedings of the Association itself. If the Government could have found it in its heart to have treated the Association as Elizabeth treated the East India Company, the difficult path to the existing prosperity of the colony would have been in comparison brief and easy.

Apart from the testimony of these principal witnesses, the entire report of evidence has permanent historical value. It throws great light on the tribal customs and the difficulties connected with the transfer of land; upon the resources of the country, not then adequately appreciated; upon the simultaneous and corresponsive development of the organs of benevolence and of acquisitiveness among the missionaries. Mr Flatt, a discarded catechist, revealed that many of them had become great landholders and stockholders: 'What meaneth this bleating of the sheep in mine ears? and the lowing of the oxen which I hear?' The most remarkable witness was a native named Nayti, who had been living some time in Wakefield's house, where he passed for a prince, but who on his return to his country was proved to be a man of low birth. His imposture, however, probably did not impair his trustworthiness as to the manners and customs of his countrymen. The last question asked him is: 'How many children will a New Zealand woman have before she kills any?' To which he replies: 'Some seven and some eight; then they begin.'

The endeavour to present a view of the condition of New Zealand at the commencement of regular British colonisation has carried us some time past the formation of the original New Zealand Association, which met for the first time at 20 Adam Street, Adelphi, on 22d May 1837, a day exactly midway between Carlyle's first lecture, 1st May, and Cooke and Wheatstone's first patent for the electric telegraph. Its origination and initial proceedings are thus described by Wakefield in his evidence before the Parliamentary Committee of 1840 :—

'We met and formed a society. The first principle which we laid down was that the society should be rather of a public than of a private character ; and that at all events no member of it should have any pecuniary interest in the object in view. The only object of the society was to bring the subject before the public and Parliament, and not to take any part as individuals in what might be the result. After putting forth to the public a printed pamphlet in which was published a statement of the objects of the society, the next step which they took was to get together a number of persons who wished to go out to New Zealand and settle there. Those persons formed themselves in a body, which may be properly called an intending colony. They were a body of people who separated themselves from society here, and formed themselves into a distinct society for the purpose of establishing themselves in New Zealand, provided the Association should succeed in its public object. As soon as this body was formed, which comprised a number of persons of some station, of good education and considerable property, the association made its first communication to the Government.'

' We must distinguish, therefore, between the Association formed for the purpose of promoting colonization, but whose members, united for a public object, were in this capacity entirely disinterested persons, and the body of actual settlers constituted under its auspices. The plan [1] proposed to the Government contemplated the annexation of New Zealand and the entrusting of its administration for ten years to a council elected by the founders, which should have full authority, subject to disallowance by the Colonial Secretary and by Parliament, to whom its proceedings must be reported.

The Association was indeed an influential body; its first chairman, Mr Francis Baring, was of worldwide fame as a banker and merchant prince; many of the directors were of the same type; others were theoretical colonial reformers like Buller, Hutt and Molesworth. A name more calculated to impress the popular imagination was then in the background. Lord Durham returned from his St Petersburg embassy on 24th June, and forthwith joined the direction. The biography of this remarkable man is in the able hands of Mr Stuart J. Reid; it will suffice for us to briefly describe him as an example of the patrician democrat whom the juxtaposition of caste and freedom have made more frequent in England than elsewhere, but of whom Alfieri is perhaps the standard type, an enthusiast for the rights of humanity in the abstract, disdainful of humanity

---

[1] The draft of the scheme will be found in the appendix to the report of the Committee of 1840, p. 163.

as impersonated in individuals, too impatient of the mass of men to make a satisfactory colleague, and, though falling short of the intellectual superiority that would have made a great leader, in every thought and action magnanimous, disinterested and sincere. He was the only statesman of the day outside of Wakefield's immediate circle who had arrived at a conception of the Imperial character of the colonies, and differed even from these in so far that, while they mainly thought of colonization as a remedy for the ills of the State, Durham took it up rather on the positive side, and dreamed and more than dreamed of reviving the glories of Elizabeth. 'Through every page of his famous Report,' says Mr Egerton, in his recent interesting volume on *British Colonial Policy*, 'there breathes a passion of Imperial patriotism, strange enough at the time.' The date of Wakefield's first acquaintance with Durham is uncertain. Had he known him in 1834 he would probably have succeeded in interesting him in the South Australian project; and as in 1835 and 1836 Durham was mostly absent on his Russian embassy, it seems not improbable that Wakefield may have visited him at St Petersburg, a conjecture slightly supported by Wakefield's possession of Russian silver utensils given him by Durham. In any case, Durham's directorship in the abortive New Zealand Company of 1825, and consequent claims to landed property in the islands, marked him out as a fit director of the new

Association; while his position as leader of the more advanced section of the Liberal party, to which almost all Wakefield's political friends belonged, and his prospect of the Premiership should this prevail, must have seemed more powerful recommendations still. But a serious drawback to his usefulness existed, for which he himself was in no way responsible.

Wakefield and his friends had a great horror of the Colonial Office, which they looked upon as a demesne of the Church Missionary Society. In endeavouring to avoid Scylla they ran into Charybdis. They addressed themselves to Lord Melbourne, the Prime Minister. Save for an honourable sense of public duty on especial occasions, Lord Melbourne was a second edition of Charles II., with more sense, discernment and shrewdness than anybody about him, and less inclination than anybody to fatigue himself with dry details. He received the representatives of the Association graciously, and turned them over to Lord Howick, afterwards Earl Grey, then Secretary at War. But for Lord Durham's connection with the Association this might have been a judicious step. Lord Howick was a very remarkable person, a true statesman and excellent administrator, whose weight of character and fearless candour made him at a patriarchal age a valuable counsellor on public affairs long after his retirement from active political life. But he had the worst temper of any statesman of his age except Roebuck, was in some measure estranged from Lord

Durham, who was his brother-in-law, and, in Wakefield's opinion, was embittered against Wakefield himself, by old misunderstandings concerning the South Australian scheme, aggravated at a later period by Lord Durham's rejection on Wakefield's advice of a plan of Howick's for the administration of Canada.[1] Wakefield's statements on this point (*Art of Colonization*, pp. 27, 28) having never been admitted or contradicted by Earl Grey, remain *ex parte*, and Grey always denied that he had given the Association reason to expect his aid. That he did become hostile is as certain as it is lamentable. An alliance between him and Wakefield would have done more for the colonial empire of Britain than any other of the many excellent things that might have been. If Wakefield could effect so much by the aid of opponents or dubious supporters of the Ministry, what might he not have achieved with the support of a Minister like Howick, who could have had *carte blanche*, the Church Missionary Society and its acolytes in Downing Street notwithstanding? Unfortunately Howick, though a most able man, was not, like Wakefield, a man of original ideas. Wakefield wrote truly of him: 'With more than a common talent for understanding principles, he has no origin-

---

[1] Wakefield writes to Lord Durham in February 1839: 'Though one should think it was just over, the time is now come for your receiving all sorts of suggestions as to the best mode of settling affairs in Canada. Every man who has a scheme will hope to persuade you to adopt a bit of it. But Lord Howick would substitute a whole plan of his own for the whole of your plan.'

ality of thought—which compels him to take all his ideas from somebody; and no power of working out theory in practice—which compels him to be always in somebody's hands as respects decision and action.' Wakefield, parentally affected towards the ideas which he had himself evolved, welcomed as an angel from heaven anybody who would help to translate them into facts. Howick, uninspired and critical, was unable to put aside the dislikes and prejudices which beset him from the first, or to see that much ought to be forgiven to the faulty persons or faulty companies by which such conceptions were to be realised. Thus he lost the fame he might have had as a builder of the Empire, and ranks only among its eminent administrators.

Durham's support, nevertheless, for a time helped the Association much in the same way as Howick's might have done. The Government, fearful of his heading an ultra-Liberal secession, was disposed to humour him in a matter so comparatively unimportant as the foundation of a colony. Before his return from Russia, a draft of the proposed bill had been submitted to Lord Howick, who took objections and proposed amendments, all of which, Wakefield declares, whether approved or not, were accepted to conciliate his support. The death of the King on 20th June, and the consequent dissolution, deferred further negotiations until the winter; but the Association was not idle, and in October a little treatise called *The British Colonization of New Zealand*, partly written and partly compiled by Wakefield, was issued from its office in Adelphi Terrace Chambers. The larger portion of the book is devoted to a description of the islands, but it has also a valuable account of the system of government proposed by the Association, a sketch of the method to be followed in the application of the Wakefield system of land sale, and an appendix (by the Rev. Montague Hawtrey) on the principles to be observed in intercourse with the natives, which Wakefield justly terms 'beautiful.' Another chapter, written by Dr Hinds, holds out hopes of the appointment of a bishop, which, to say nothing of the attendant spiritual advantages, 'will obviously increase the respectability of the colony.' No religion and no respectability, however, could conciliate the missionary party. Mr Dandeson Coates attacked the Association and its scheme in the two pamphlets already referred to, to which Wakefield replied in another (dated 12th December), pointing out that colonization of a very undesirable sort was proceeding already, and that Mr Coates virtually proposed a scheme of colonization himself.

Mr Coates's influence with Lord Glenelg appeared to be paramount when, on 9th December 1837, a deputation from the Association was again received by Lord Melbourne, and this time Lord Glenelg was present. 'Lord Melbourne, who appeared to have forgotten what had passed on the former occasion, referred to Lord Glenelg. Lord Glenelg, without any reference to what had passed before, stated, partly from memory and partly by reading from a paper, a number of objections, which, if they had been valid, would be quite fatal to the scheme. He objected to it on almost every possible ground. It appeared then to the members of the Association that they had been rather hardly treated in being allowed to proceed as they had done in encouraging the public to prepare a colony for emigration to New Zealand. One of them was described to Lord Melbourne as having taken steps with a view to emigration, and as being likely to suffer very seriously from now finding himself not able to carry his plan into effect. Lord Melbourne, not knowing that he was present, said that he must be mad. The gentleman got up and said that he was the madman. All this excited a good 'deal of feeling.' Within a week, however, a complete change seemed to have come over the mind of the Government. Lord Glenelg received another deputation at the Colonial Office, to which he declared that the Government would grant the Association a charter of incorporation on condition of its transforming itself into a joint-stock company. To this the directors, who had made it the very foundation of their scheme that they should have no pecuniary interest in it, declined to agree.

The objection was doubtless sincere, yet it can be no breach of charity to conjecture that even stronger objections may have been thought to apply to other propositions of Lord Glenelg's conveyed in a letter to Lord Durham, dated 29th December. The first portion of this letter, by admitting, on the strength of despatches stated to have been just received, the absolute necessity of establishing British authority in New Zealand, threw the case of the Church Missionary Society overboard, but it went on to restrict the Association's area of occupation, to reserve the right of incorporating new companies, and to prohibit purchases of land from the natives without the assent of a Government Commissioner—a reasonable proposal if the Government and the Association worked hand in hand and agreed on first principles, but which might otherwise nullify its power to make any investments. An able reply signed by Durham, but evidently drafted by Wakefield, was returned next day; and after further correspondence between the two peers, which Wakefield says was too confidential to be made public, the Association determined to introduce a bill to carry out its objects on their original basis. In taking this step it professed itself confident of the support of Lord Howick, who, having seen the original draft of the project (and not, as he afterwards mistakenly alleged, an abstract of it), and having returned it with amendments accepted by the Association and incorporated in their new bill, was thought to have incurred a moral obligation to support it. He denied the existence of any such obligation. Wakefield had apparently the best of the argument before the Committee of 1840; it nevertheless appears to us that the expectation of Lord Howick's support was a kind of Mambrino's helmet which the Association put up for a show, but took care not to test. The bill was not introduced until June 1838, when Lord Durham and Wakefield were both in Canada. It was thrown out by 92 to 32, Lord Howick and Sir George Grey leading the opposition on behalf of the Government. As this destroyed all hope of the scheme being adopted in its original and preferable shape, the Association determined to dissolve, and reconstitute itself as a joint-stock company.[1] All its expenses had hitherto been defrayed by Dr Evans and Wakefield from their private means, and had amounted to about a thousand pounds apiece. Compensation was voted to them. Evans, who had a family, very justifiably accepted it. Wakefield declined to receive a penny.

The chief ostensible ground on which the Government had opposed the bill of the Association had been 'the want of an actual subscribed capital,' to obviate which it was necessary for the Association to condescend to the status of a joint-stock company.

---

[1] In Thomson's *Story of New Zealand*, it is stated, on the authority of an anonymous colonist, that this dissolution was occasioned by a dispute, developed at an entertainment given by Lord Durham to the Association, whether the administration of the company's settlements in New Zealand should be conferred upon Wakefield or Major Campbell. The groundlessness of the tale is proved by the fact that both Wakefield and Lord Durham were in Canada at the time.

Durham and Wakefield were still in Canada, but provision had no doubt been made for the emergency. In October the 'private and confidential' prospectus of the New Zealand Colonization Company was issued, with a paid-up capital of £250,000, and power to extend it to half a million. The names on the directorate were principally of City men, and the element of colonial reform was barely represented. In fact, the mission of this new company was no more than to form a rallying point for intending emigrants, and prepare the next year's expedition. Much subterranean activity was no doubt rife, but the company made no overt demonstration until March, by which time interesting incidents had occurred. Much had been heard before the Lords' Committee of the proceedings of a French adventurer, the Baron de Thierry, who had claims to land in New Zealand, worthless in themselves, but quite good enough for the French Government to buy if it desired to set up a claim to the country. The Baron's brother, seeking support in England, called upon Mr Angas, of South Australian reputation, who, justly alarmed at what he elicited, wrote to Lord Glenelg, forcibly pointing out the necessity of prompt action. His advice was to proclaim British authority in New Zealand without further delay, and the neglect with which it was treated affords, unintentionally on his part, for he was no friend to the New Zealand Company, the fullest justification of the latter's subsequent action.[1] The feeble Glenelg was removed by his own colleagues in February, and was succeeded by Lord Normanby, a nobleman who had earned an enviable reputation for tact and conciliatory spirit as Lord Lieutenant of Ireland, and might therefore have made an excellent colonial governor, but was far below the calibre of a Secretary of State. On 4th March the Colonization Company addressed him, pointing out that the conditions required by Government had been complied with, to which Lord Normanby replied that they had been rejected once, and that the Government was free from all responsibility. In plain English, the Government had broken with Lord Durham, and were no longer afraid of him. Silence ensued until 27th April, when the company, now developed into a 'New Zealand Land Company,' formed by the amalgamation of the Colonization Company, the old Association, and the Company of 1825,

---

[1] *Hodder's Life of G. F. Angas*, pp. 208-212. The real motive of the Government's opposition, *vis inertiæ* and horror of colonial extension apart, is naïvely intimated in a passage from Mr Angas's diary: 'If it were possible to get a hundred *pious* persons to advance £1000 each, I think Lord Glenelg would give them a charter.' Dr Dunmore Lang, the eminent New South Wales colonist, published four letters to Lord Durham recommending immediate annexation, and the honour of preserving New Zealand for Britain is awarded to him in the *Dictionary of National Biography*. But as his pamphlet was published in July 1839, and the company's expedition had sailed in May, he was but knocking at an open door as concerned Lord Durham, although his letters were no doubt serviceable as a stimulus to public opinion.

Lord Durham in its chair, and a paid-up capital of a hundred thousand pounds in its pocket, gave a splendid dejeuner, accompanied with much oratory, at Lovegrove's Tavern at the West India Dock. On 29th April the Colonial Secretary was the dismayed recipient of a communication informing him that he was aware that the company intended to form a settlement in New Zealand, which information his Lordship declared to be great news to him. It further stated that the first ship was actually to sail upon 1st May, and requested letters commendatory to the Governors of New South Wales and Van Diemen's Land. This application, as was probably intended, forced Lord Normanby's hand, and compelled him to almost pledge the Government to obtain territorial rights over New Zealand by negotiation with the natives; while declaring that meanwhile the Company could not be recognised, and that no guarantee could be given for the validity of its land purchases. The good ship *Tory*, of 400 tons, armed with eight guns and with thirty-five souls aboard, none the less sailed from London on the 5th May, the anniversary of the memorable day that ushered in the French Revolution, and of the death of Napoleon. She carried among other passengers Colonel William Wakefield, agent of the Company, late of Lancaster Castle, but more recently still of the Portuguese and Spanish services, where he had won honour as a brave and able soldier; Wakefield's son, Edward Jerningham, who had in the preceding year accompanied his father to Canada, a youth of more ability than conduct, notwithstanding the steadying influences of Bruce Castle School and King's College; Dieffenbach, afterwards famous as a naturalist; and that poor bedizened daw, 'Prince' Nayti. The commander, Edmund Chaffers, had been master of the *Beagle* in the memorable six years' voyage through which Fitzroy carried Darwin. The expedition was merely a precursor of the despatch of the general body of emigrants, which was to follow in time to effect a junction with it at Port Hardy, in Cook's Straits, by 10th January 1840, the height of the New Zealand summer.

The *Tory* sailed from London, as has been seen, four days after the appointed time, a delay doubtless inevitable, for the Company's directors and the power behind them [1] must have well known that no time was to be lost. She cast anchor at Plymouth, and as she did so a stout, fresh-complexioned, middle-aged gentleman, with a countenance expressive of intelligence and resolution,[2] left London in a post-chaise, driving rapidly to the south-west. This was no other than Edward Gibbon Wakefield, whom rumours had reached that Government intended to stop the departure of the vessel. He urged the *Tory* off, and she

[1] Wakefield did not become a director till some time afterwards.
[2] 'A countenance expressing in turn a sort of playful cunning, warm sensibility, clear insight and firm, resolute purpose.'—THORNTON HUNT.

sailed unmolested on 12th May. Whether Government could have worked itself up to an act of such courageous cowardice cannot be known. If it had, what a theme for epigram at the expense of a country that stopped the *Tory* and did not stop the *Alabama!* In any case, Wakefield's vigorous action was the fitting crown of a series of vigorous actions which won for our Queen as bright a jewel as any of her diadem, and saved the Britain of the South from becoming a French convict settlement, a nuisance hateful to God and man, only to be abated at the cost of a bloody war.

While the *Tory* was ploughing the waves, the Company was not idle on shore. Their prospectus had already appeared on 2d May. On 14th May they held a meeting, the agenda for which, extant on a sheet of paper in Wakefield's writing, afford the liveliest picture of the Hero as Company Promoter. The most important of the nine items also convey the Company's apology for its energetic action :—

'To suggest, in general terms, the expediency of vigorous action as the best means of inducing Parliament to legalise and regulate the colonisation of New Zealand; showing that nothing will be done by Government unless individuals act, and how nearly all the colonies of England originated in the activity of individuals; explaining the necessary preoccupation and indifference of Government, and the necessity for legislation which arises when numbers emigrate directly from England to establish themselves in a distant country.

'A despatch from the Governor to the Colonial Secretary explanatory of the state of the question, pointing out the reasons for legislating, suggesting the best mode of proceeding for national purposes, and asking for an interview for the directors.'

Lord Durham accordingly wrote on 22d May soliciting an interview with Lord Normanby. Deputations were received on 1st June and 13th June; yet Lord Normanby thought himself justified in stating on 12th August that he had 'no knowledge of the proceedings of the New Zealand Company.' They had in fact stirred him up to announce by a letter to the Treasury on 13th June his intention 'of adding certain parts of the islands of New Zealand to the Colony of New South Wales as a dependency of that Government,' and of exalting Captain Hobson, R.N., the new British consul, known for gallantry in the West Indies, and as the layer-out of Melbourne, to the dignity of Lieutenant-Governor. Circumlocutionary correspondence between the Treasury, Colonial Office and Foreign Office delayed Hobson's appointment until 14th August, two days before the *Tory*, which had enjoyed a splendid run without sight of land save a distant part of the Canaries, 'saw the high land of New Zealand.' She anchored at Port Nicholson, on the northern side of Cook's Strait, on 20th September. Hobson left England shortly afterwards, and arrived in the Bay of Islands on 29th January 1840. The instructions given to the leaders of the rival expeditions, and the proceedings of each, will be best related in a subsequent chapter. The narrative will be a joyful history in so far as it records that the one absolutely indispensable object was accomplished by New Zealand being preserved to the nation and becoming the home of prosperous colonists ; a lamentable one in so far as it recites the disfigurement of what might have been an ideal chapter in colonization. The fault lay entirely with the Government, an excellent administration in many respects, but neither sufficiently large-hearted to meet the Association in a generous and confiding spirit, nor (which would have been equally indispensable) sufficiently resolute to subject its doings to the control of a strong but sympathetic representative of the Crown. It let things drift until they could drift no longer, and then in a panic created an authority antagonistic to the original colonists, the source of endless dissension, scandal and damage, material and moral. Abler men suceeeded Lords Glenelg and Normanby at the Colonial Office, but they could never get out of the groove traced for them when their predecessors compelled the high-principled and disinterested directorate of the New Zealand Association to descend to the level of a joint-stock company.

CHAPTER VI

WAKEFIELD IN CANADA WITH LORD DURHAM IN 1838—RECALL OF THE MISSION—THE DURHAM REPORT—WAKEFIELD'S SUBSEQUENT VISITS TO CANADA.

CHRONOLOGY, or once at variance with her sister History, bids us interrupt the narrative of New Zealand colonization and turn to that remarkable episode in Wakefield's life, his mission to Canada in 1838 as, together with Charles Buller, the confidential adviser of Lord Durham. It is an episode brilliant indeed as regards its momentous consequences to the Empire, but obscure as concerns Wakefield's personal share in it. To the public eye the mission for a while appeared a failure; and yet a real victory was won—the victory of a few ideas which arose silently in the minds of at most three persons, and shaped a State paper which shaped the destinies of the British Colonial Empire. The actual authorship of the Durham Report may perhaps in some degree admit of elucidation, but the origination of the ideas which gave it birth can never be accurately determined. Durham, Charles Buller, Wakefield had in common the attribute of magnanimity. None of them ever sought to deprive a colleague of a particle of merited honour. As, however, Wakefield's ostensible share in the transactions of Durham's Canadian mission was of necessity much less conspicuous than Durham's or Buller's, it is but redressing the balance to point out that he avowedly stood in the position of instructor to the other two, who in colonial affairs were proud to be accounted his disciples. This needs to be borne in mind, for the indications of his direct agency are of the slightest. It is also to be remembered that whatever may have been his share in inspiring that Magna Charta of the colonies, the Durham Report, this was not the work that he was sent out to accomplish; he was rather expected to apply the Wakefield system to the Crown lands. In truth, the scope of the Durham mission became greatly enlarged, and while it for a while seemed a failure as concerned the minor objects which it was despatched to effect, it was preparing the greatest of successes in a higher sphere. Durham, Buller, Wakefield might all be compared to Saul, the son of Kish; hunting the strayed asses of Canadian disaffection, they found the kingdom of Responsible Government.

It will be necessary to preface the story of Lord Durham's mission and its results with a brief account of the occurrences which had rendered it indispensable.

The difficulties which Lord Durham was sent out to settle were of ancient date, and might be traced back to an avowedly healing measure. This was the re-enactment in 1774 of the French civil law, which the British conquest in 1763 had temporarily annulled. The Act—though drafted with such carelessness as to have for a while deprived French Canadians of *habeas corpus* and trial by jury—produced on the whole a good effect, and served to maintain order during the American revolutionary war. Among its consequences, which may or may not have been intended, was the diversion of the stream of British immigration from Lower to Upper Canada, thus perpetuating the French type which Lower Canada retains to this day. In 1791 the colony was divided into two provinces, and a separate legislature established in each. The Lower Canadian House of Assembly being in consequence almost entirely French, it was sought to balance this by a nominated legislative council almost entirely English. Difficulties naturally arose, and the claims of the Lower House to the right of prescribing the appropriation of the revenue led to continual disagreements. In 1828 the most serious grievances of the Canadians were removed, but only with the effect of showing that a spirit of revolt had taken possession of them, and that the redress of wrongs, originally a *bona fide* object of agitation, had become the mere stalking horse of revolution. This attitude compelled the Commons to reject the not unreasonable demand for an elective legislative council, preferred in 1837, which, so long as the two provinces remained disunited, could only have prefaced further agitation. Yet the French Canadians certainly did not wish to be absorbed into the United States, and they can hardly have fancied themselves able to stand alone.[1] The object of the discontented Anglo-Canadians in the Upper Province, who had sufficient reason to complain of the 'family compact,' or rather ring of politicians which, omnipotent in the Legislative Council, engrossed every place of trust and profit, was, on the other hand, annexation to the United States. From October 1832, the Assembly of Lower Canada stopped the payment of the salaries of the civil servants. In October 1837, insurrection broke out in Lower Canada; and in December in Upper Canada. Both were easily repressed, in great measure by the assistance of loyal volunteers. A more alarming symptom was the assemblage on the United States frontier of bands of American sympathisers, who in some instances actually invaded the colony, although they were soon expelled. The Home Government, rightly considering that the situation demanded vigorous measures, suspended the Canadian constitution, and announced their intention of sending Lord Durham out as Governor-General of the five British provinces, and also as Lord High

[1] I have put the question, 'What did the "habitans" want?' to a hundred people, French and English, and never could obtain a satisfactory answer. They all said, 'No one knows; it was neither more nor less than madness.'—Godley, *Letters from America*, vol. 1, p. 78.

Commissioner, clothed with extraordinary powers for the settlement of questions pending in the Canadas.

The reason which led the Government to select Lord Durham for what O'Connell might have called the 'Head-Pacificatorship' of the Canadas was correctly stated by the *Quarterly Review*. 'They did not know what else to do with him.' It was equally dangerous to take him into the Cabinet, or to leave him out. Within, he would have been an imperious and uncomfortable colleague; without, he was very likely to put himself at the head of the more advanced section of the Liberal party, which, though entirely unable to form a government, was quite capable of upsetting one. Ministers, therefore, justly reasoned that, from a party point of view, nothing but good could come of Lord Durham's appointment to Canada. If he succeeded, the credit would largely redound to the Government, and the thorough settlement of the contingent problems would be a matter of sufficient magnitude to detain him abroad for several years. If he failed, he would return discredited and harmless. Canada was simply a tub thrown to a whale.

It may well be doubted whether, with the exception of Lord John Russell, any of the Ministers thought Lord Durham the fittest man to be entrusted with the government of Canada at such a crisis. And yet, granted one essential condition, he really was so. He had the stainless character, the high spirit, the courage, the disinterestedness, the patriotism, the imperial instinct, the industry necessary for a great Governor-General. His defects were incapacity for the management of men, and inexperience in administrative business. His haughtiness and sensitiveness disqualified him for the arts which the most high-minded politicians find indispensable in self-governed communities, and the delicacy of his health had hitherto debarred him from laborious office. These were defects which able counsellors might do much to remedy. Good advice was the one thing needful, and the general success of Durham's measures proves that he knew where to find and how to receive it. The one error in administration he committed was, as we shall see, in nowise discreditable to him, but arose from a generous confidence that the public good would for once be allowed to prevail over legal technicalities.

The men in whom Durham's confidence was chiefly reposed were Charles Buller and Edward Gibbon Wakefield. To the appointment of Buller as his chief secretary no objection could possibly be made; his character was rated even more highly than his ability. The son of an Indian judge, he had in his youth enjoyed the instructions of a very exceptional tutor, Thomas Carlyle; and, as a brilliant young Cantab, had qualified for a legislator by becoming an 'Apostle.' Elected to Parliament at an early age, he had distinguished himself by the liberality of his sentiments, the effectiveness of his oratory, and the geniality of his humour. He had already rendered a great public service as chairman of the Public Record Commission. He had studied colonial questions under Wakefield's guidance, and the strength and durability of the attachment with which the latter inspired him are among the soundest guarantees of his own worth.

Wakefield, of course, was far from standing in the same position; it had not yet been thought expedient that his name should appear on the board of the New Zealand Company; and Durham must have been well aware that his employment in any capacity would expose the Canadian administration to damaging attacks. The advantage, nevertheless, outweighed the objection, and Durham courageously acted as he deemed right in the public interest. Wakefield remained intimately associated with him throughout his mission, and we have Durham's own word that he would have been appointed Commissioner of Crown Lands but for the interposition of the alarmed Ministers at home. No such vindication can be offered for another appointment which created more scandal than could have been occasioned by the bestowal of any office upon Wakefield, and could not be justified on the ground of the indispensableness of the recipient. Mr (afterwards Sir) Thomas Turton, under-secretary and legal adviser, appears to have been an able lawyer, but possessed no such monopoly of legal knowledge as could render it necessary to search the bar of England for the one barrister who had been divorced by the House of Lords on the ground of incestuous adultery. The causes of this unfortunate step will be most fitly investigated by Lord Durham's biographer. Two have been assigned—one the chivalrous but (in a public matter) reprehensible generosity which led Durham, having once rashly named Turton, to stand by an unfortunate friend and former schoolfellow; the other, a blunder of the Treasury's which led him to think that the nomination could not be retracted. As so often happens, the defensible appointment was prevented, and the indefensible retained.

Durham should have been doubly cautious, for he knew that he was leaving in his rear a bitter, unscrupulous and most formidable enemy. Lord Brougham had never forgiven his brilliant oratorical campaign in the autumn of 1834, when in speech after speech he castigated the erratic Chancellor veering to the Tories. Brougham now had his absent adversary at a terrible disadvantage, and no consideration of candour or patriotism could mitigate his virulence. His animosity towards the Ministry who had ostracised him was even more intense than his animosity towards Durham, and he revelled in his ability, now to wound them through Durham's side, now to salve their hurts with the gall of his contemptuous patronage. The attitude of this distinguished personage towards the Melbourne Ministry for several years was precisely that of a cat to a mouse. Seldom indeed can it have happened that a public man neither trusted nor respected by anybody, without a single avowed follower in the country, should make so conspicuous a figure before the world, and exercise such real influence upon the course of affairs. The secret was the nice balance of the contending political parties. The moment that a strong Government appeared which neither feared nor needed him, Brougham sank into insignificance.

The Government bill for suspending the Canadian constitution and granting extraordinary powers to a Lord High Commissioner was introduced into the Commons on 16th January, and passed the Lords on 6th February, after having been 'greatly mauled and worried' by Sir Robert Peel in the Lower House, and by Lord Brougham in the Upper. The Duke of Wellington might easily have thrown it out, but, as ever with him, patriotism prevailed over party spirit. During the debate in the Commons, the note of responsible government for the colony, the ultimate solution of the problem, was sounded by Mr Warburton, but mainly on the ground that such a concession must produce absolute separation, the consummation desired by the speaker. The act provided for the suspension of the constitution of Lower Canada until November 1840, and for the interim appointment of a special legislative council by the Governor under the authority of the Crown. The Governor's powers were imperfectly defined, and it was to be foreseen that any attempt on his part to exercise them vigorously would lead to attacks from the Opposition which a feeble Government, dependent upon an exiguous Irish and Scotch majority, was not likely to resist.

Durham, however, nothing daunted, sailed on 24th April, and arrived at Quebec on 29th May, accompanied by Buller and other members of his suite. Wakefield appears to have arrived somewhat later. Lord Glenelg, the Colonial Secretary, had believed that he was already on his way to Canada by 4th May. The statement is made in a private letter from Glenelg to Durham, requesting that Wakefield 'may have no regular appointment under the Crown. You may well believe that it is not with any wish to injure Mr Wakefield that we make this request. He is a clever man, and may, I have no doubt, be very usefully employed, and of course there could be no objection to his employment unofficially. We cannot help feeling, however, that to give him an official station in the province might produce much dissatisfaction and embarrassment.' This would not seem to have been apprehended from any question as to private character, but from the antipathy of the French Canadians to Wakefield's views on colonization, as afterwards expressed by Roebuck in a letter to the

Spectator. 'One of the chief disputes between the Executive and the House of Assembly had risen respecting the management of the waste lands of the country, and the application of the funds derived from them. Respecting this matter, Mr Wakefield had made himself exceedingly busy in England—had proposed a new theory and proposed to withdraw the lands from the surveillance of the people of the colonies altogether, and to convert the funds into the means of deporting the pauper population of England and Ireland.' Roebuck adds that Wakefield was employed in making a report upon the waste lands of the colony, no doubt the basis of the elaborate paper on the same subject by Charles Buller in Appendix B to the Durham Report. Glenelg's remonstrances with Durham on Wakefield's anticipated appointment were reinforced by a letter which, a few days after Durham's arrival in Canada, he received from Lord Melbourne, referring, as would appear, to Turton's appointment also. To this, as regarded Wakefield, he replied as follows [1]:—

'*June* 15, 1838.—As for Mr Wakefield, your letter arrived before him, and I have therefore been able, without compromising my own character and independence, to comply with your desire. He holds no employment or official situation whatever, nor

---

[1] We are obliged to Mr Stuart J. Reid for the communication of Lord Glenelg's letter, and of Durham's replies to him and Melbourne. Melbourne's own letter seems not to be forthcoming.

will his name appear before the public at all. "Oh, no! we never mention him; his name is never heard." Really, if it were not very inconvenient, all this would be very ludicrous. But I am placed in a very painful situation. I am called to perform an almost superhuman task. You provide me with no, or most inadequate, means from yourselves, and you then interfere with the arrangements I make to supply myself with the best talent I can find.'

On the same day Durham thus replied to Lord Glenelg :—

'I had intended to have named Mr Wakefield a Commissioner of Inquiry into the Crown Lands, Emigration, etc., but in consequence of your letter have given up all thought of it, and Mr Wakefield will hold no official situation of any kind under me or the Government.'

Wakefield, nevertheless, remained in Canada, and continued to render efficient service during the entire period of Lord Durham's mission. The ostensible Chief Commissioner of Crown Lands, Charles Buller, was discharging the more onerous duties of Chief Secretary, and was, moreover, Wakefield's *alter ego* in matters of land and emigration. If, however, Wakefield received any remuneration, it must have come out of Durham's own pocket.

Durham's first act had been to dismiss the Executive Council he found, and to instal one chiefly composed of his own immediate followers, a step fully justifiable on the ground assigned, that, under the existing exceptional circumstances, 'the administration of affairs should be completely independent of and unassociated with all parties and persons in the province.' Wakefield, of course, was not a member of this council, nor had it been intended that he should be; but he was undoubtedly consulted on all important occasions. Within a few weeks of his arrival, Durham had initiated several important and healing reforms, three of which, a land commission, a registry of titles, and the commutation of feudal tenures, lay within Wakefield's especial sphere.

There is a book in New Zealand given to Wakefield by Lord Durham, with an inscription testifying that he had never erred except when he rejected Wakefield's advice. If, then, Durham considered his famous Ordinance of 28th June an error, it was promulgated in opposition to the advice of Wakefield, but it is quite probable that neither regarded it in that light. In one point of view, the Ordinance ruined Durham's mission by providing his antagonists at home with a point of attack, and cowing his feeble friends. From the standpoint of reason it was wise and right. The question at issue bore no relation to the high matters of policy which Durham had been sent to Canada to determine. It simply regarded the fate of the captured rebels whom he found awaiting trial. Their offence was notorious, but was virtue in the eyes of the majority of their countrymen. An ordinary French Canadian jury would have acquitted them forthwith ; to obtain justice, recourse must have been had to the odious method of a packed tribunal. The prisoners themselves had fully expected this course to be resorted to, and were unspeakably relieved to find that Lord Durham proposed to send them out of the country without trial. They gladly accepted what they rightly considered an act of signal clemency, and, if only the British Parliament had not been sitting, all would have been well. But the legality of Durham's Ordinance banishing the prisoners —though much might be said on its behalf even on that ground—was not altogether so clear as its expediency, and one detail was obviously *ultra vires*— their exile to Bermuda, where Durham had no jurisdiction to send them, and the Governor none to detain them. A strong Government would have immediately cured the irregularity by a short Act of Parliament, and even a weak Government might have seen that it was better to resign on such a question than to allow its course to be dictated by its enemies. Not so Lord Melbourne's administration, which, disallowing Durham's Ordinance, was compelled to pass an indemnity bill, forced upon it with every circumstance of humiliation by Lord Brougham, who, as was said at the time, 'determined on involving in one common misfortune and disgrace the Ministers and their Governor-General, not only accomplished the fall of Lord Durham, but so contrived that all the odium of the transaction should attach to the Ministers themselves.' On 9th August, Melbourne announced the disallowance of the Ordinance. Durham's first intimation of it was from the columns of an American newspaper. Buller saw from the expression of his face that he had received a violent shock. The official despatches arrived a few days later, and on 25th September he sent in his resignation. On 9th October he issued a proclamation, certainly ill-judged, which gave the Government an excuse for summoning him home. He escaped this mortification by having already left the colony without having been recalled, or having obtained the Royal consent, an act undoubtedly liable to grave criticism, and of which more would have been heard if the despatch dispensing with his services had not already been upon its way. He quitted Quebec on 1st November, and two days later an insurrection exploded, which was suppressed without difficulty by his provisional successor, General Colborne. The despatch announcing his immediate return was brought to England by his aide-de-camp, Captain Dillon, who, accompanied by Wakefield, sailed from New York on 25th October. Rough weather compelled them to transfer themselves to a fishing boat off the coast of Ireland, and they experienced some peril in getting to land.

Durham's return interrupted several important measures in the preparation of which it found him engaged, which, as they were doubtless agreeable to the recommendations of his Report, must have given him a high place among colonial legislators. Apart from these and the memorable Report itself, the chief fruit of his meteoric administration was the evidence it yielded that an English Governor could be popular in Canada. He went on steadily rising in popularity throughout the whole of his rule, and enjoyed the full sympathy of public opinion in his conflict with the Ministry at home. Three thousand of the most respectable inhabitants of Quebec attended him to the place of embarkation, and his popularity in Upper Canada was even greater. It must be a question how far he had gone out to the country with any definite views respecting the French Canadian grievances. Wakefield, in a remarkable letter to the *Spectator*, published on 24th November in reply to letters from Roebuck, the salaried agent of the French Canadians, says that he for his own part had been a strong Canadian sympathiser, but, as a result of an extensive acquaintance with the leading men among them, had been led to change his views. This is important, as it leads to the recommendation for the union of the British North America provinces as a means of controlling the French element by the English, which is one of the most important features of the Durham Report. A journey to Saratoga, undertaken without Lord Durham's knowledge, in the vain hope of meeting the exiled Canadian leader, Papineau, and mentioned in this letter, is the only vestige of Wakefield's political activity during Durham's mission. Thomas Slingsby Duncombe, who kept a diary of his visit to Lord Durham, mentions him repeatedly, but only as an amateur in mesmerism.[1]

Durham arrived off Plymouth on 26th November after a tempestuous passage, and it was four days more ere the weather moderated sufficiently to allow his landing. The reception he encountered was more in accordance with Wakefield's original expectations than with his subsequent conclusions, if Greville is warranted in attributing to him the admission upon his own arrival 'that he had never been so amazed in the course of his life, and owned that they had all expected to make a very different impression, and to be hailed with great applause.' Durham *was* hailed with great applause, yet it is incontestable that the bad taste of his proclamation making known the disallowance of his Ordinance had created very unfavourable comment, and that the public feeling at one time is accurately expressed by a celebrated passage in Mill's Autobiography : 'Lord Durham was bitterly attacked on all sides—inveighed against by enemies, given up

---

[1] Wakefield was a powerful magnetiser. 'I recollect,' says Mr Allom, 'a story he told me of his being at an evening party where he had mesmerised a young lady, but was struck with horror on finding that he could not revive her. He jumped into a cab and went in search of his friend Dr Elliotson. After some hours' search Elliotson was found, and they returned in company, and Dr Elliotson succeeded in reviving the lady.'

by timid friends, while those who would willingly have defended him did not know what to say. He appeared to be returning a defeated and discredited man. I had followed the Canadian events from the beginning; I had been one of the prompters of his prompters; his policy was almost exactly what mine would have been, and I was in a position to defend it. I wrote and published a manifesto in the [*London and Westminster*] *Review*, in which I took the very highest ground in his behalf, claiming for him not mere acquittal, but praise and honour. Instantly a number of other writers took up the tone. I believe there was a portion of truth in what Lord Durham soon after, with polite exaggeration, said to me—that to this article might be ascribed the almost triumphal reception which he met with on his arrival in England.' The *Spectator* of 24th November made copious extracts from advance sheets of this article, which other journals had also received; there was, therefore, time to influence public opinion. Mill's generous temper lent fire to his generally measured and sober advocacy, and his essay was admirably calculated to effect its object. A powerful defence of Lord Durham on every point on which his conduct had been impugned was thus summed up :—

'He has been thwarted, but he has not failed. He has shown how Canada ought to be governed; and if anything can allay her dissensions, and again attach her to the mother country, this will. He has at the critical moment taken the initiative of a healing policy. He has disposed of the great immediate embarrassment —the political offenders. He has shown to the well intentioned of both sides an honourable basis on which they may accommodate their differences. He has detached from the unreasonable of one party their chief support—the sympathy of the United States, and it is reserved for him to detach from the unreasonable of the other the sympathy of the people of England. He comes home master of the details of those abuses which he has recognised as the original causes of the disaffection; prepared to expose these as they have never before been exposed, and to submit to Parliament, after the most comprehensive inquiry which has ever taken place, the system on which the North American colonies may be preserved and well governed hereafter.'

This promise and vow of his political sponsor Durham amply redeemed by his famous Report of the following year, which has become the accepted exposition of the principles which should guide the mother country in her dealings with her colonies. The effect of the document was enhanced by the sensational method of its publication. While Ministers were still hesitating what to do with it, the most important portion appeared (8th February) in the *Times*. With the same decision which he afterwards showed in anticipating the probable resolution of Ministers to stop the pioneer vessel of the New

Zealand Company, Wakefield precipitated the Report into print to save it from mutilation. According to the testimony of Sir Richard Hanson, afterwards Chief-Justice of South Australia, then one of Durham's secretaries, adduced by Henry Reeve in his edition of the Greville Memoirs, his motive was jealousy for the integrity of the portion which he had himself written, respecting which Durham seemed inclined to make concessions. In this case he must have acted without Durham's sanction, and this agrees best with Durham's language in the House of Lords. According to a tradition in the Wakefield family, however, the sanction *was* given, and when Durham seemed disposed to recall it he was answered, 'My lord, it has gone already.' In any case, there can be no question that Wakefield rendered a great service to the country. The Report must eventually have crept into light as originally written, for two thousand copies had been privately printed, but it must have lost much of its effect if it had been mutilated or delayed. Hanson took it to the *Times*. The best justification for the step will be found in the words of Lord Melbourne: 'He did not think the noble earl had any right to conclude that his Report in full would be laid before Parliament, but Government had now no discretion in the case.'

The current belief respecting the authorship of the Durham Report was thus epigrammatically expressed at the time: 'Wakefield thought it, Buller wrote it, Durham signed it.' 'Written,' says Stuart Mill, 'by Charles Buller, partly under the inspiration of Wakefield.' According to Sir R. Hanson's account as communicated to Henry Reeve, Buller wrote the whole except two 'paragraphs' on Church and Crown Lands. But this certainly much underrates Lord Durham's share. Mr Egerton, in his history of British Colonial Policy, justly remarks that the style is unlike that of the elaborate Report on Crown Lands in the appendix, to which Buller's name is attached. It may be added that a large part of it strongly resembles the style of the proclamation of October announcing the disallowance of the Ordinance, which bears throughout the impress of strong personal feeling, and which it is scarcely probable that the high-spirited Durham would have delegated to a subordinate. This remark is especially applicable to the most important portions of the Report—the preamble, the section on Lower Canada, and the general summing up and statement of remedies proposed. These wear a character of patrician dignity and hauteur not easily assumed save by one to the manner born. The evidence for Buller's share in the authorship is nevertheless too strong to be set aside.[1] Miss Martineau, the last person to detract a leaf from Durham's chaplet, says of Charles Buller: 'It is under-

[1] The *Quarterly Review* seems to have been of opinion that the Report wrote itself. 'We suspect, and shall be glad if our suspicion be confirmed, that in Lord Durham's execrable Report Mr Buller had as little hand as Lord Durham himself.'

stood that the merit of the celebrated Report is mainly ascribable to him.' Perhaps the most probable view is that portions were rewritten by Durham from Buller's original draft, which would involve the retention of much of his wording. The section on Upper Canada may be entirely his. The recommendation for the union of the provinces almost certainly emanated from Wakefield—' the person who puts in the jewel into Lord Durham's Report,' says a spiteful opponent. If he wrote any part of the Report on Church and Crown Lands, he wrote the whole; and the probability is that by 'paragraphs,' if he really used the word, Sir R. Hanson meant 'sections.' However these points may be determined, an equal share of the credit of the Report belongs to all concerned. It may well be that Durham was guided by his advisers to truths which he would not have discovered without them, but discernment in the choice of counsellors is one of the surest marks of ability in a ruler, and it is manifest that all the recommendations which he sanctioned had been intelligently considered and approved by him.

The great value of Lord Durham's Report was that the principles justly recommended as effective for the pacification of Canada were such as, once accepted there, must be admitted as applicable to the colonies of the entire Empire, those only excepted which might be peopled by inferior races. In a masterly survey of the existing condition of affairs, Durham makes the same admission as we have seen Wakefield make in his letter to the *Spectator*—that he had been mistaken as to the causes of French Canadian discontent. The ostensible grounds of complaint were just, but the redress of these would have done little to appease the quarrel, which really sprang from hatred of the English nationality, and fear of being absorbed by it. 'I expected to find a contest between a government and a people—I found two nations warring in the bosom of a single state. I found a struggle, not of principles but of races; and I perceived that it would be idle to attempt any amelioration of laws or institutions until we could first succeed in terminating the deadly animosity that now separates the inhabitants of Lower Canada into the hostile divisions of French and English.' The remedy proposed was to give the French Canadians Responsible Government[1]—not the mere mockery they already possessed, which left their elected representatives without influence, but the same effective control over the Ministry of Canada as the British Parliament exercised over the Ministry of Britain. As a counterweight, all the five British American provinces were to be united; disloyal and factious tendencies among the French were to be checked by a majority to the legislature attached to the British connection, and the two races, thus acting together,

[1] The subject was further developed in *Responsible Government for the Colonies*, 1840, an able pamphlet mainly written by Charles Buller, though Wakefield appears to have had a hand in it.

were to learn their real community of country and of interest. 'I admit,' writes Durham, 'that the system which I propose would, in fact, place the internal government of the colony in the hands of the colonists themselves ; and that we should thus leave to them the execution of the laws of which we have long entrusted the making solely to them.'

That this statement, now a commonplace, should then have been thought alarming, indicates most forcibly the progress of political enlightenment since that day, and the extent of the national obligations to Durham and his coadjutors. The prevalent theory of the day—inconsistent with contentment or good government in Canada or any colony out of its infancy—was fairly enough indicated by the *Quarterly Review* in an article whose waspishness and italics bespeak the pen of Croker : ''The fundamental error is this, they forget that Canada is a *province*—a *colony*. They measure it by a scale of doctrines which are applicable only to a national and independent *sovereignty*.' The idea in the writer's mind manifestly is that a colonist is from the nature of the case inferior to a citizen of the mother country : that a colony may have a legislative assembly to play with, but must not have a responsible ministry to work with. Responsible government, aye or no, that was the question. The Quarterly Reviewer had no doubt as to the momentous character of the decision about to be taken. 'If this rank and infectious Report does not receive the high, marked and energetic discountenance and indignation of the Imperial Crown and Parliament, British America is lost.' A magnificent contribution to the literature of unfulfilled prophecy! which nevertheless represented the views of the bulk of the Tory party, though probably not those of its most intelligent leaders. To the restraining influence of Peel and Wellington, and to Lord John Russell's advocacy of Durham's views in the Cabinet, must be ascribed the absence of any great party contest on the subject in the session of 1839. A mighty catastrophe had been expected. Durham, another Samson, was to have buried himself in the ruins of the Ministry, but the session left them both erect. The doctrines of the Report, meanwhile, were gradually filtering into men's minds, and Parliament had scarcely risen ere Lord John Russell's instructions to the new Governor, Poulett Thomson, afterwards Lord Sydenham, made tentative approaches to the principles of responsible government. Durham and his advisers had outrun their age by thirty years in proposing the union of all the North American colonies, but the union of Upper and Lower Canada (now Ontario and Quebec) was achieved in 1840 by the adroitness of Poulett Thomson, who had departed primed for his task by numerous interviews with Durham. Lower Canada was not then in the enjoyment of representative institutions, and Upper Canada was wisely being allowed more representatives than its share, a concession which would not have been necessary if Durham's plan of fusing all the North American colonies had been adhered to. Much friction remained to be overcome, but a succession of able and prudent Governors-General have so cemented the relations between the mother country and the colony that while the desire, whether for absolute independence or for absorption into the United States, has almost died out on the one side, the unworthy craving to abdicate our North American Empire is even nearer extinction on the other. The new constitution was signed by the Queen on 23d July 1840, five days before the death of Durham, almost whose last words were: 'The Canadians will one day do justice to my memory.' He could not foresee how far beyond Canada would extend the influence of his Report, 'the most valuable document in the English language on the subject of colonial policy' (Egerton); how it would mould the relations of the mother country with colonies yet uncreated; and how the last days of his ablest counsellor would be devoted to battling for responsible government on the other side of the world.

Wakefield twice returned to Canada, and for brief intervals actively participated in its politics. He was there from December 1841 to the winter of 1842, and again from September 1843 to January 1844. He says in the *Art of Colonization* that he had expectations of obtaining a permanent position in the colony, but does not state what it would have been. His visits seem to have had some connection with the affairs of a land company, and also with canal and railway legislation, and it was probably with a view of furthering these projects that in November 1842, 'having taken a very active part in promoting that change' [the admission of the French Canadians to a share in the administration] 'under Sir Charles Bagot' [Lord Sydenham's successor] 'I was elected a member of the Assembly by an important county of Lower Canada,' *i.e.*, Beauharnois, through which the canal was to be run. The majority was 737, entirely made up of the votes of three French Canadian parishes. Colonial politicians are not always regardful of social amenities, and at the time of Wakefield's election his opponents made the freest use of the bygone unfortunate circumstances in his life. He read all the attacks, and tossed them one after the other across the room to his secretary, Charles Allom, afterwards an officer in the Indian army, with the remark, 'Send that to your mother.' During both visits he acted as correspondent to the *Colonial Gazette*, and his letters will be found full of interest. In 1843 he took a conspicuous part in Canadian politics as a Member of Parliament, and one more important, though unacknowledged, as the secret adviser of Sir Charles Metcalfe, the Governor-General. In December 1843 he moved an amendment of portentous length, and supported it by a speech which Mr Dent, the diligent and judicious Canadian historian of this period, calls 'argumentative and able.' From the summary he gives it would appear well entitled to this character, although of Wakefield's oratory he remarks : ' As a public speaker he appealed to the reason rather than to the imagination, and there was little of the *ad captandum* orator about him. He was better calculated to impress educated men than the public at large, and by consequence was not well fitted for the labours of an electoral campaign, although he possessed many rare qualifications for a legislator.' It harmonises with this account that those who have heard Wakefield speak in public recollect his ' dallying with his golden chain,' like the chancellor in Tennyson's 'Sleeping Beauty.' ' Though not much accustomed to speaking in public,' says one who had heard him in New Zealand, ' his language was powerful and impressive ; though never fluent, he was never tedious ; and when roused by passion he displayed latent powers which early cultivation and exercise might have raised to those of a commanding orator.'

The all-engrossing question during Wakefield's third visit to Canada was the conflict between Sir Charles Metcalfe, the Governor-General, and his Ministers, which for long after Wakefield's departure kept the country without a government. Wakefield sided with Sir Charles, in consequence, Mr Dent thinks, of the hostility of Ministers to his plans of colonization. Mr Dent, however, who is the very model of a fair-minded historian, adds that he became one of Sir Charles's most trusted advisers; and it would not be easy to produce a higher testimonial to character than the confidence of Sir Charles Metcalfe. The controversies of that day are now matters of history, but they retain a permanent importance for the biography of Wakefield as the parents of two of his most remarkable literary productions, one most creditable to his moral nature, the other to his intellectual. The author of the noble character of Sir Charles Metcalfe, 'whom God made greater than the Colonial Office,'[1] was assuredly not insensible to the beauty of virtue, his pen is steeped in genuine veneration for 'the Christian gentleman, of whom it is not enough to say that nothing would persuade him to take an unfair advantage; he can hardly persuade himself to take a fair one:'—the impersonation, the writer evidently feels, of a higher ideal than it is given to himself to attain. It is believed that the publication of this pamphlet prevented Sir Charles Metcalfe's recall. Far more important, however, is another production which perhaps has never been mentioned in a book from the day of its publication

---

[1] *A View of Sir Charles Metcalfe's Government of Canada.* By a Member of the Provincial Parliament. London, 1844. The author of a violent pamphlet against Wakefield, not willing that he should have the credit of a fine saying, altered 'God' in the above quotation into 'Government'!

to the present—an essay, nevertheless, of such wisdom, insight and vigour that the present writer would deem all the pains bestowed on this biography well bestowed if they had accomplished nothing else than its retrieval from oblivion.

Fisher's Colonial Magazine for July 1844 contained forty-five octavo pages of excruciatingly small print, entitled 'Sir Charles Metcalfe in Canada,' and attributed in the general preface to 'an eminent public character,' but Wakefield's authorship is patent in every line. About half of it is occupied with the ephemeral affairs of Sir Charles Metcalfe's administration, the rest is a magnificent essay on Responsible Government, attacking the fallacies which then prevailed as to the right of the mother country to keep her colonies in leading strings, expounding the principles of the British Constitution itself, and showing with what ease and safety they admit of application to the colonies. The special evils of the denial of representative institutions to colonies under the sway of a Governor and an official clique are vigorously exposed; nominated councils and civil lists independent of popular control come in for their share of censure; and the scheme of giving the colonies direct representation in the Imperial legislature is discussed and rejected. The superiority of the English system to republican democracy is asserted, and the argument involves a most acute examination of the inevitable, and therefore incurable, defects of the constitution of the United

States. Though there is no direct reference to Ireland, the impossibility of any system of Home Rule, short of an absolute legislative separation, is pointed out by anticipation. The soundest rules for permanently attaching the colonies to the mother country are laid down; and towards the conclusion, the local affairs of Canada disposed of, the author's imperial instinct finds expression in a prevision of the probable future relations between Britain and her colonial empire :—

'True it is, that the wide continents we are colonising promise at some distant day to maintain communities too powerful for the precise colonial relation, even as I have been describing it, to continue for ever to subsist between them and the people of these islands. But that period is distant, though inevitable. All we can certainly know is that it will come; that at some future time our colonies, powerful as the parent state or more so, must either, through mismanagement, have become independent states more likely to be its enemies than its hearty friends, or else through a wise foresight have been kept closely bound to it—confederacy in some shape by degrees taking the place of the old bond of union—the British nation continuing still united so far as perpetual peace, mutual ·good understanding, freedom of commerce and identity of foreign policy can unite it—these islands still its metropolis, though their people be no longer the admitted holders of its whole imperial power. All we can do is to take care of the present and near future. The future that is far off will take good care of itself. For this age and the next it is enough to know that colonies, built up by our own people, and gifted with our own free institutions, must be bound alike by the natural feelings and the commercial wants of their people, to ourselves and our policy, no less than to our trade; that neither the one tie nor the other need we, nor yet if we are wise shall we, ever let go or loosen.'

In another remarkable passage Wakefield refutes by anticipation the groundless objection to his system, so frequently brought forward since his death, of its having been contrived in the interest of an oligarchic plutocracy, and designed to stereotype the social inequalities which prevailed in the parent country. He was, indeed, desirous that all classes, the higher as well as the lower, should have their share of the opportunities for expansion afforded by our colonial empire; he wished for a large infusion of refinement and culture to keep colonial life, public and private, at a high level; he believed, and time has justified him, that the colonies could be withheld from setting up as independent republics, and welcomed every influence tending to retain them within the imperial system; but he never believed that all the institution and all the class distinctions of Great Britain and Ireland could be replanted at the Antipodes. After enumerating some of the more obvious causes which render it 'impossible to establish in a dependency the literal and exact transcript of the political institutions of an independent state,' he continues :—

'It is clear enough, then, that in attempting to give to our colonies political institutions essentially modelled upon our own, it is idle to think of their adopting all our aristocratic peculiarities, be they ever so cherished and venerable, whether in Church or State. In the one or two of our most recently planted settlements' [South Australia and New Zealand] 'where pains have been taken in the first instance to transplant an organised society of rich and poor, landholders, merchants, tradesmen, artisans and labourers all together, and to have them carry at once with them from home into the wilderness their church and schoolhouse, a state of things promises to grow up more like our own than is to be found in our older colonial possessions. But no such marked inequalities of rank as prevail at home can by any chance be made a lasting feature of the social state, even in colonies so founded. As to hereditary rank, with here and there perhaps a solitary exception, it is a thing not to be thought of. The political franchise, too, must be more extended, and representation more clearly apportioned to population than with us. And as regards privileged church-establishments, every colony had need be allowed altogether its own way. If it wants them, they are easily to be had. If not, it will be worse than folly to try to force it to put up with them.'

Some six months before the publication of this essay Wakefield had been recalled from the pleasant occupation of exercising *irresponsible* government in Canada as the secret counsellor of Sir Charles Metcalfe by an event at once distressing to his private affections and sinister for the interests of the New Zealand Company —the death of his brother Arthur in the massacre of Wairau in the preceding June. There was then no direct communication between New Zealand and America, and the ship that brought the heavy news had left the spot of the globe which then held Wakefield far behind her, as she ploughed the second great ocean on her path towards London, where the tidings took ship again, and overtook him after making more than half the circuit of the globe. He immediately returned to England, which he reached in a state of the deepest depression. His personal fascination, so potent with all, was most deeply felt by children and the young. Mrs Storr, then little Miss Allom, who, in her own words, would have been glad of an opportunity of dying for him, remembers him as he sat lost in gloom at the end of the drawing-room in Hart Street, Bloomsbury. She nestled against him trying to sooth him, and her mother called her away. 'Let her be,' answered Wakefield, 'let her be!'

CHAPTER VII

THE PLANTING OF NEW ZEALAND—THE COMPANY'S INSTRUCTIONS TO ITS AGENTS—COLONEL WILLIAM WAKEFIELD—HIS LAND PURCHASES—NATIVE RESERVES—TREATY OF WAITANGI—FRUSTRATION OF FRENCH DESIGNS UPON THE COLONY

THE Durham Report became a more important factor in the history of Britain's colonial empire than even the Wakefield system, yet the Canada expedition was no more than a brilliant episode in the life of Durham's counsellor. We must follow him back to New Zealand, the colony of his predilection, although for long he is not more immediately visible in the events occurring upon the islands than the dramatist whose pen has filled the theatre, but who never appears in person upon the stage.

The pioneers of the *Tory* left England amply provided with instructions from the Company, throughout the greater part of which Wakefield's manly style is easily recognisable. These it is not too much to characterise as models of wisdom as concerned the direction of the Company's affairs, and of fairness as regarded the rights of the various classes affected by the undertaking. They were so framed as not merely to prescribe rules of action, but to answer many of the most specious objections against colonization in New Zealand, and against the measures which it was absolutely necessary to adopt if colonization was to be effectively carried out. Those most anxiously weighed and carefully expressed related to that interference with aboriginal claims which cannot possibly be avoided if the white man is to fulfil his mission of civilising the earth, but which every just and humane person desires to reduce to a minimum.

The language of the New Zealand directors breathes this spirit of justice and humanity.

'The chief difficulty,' they say, 'with which you may have to contend is that of convincing the natives that the expedition under your orders has no object hostile to them. They are necessarily suspicious in consequence of the ill-treatment which they have often received from Europeans. We recommend that you should on every occasion treat them with the most entire frankness, thoroughly explaining to them that you wish to purchase the land for the purpose of establishing a settlement of Englishmen there; and you will abstain from completing any negotiation for a purchase of land until this, its probable result, shall be thoroughly understood by the native proprietors and by the tribe at large. Above all, you will be especially careful that all the owners of any tract of land which you may purchase shall be approving parties to the bargain, and that each of them receives his due share of the purchase money. You will fully explain that the Company intends to dispose of the property to individual settlers expected from England, and that you purchase, if at all, on the same terms as have formed the conditions of private bargains for land in other parts of the islands.

'But in one respect you will not fail to establish a very important difference between the purchases of the Company and those which have hitherto been made by every class of buyers. Wilderness land, it is true, is worth nothing to its native owners, or worth nothing more than the trifle they can obtain for it. We are not therefore to make much account of the inadequacy of the purchase money according to English notions of the value of land. The land is really of no value, and can become valuable only by means of a great outlay of capital on emigration and settlement. But at the same time it may be doubted whether the native owners have ever been entirely aware of the consequences that would result from such cessions, as have already been made to a great extent, of the whole of the lands of a tribe. Justice demands, not merely that these consequences should be as far as possible explained to them, but that the superior intelligence of the buyers should also be exerted to guard them against the evils which, after all, they may not be capable of anticipating. The danger to which they are exposed, and which they cannot well foresee, is that of finding themselves entirely without landed property, and therefore without consideration, in the midst of a society where, through immigration and settlement, land has become a valuable property. Absolutely they would suffer little or nothing from having parted with land which they do not use and cannot exchange; but relatively they would suffer a great deal, inasmuch as their social position would be very inferior to that of the race who had settled amongst them, and given value to their now worthless territory. If the advantage of the natives alone were consulted, it would be better perhaps that they should remain for ever the savages which they are. This consideration appears never to have occurred to any of those who have hitherto purchased lands from the natives of New Zealand. It was first suggested by the New Zealand Association of 1837; and it has great weight with the present Company. In accordance with a plan which the Association of 1837 was desirous that a legislative enactment should extend to every purchase of land from the natives, as well past as future, you will take care to mention in every *bookabooka*, or contract for land, that a proportion of the territory ceded, equal to one-tenth of the whole, will be reserved by the Company, and held in trust by them for the future benefit of the chief families of the tribe.

'The intended reserves of land are regarded as far more important to the natives than anything which you will have to pay in the shape of purchase money. At the same time we are desirous that the purchase money should be less inadequate, according to English notions of the value of land, than has been generally the case in purchases of territory from the New Zealanders. Some of the finest tracts of land, we are assured, have been obtained by missionary catechists and others who really possessed nothing, or next to nothing. In case land should be offered to you for such mere trifles as a few blankets or hatchets, which have heretofore been given for considerable tracts, you will not accept the offer without adding to the goods required such a quantity as may be of real service to all the owners of the land. It is not intended that you should set an example of heedless profusion in this respect; but the Company are desirous that in all their transactions with the natives the latter should derive some immediate and obvious benefit by the intercourse.'

These instructions are indeed admirable. They grapple at once with the difficulty of the apparent inadequacy of the price at which the uncultivated lands of a people destitute of the circulating medium must be acquired, and indicate the means by which the bargain may notwithstanding be made as advantageous to the sellers as to the buyers. When at a later period Sir George Grey, the Maori's friend *par excellence*, made extensive acquisitions of land in the Middle Island, he acted entirely in their spirit, and could do no otherwise. Much, however, depends upon the character of the agent entrusted with the execution of instructions drafted at the other side of the world. Colonel Wakefield's antecedents might have been deemed unfavourable. We have become acquainted with him as a member of the giddy society at Paris among whom the Turner plot was hatched, and as punished for his complicity with a penalty not less severe than that meted out to his brother. He had himself eloped with his wife, the daughter of a baronet, and had been seriously embarrassed in his circumstances, both before and after the Turner episode and its consequences. On the other hand, those who knew him, or have retained the tradition of him, unanimously express amazement at his participation in such a transaction, and declare that this could only be attributed to the contagion of the Parisian circle, and to the irresistible magnetic influence which Edward Gibbon exercised upon most men, and especially upon a brother seven years younger, and particularly open to it from having been attached to him at the Turin embassy while a mere youth. In maturer life William appeared not more shrewd than trustworthy. He had fought for freedom in Spain and Portugal, where he had been especially distinguished for coolness, and was about to distinguish himself in New Zealand by munificent generosity. We shall see that he retained the confidence of the Company through nine most difficult years, and his name is still cherished by the descendants of those whose hardships were shared by him. In such a conflict of evidence, it is fairest to resort to the testimony which the man has unconsciously bequeathed concerning himself, and this is wholly in his favour. In the portions of his correspondence which remain, Colonel Wakefield appears the tender father, the careful guardian, the steady friend, the loyal servant of his employers, just and firm in his dealings with all men.

Intellectually, William Wakefield is described by Mr Gisborne (*New Zealand Rulers and Statesmen*) as 'a pale copy of his brother.' This may be in so far true, that William made no pretence to originality of genius, but he was as much the hand of the New Zealand Company as Edward Gibbon was its brain. Among the hosts of ideas which Edward's creative mind was perpetually emitting, a certain proportion were almost inevitably unsound; he was not always careful to sift these out, and sometimes damaged himself and his cause by advancing arguments or proposals obviously untenable. William, on the other hand, was a man of close reserve, and of that peculiarly baffling secretiveness which is not synonymous with taciturnity. 'His manner,' says Mr Gisborne, 'was attractive, and, in outward appearance, sympathetic, but the inner man was out of sight and hearing.' 'Of medium height,' says Mr Crawford, 'compactly built, fair in complexion and Saxon in appearance and temperament, astute and reticent, he had seen much of the world, both British and foreign, and could make himself a very pleasant companion. People said he was always so, *except when spoken to on business.*' His general conduct of affairs attests his eminent talents as an organiser; and his official despatches and journals, which ought to be reprinted in a volume, are excellent reading.[1]

Among other important points, the instructions given to Colonel Wakefield contemplated the choice of a metropolis for the future colony. 'You should endeavour to make an extensive purchase on the shores of that harbour, which, all things considered, shall appear to offer the greatest facilities as a general trading depot, and port of export and import for all parts of the islands, as a centre of commerce for collecting and exporting the produce of the islands, and for the reception and distribution of foreign goods. In making this selection, you will not forget that Cook's Strait forms part of the shortest route from the Australian colonies to England, and that the best harbour in that channel must inevitably become the most frequented port of colonized New Zealand. That harbour in Cook's Strait is the most valuable, which combines with ample security and convenience as a resort for ships the nearest vicinity to, or the best natural means of communication with, the greatest extent of fertile territory. So far as we are at present informed, Port Nicholson appears superior to any

[1] They will mostly be found in the appendix to the report of the Parliamentary Committee of 1844.

other.' This answers Mr Reeves's criticism, at first sight cogent, that the Company should have confined its operations to the Middle Island, where natives were few. It is true that such a course would have relieved it from many of its embarrassments, although, after all, the greatest disaster it ever encountered occurred in the Middle Island, but would have thrust it into a corner, and left the choice of the metropolitan site to others. No important town has ever arisen on the southern shore of Cook's Strait. Colonel Wakefield, nevertheless, was directed to obtain land 'around one good harbour, at least, on each side of Cook's Strait.' He was further enjoined to keep a journal, to inform the Company of every minute particular, to afford every assistance to the scientific members of the expedition, 'to show all missionaries the respect deserved by the sacrifice they have made as the pioneers of civilisation,' to have divine service on Sunday, and abstain, as far as possible, from work on that day, not so much from scruple, as because the natives, no great workers on week days, deemed the Englishman who worked when he might have rested the most degraded of mankind. Two of the instructions are especially remarkable :—

'We must now mention another rule which you will not fail to impress on all your subordinates; namely, the propriety of carefully avoiding anything like exaggeration in describing the more favourable features of the country. Let the bad be stated as

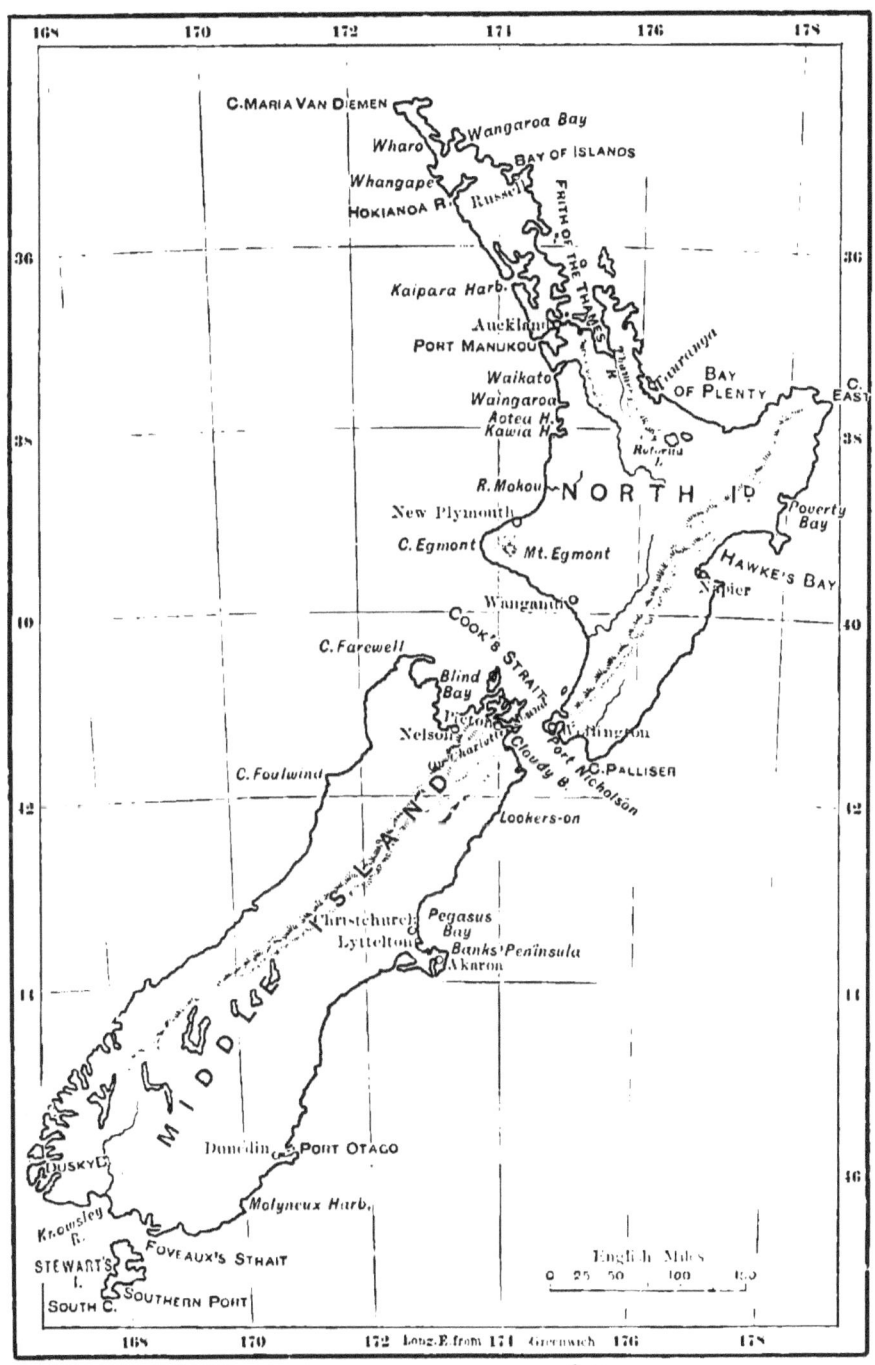

MAP OF NEW ZEALAND, 1837.

(*Showing progress of settlement up to 1850.*)

plainly and fully as the good ; so that the Company, hearing the whole truth as well as nothing but the truth, may run no risk of misleading others.

'You will consider any act of aggression or affront from any of the Company's servants towards any native of New Zealand as a sufficient reason for immediate dismissal from the Company's service, and in the most public manner.'

Colonel Wakefield's expedition, as already stated, sighted New Zealand on 16th August ; and Captain Hobson reached the Bay of Islands on 29th January 1840. The first considerable body of emigrants had already arrived at Port Hardy on 22d January and proceeded to Port Nicholson to take advantage of the land purchases which Colonel Wakefield had been industriously making. The two rival authorities were thus in presence, although the distance between the Bay of Islands and Port Nicholson for some time prevented actual contact. Before leaving England, Hobson had addressed a letter to Lord Normanby, pointing out eleven defects in his instructions. He had obtained scant satisfaction, but a clearer conception of the exigencies of the case compelled Lord John Russell, Lord Normanby's successor, to modify these instructions in several respects. At the same time the Company were obliged to beat a retreat upon an important point. Their intending colonists, finding themselves bound for a land where, in consequence of the obstinate refusal of the British Government to assume sovereignty, no legal jurisdiction over members of its body existed, endeavoured to cure the defect by a voluntary association, and a court elected by mutual consent. This righteous determination was announced with much solemnity on the sailing of the expedition from Blackwall (September 1839), but the Company soon learned with consternation on the highest legal authority that 'if one of the parties to the agreement should commit a murder or an assault, and should be executed or imprisoned accordingly, all the parties to the agreement would be liable to a prosecution for murder, or an action for false imprisonment.' The directors, who had themselves prompted the colonists' action, could but send after them 'their earnest advice and anxious hope that the agreement may not be put in force by anybody.' Lord John Russell should have lost no time in proclaiming British sovereignty, but he still left action to Governor Hobson, nor was he impressed by an able statement, evidently drafted by Wakefield, of the rights of the British Crown, and the imminent danger of French aggression in New Zealand, which the company addressed to Lord Palmerston 'as belonging to the Foreign Department of Her Majesty's Government.' He referred it to Lord John Russell, who took four months to answer,[1] and at last, under pressure

[1] *Foreign Office*, 11th March 1840.—Lord Palmerston desires me to refer you to my letter of the 15th November last, and to request that you will move Lord John Russell to favour him with a reply to that letter.—*Correspondence relative to New Zealand*, p. 68.

from Palmerston, whose view of the matter was probably widely different, replied by an enumeration of formal difficulties which five minutes could have brushed away.

Colonel Wakefield, meanwhile, if indulgence in a graphic but familiar expression may be permitted, had been as busy as the devil in a gale of wind. He had, as we have seen, anchored at Port Nicholson on 24th September. On 27th September he bought, for a liberal assortment of all sorts of articles, from muskets down to shaving brushes, the port and the adjoining territory; on 24th October he concluded a similar purchase on the southern side of the Strait; and on 8th November he purchased large tracts upon both, acquiring altogether, or supposing himself to acquire, a territory about the size of Ireland. The districts acquired were respectively entitled North and South Durham, names afterwards disused. He had, indeed, no time to lose. The hesitations of the Home Government had advertised the profits which speculators might hope to make in New Zealand, and nothing but the swift voyage of the *Tory* and his own promptitude enabled him to baffle a shoal of Australian land-sharks. While he was negotiating, a small trader arrived from Sydney with 'deeds from various merchants to be filled up by the chiefs' names,' *more Batmanico*, and of course lacking in the reserve of land for the benefit of the natives as prescribed by the regulations of the New Zealand

Company.[1] Colonel Wakefield wrote with perfect truth: 'It must be remembered that nine-tenths of the land is without an inhabitant to dispute possession, and that the payment I have made to the owners is large when valued by the standard of exchange known amongst them, and perfectly satisfactory to the sellers.' Well it might be, for the literary capabilities of the New Zealanders had been recognised by an allotment of slates and pencils, and a gross of Jews' harps had been contributed to stimulate any latent taste for music. There was, nevertheless, a grievous flaw in the title which Colonel Wakefield conceived himself to have acquired; the sellers, according to New Zealand ideas, had no right to sell. To Europeans long ago emerged from the savage state, it seems almost incomprehensible that societies should exist where co-operative associations cannot be bound by the majority, and where no individual has the least bit of land that he can call his own. But such was actually the case in New Zealand. No land purchase could be considered safe unless every adult male of the tribe had been consulted and had given his sanction, even though he were the captive of

---

[1] 'Mr John Wright, settler at the Bay of Islands, has a property of which three of the boundary lines are well defined, but the fourth boundary line being "as far as the said John Wright shall think proper," it will be a matter of some difficulty for future doctors of the civil law in New Zealand to decide where that boundary shall be.—LANG, *New Zealand in* 1839.

another clan, or serving on board a whaler, or fulfilling an engagement with Mr Barnum. Such a condition, all but impossible of fulfilment in any case, was most manifestly so in the circumstances of haste under which Colonel Wakefield acted. The inevitable neglect led to a host of evils—misunderstandings and consequent wars with the natives, quarrels between the representatives of the Company and the Crown, the infliction of grievous hardships upon innocent settlers by the invalidation of titles upon which they had every right to rely, and the extent to which bargains, believed to be concluded, were opened and reopened *ad infinitum*. Mr Reeves is perfectly justified in remarking that 'the first occupation of New Zealand was rushed, and, like everything else that is done in a hurry, it was in part done very badly. The settlement of the North Island should not have been begun until after an understanding had been come to with the Imperial authorities and the missionaries, and on a proper and legal system of land purchase.' But this was no fault of the Company, which had been vainly trying to come to an understanding with the Government and the missionaries ever since June 1837, and had at last been goaded into activity by the imminent danger that French annexation would be the consummation of all things. The very step into which, to the nation's unspeakable advantage, they drove the Government, of proclaiming British sovereignty, might have been their own ruin. Though the subsequent action of the Government's representative in annulling all land transactions previous to the annexation could have been foreseen by no one, it was to be expected that as soon as the authority of the Crown was proclaimed in New Zealand, all subsequent alienations of land would be prohibited, and that, consequently, if the Company did not anticipate this step by extensive purchases, it would be unable to fulfil its obligations to the large body of emigrants for whom it had undertaken to find settlements, most of whom were already actually on their way. This, even more than the dread of the speculative land-sharks from Sydney, explains the preternatural purchasing power of Colonel Wakefield, to whom the cognomen of 'Wideawake,' into which his family name was altered by the Maoris, was to a great extent applicable, and would have been even more so if he had surmised that the crafty New Zealand chiefs knew more about New Zealand land titles than he did, and were chuckling even then at the prospect of selling their land again and again, even unto seventy times seven.

The commercial intercourse of civilised nations and barbarians, especially as concerns dealing with land, raises difficult problems for the jurist and philanthropist. The maxim, 'property has its duties as well as its rights,' applies to savage quite as much as to civilised man. It cannot be admitted that a tribe of cannibals has a right to retain large tracts of the earth's surface, on or near which they happen to have established themselves, in an unproductive and useless condition. It is the duty and the very *raison d'être* of the civilised man to develop the resources of the earth, and if he neglected this he would be punished by the ills that follow in the train of over-population at home. Yet, as a civilised tenant cannot well settle under a cannibal suzerain, he must in some manner acquire his land unless he can first civilise his landlord. The latter experiment was tried in New Zealand by the missionaries, and failed because it was impossible to shut out other European influences of a pernicious nature, insomuch that civilisation was far outrun by depopulation. Traders and land speculators had their own methods, which may be defined as taking advantage of the ignorance of the savage, and buying him out for a song. Equity and humanity must alike disapprove; yet part of the disapprobation with which such proceedings have been visited arises from an erroneous conception of the rights of property among barbarians. There was commonly no development, no reclamation, not even any occupation to establish a title morally valid. Large tracts spoken of as though they had been transmitted from father to son since the arrival of the first inhabitants, with title-deeds tattooed upon the persons of the natives, were utterly waste and entirely worthless to the nominal possessors, conferring no advantage or privilege but the right of shooting rats. The natives, except as regarded the land actually brought under cultivation, were not proprietors but squatters, with rights comparable to that possessed by an English cottager of grazing his donkey upon a common. So opines Vattel, first among the expounders of the law of nations. It is sufficiently ridiculous to observe the deference paid to such shadowy pretensions, so long as the claimant is black brown or red, by writers who would oust the white proprietor in every country who has complied with every legal and moral condition of ownership, by open violence or the more cowardly device of an oppressive land tax. This deserves no other name than cant; but it is no less certain that every *bonâ fide* claim, however indefinite, ought to be fully acknowledged and satisfied to its full worth. But how is this compensation to be made? There is something shocking to refined feeling in acquiring the possessions of poor ignorant people for trinkets and cloth, or even for tools and weapons. It is true that these commodities have an immense value in their eyes, but the civilised purchaser knows well that this value is partly fictitious, and that the really useful part of the consideration he tenders will wear out in time and leave nothing to replace it. Money multiplies itself, but money in the then condition of the natives would have been useless to them and incomprehensible. The New Zealand Company met the difficulty in the only way in which it can be met, by the reservation for the natives of a portion of their land, which, though comparatively small, could, through the development of the country by European colonization, come to be far more valuable to them than the whole. Wakefield put the matter into a nutshell before the Committee of 1840:—

'The terms were, a payment, in the first instance, of various goods, such as the natives require, but which the Company regard as a merely nominal price. They have paid for their lands a much higher price than has commonly been paid by other purchasers in the first instance ; but the consideration which they offer to the natives, and which they regard as the true purchase money of the land, is the reserved eleventh, which eleventh, by means of the expenditure of the Company, acquires, in a very short time, a higher value than all the land possessed before. I feel myself quite satisfied that if the measure were to proceed in the best way, every acre of the land reserved would be worth at least thirty shillings ; so that there would be an endowment of three millions sterling in the course of time as a native provision.'

Mr Buller (not Charles Buller) pertinently inquires :—

'What security is there that the natives will have the benefit of it?

'There is no security at present, because the Government has hitherto refused to let law be established in New Zealand, so that it is impossible to create a trust. The Company are very desirous of placing this land in trust for the benefit of the natives. They have considered the subject a good deal, but they have found great difficulty in defining, till they have better information, what the trusts ought to be. Their objects in reserving these lands has been to preserve the native race. They believe that it will be impossible to preserve the native race, that the native race in New Zealand will undergo the same fate which has attended other people in their situation, unless their chief families can be preserved in a state of civilisation in the same relative superiority of position as they before enjoyed in savage life; and with this view the Company is desirous of investing them with property. But if it placed the property at once at their disposal, they would sell it for a trifle. It became, therefore, necessary to create a permanent trust. That the Company will do as soon as they possibly can; and in the meantime they have appointed a commissioner, whom they have sent out for the purpose of preserving, letting and taking care of those lands.'

These roseate anticipations, of course, were based on the supposition that the Company's purchases would not be interfered with, and when they were cut down from twenty millions of acres to two hundred and eighty-three thousand, the possibility of forming any considerable fund for the benefit of the natives came to an end.

There seems no reason to charge the New Zealand Company with indifference to the well-being of the native race. The one fault was the want of due inquiry into the validity of the titles supposed to be conveyed by the native vendors ; and this was forced upon Colonel Wakefield by the necessity for extreme dispatch, lest the Company should in the meantime be deprived of all purchasing power. Far otherwise would it have been if, instead of stealing away from a hostile and jealous Government, the *Tory* had sailed under Government auspices, and with an Imperial Commissioner on board.

The Imperial Commissioner who did sail, and who, through no fault of his own, sailed into the north of the colonists' opinion, had arrived at the Bay of Islands. Captain Hobson had touched at Sydney, where he took council with the resolute and autocratic Governor, Sir George Gipps, his immediate official superior, who on 14th January issued a proclamation annulling by anticipation all purchases of land that might be made after that date. Hobson's instructions did not allow him to take the simple and common-sense course of proclaiming the sovereignty of Great Britain by right of discovery, though Captain Cook had done as much seventy years previously. It was necessary to obtain a treaty of cession from the natives, who were convened for the purpose at Waitangi (*Sounding Water*, so called from a cascade). Had they refused, as they were very near doing at the instigation of the Roman Catholic missionary bishop, the Governor would have been placed in the most painful and ludicrous position, and would have had no *locus standi* in the islands. Happily they yielded under the influence of the famous English missionary, Henry Williams. The treaty was signed on 6th February,[1] but four months were spent in obtaining the concurrence of native chiefs in other parts of the islands. It was not until 17th June 1840 that British sovereignty was proclaimed in the Middle Island. Had the French been more alert, this delay would have had serious consequences. But it was not until July that a French frigate, *L'Aube*, appeared at the Bay of Islands with orders to take possession of Akaroa in the Middle Island. Had not Wakefield compelled the British Government to send Hobson out, or had the treaty of Waitangi fallen through, there would have been nothing to prevent this, for the Government had repudiated their perfectly valid title by right of discovery, and could have alleged no other. The

---

[1] A diary recording the progress of the negotiations from day to day was kept by the Rev. W. Colenso, and was published at Wellington in 1890. Mr Colenso expressed his doubts whether the chiefs understood what they were signing, but His Excellency thought he had done as much to enlighten them as could be expected from anybody ignorant of their language.

Middle Island might then have become another New Caledonia. Even as it was, France could have set up a claim of pre-emption in 1838 by a French whaling master, who had actually paid one hundred and fifty francs as earnest money. Hobson, however, divined the French captain's intention, and hurried Captain Owen Stanley in the *Britomart* to the spot. Stanley beat the French frigate by four days, and the sight of the British flag flying scared *L'Aube* to sea again. She, nevertheless, disembarked some intending settlers, who eventually, for the most part, migrated to the Marquesas.

In this lame fashion did New Zealand eventually hobble into the ranks of the British colonies and the Maories become British subjects. Apart from these results, the treaty of Waitangi was no matter for congratulation. It could not have been obtained at all without an enormous and uncalled for concession, the recognition, in spite of Vattel, of the absolute right of seventy thousand savages to sixty-six millions of acres of valuable land, by far the greater part of which they had never occupied, and were incapable of turning to account in any way. This carried the recognition of the tribal tenure along with it, and native sovereignty and native jurisprudence together opened a Pandora's box of ills for the unfortunate settlers, thus powerfully described by the present Agent-General for New Zealand, the Hon. W. P. Reeves:—

'Had Captain Hobson been able to conceive what was entailed in the piecemeal purchase of a country held under tribal ownership, it is difficult to think that he would have signed the treaty without hesitation. He could not, of course, imagine that he was giving legal force to a system under which the buying of a block of land would involve years of bargaining, even when a majority of its owners wished to sell; that the ascertainment of a title would mean tedious and costly examination by courts of experts of a labyrinth of strange and conflicting barbaric customs; that land might be paid for again and again, and yet be declared unsold; that an almost empty wilderness might be bought first from its handful of occupants, then from the conquerors who had laid it waste, and yet after all be reclaimed by returned slaves or fugitives who had quitted it years before.'

It is now easy to discern what the Government ought to have done. Instead of thwarting the original New Zealand Association, they should have reposed a generous though not a blind trust in it. They should have at once incorporated New Zealand in the Empire, and ruled it through the Association, enjoying the status and subjected to the restraints of a chartered company, and under the surveillance of an agent of the Government. They should have provided a law-making power which might at a stroke have got rid of the nuisance of tribal titles to land, while the executive should have seen that the real interest of the natives did not suffer. The administration, apart from the Association's share in it, should from the first have been in stronger hands than those of a captain in the navy, taking orders from the Governor of another colony. A first-rate man should have been chosen, strong in ability and devotion, able to overawe, if need were, both natives and colonists, and not unprovided with naval and military force. The England of Victoria, no less than anciently the England of Elizabeth, had many rising young men competent for such a mission, enthusiastic at the prospect of building a new State, and to whom three or four years of such experience would have been invaluable. The envoy would have returned an accomplished Colonial Minister, and qualified for activity in any sphere. What if the choice had fallen upon William Ewart Gladstone?

CHAPTER VIII

SETTLEMENT OF WELLINGTON — ILL-JUDGED PROCLAMATION OF GOVERNOR HOBSON—AUCKLAND MADE THE SEAT OF GOVERNMENT—THE COMPANY AND THE COLONIAL OFFICE—MASSACRE OF WAIRAU — GOVERNORS FITZROY AND GREY— WAKEFIELD'S ILLNESS

GOVERNMENTAL mismanagement had created two rival authorities in New Zealand, one clothed with the attributes of legality, the other representing the brain and muscle of the colony. Before Captain Hobson could take any steps to assert the supremacy with which he had undoubtedly been invested, the pioneers of the *Tory* had been reinforced by the arrival of six emigrant ships between 22d January and 7th March, bearing the choicest contingent of colonists, the South Australian excepted, that had come to form a British settlement since the days of the *Mayflower*, and superior to the Pilgrim Fathers in their average standard of culture, and as representatives of all classes of the nation. All landed at Port Nicholson. The history of the infant settlement, almost from day to day, may be read in Colonel Wakefield's reports and in Edward Jerningham Wakefield's *Adventures in New Zealand*, a book which will always hold a distinguished place among English books of travel, notwithstanding an atmosphere of controversy conducted with questionable taste and temper, and an unevenness mainly attributable to its having been compiled from letters written home. 'Then between thirteen and fourteen years of age,' says Mr Albert Allom in his delightful pamphlet of reminiscences of Edward Gibbon Wakefield, 'it was my great happiness to be sent for on every arrival of despatches, in order that I might have the first perusal of the diary of E. J. Wakefield, giving an account of the expedition of Colonel Wakefield which founded Wellington.' Colonel Wakefield would undoubtedly be worshipped by the present race of Wellingtonians as a hero, did the Hellenic dispensation still obtain. After one abortive attempt at location, the city was founded in its present picturesque but confined situation, compared by Lord Lyttelton to that of Ilfracombe, cramped and hemmed in by furzy hills, but with deep water to the shore, and with the magnificent central position which has made it, though but fifth among New Zealand cities in population, the capital of the country. It was originally called Britannia, but Edward Gibbon Wakefield, among whose virtues gratitude held a conspicuous place, remembered the service which the Duke of

Wellington had rendered to the South Australian colonists, and how the intended acknowledgment had been thwarted. By his interposition, and as a personal favour to himself, the city received the name of Wellington.

For a short time affairs at Wellington went on propitiously. Up to the date (4th June) when Lieutenant Shortland, Colonial Secretary, arrived to proclaim the Queen's sovereignty, and put an end to the provisional state of things which had hitherto obtained, 'nearly fifteen hundred English people and four hundred untutored savages had lived for five months without any serious breach of the laws, to which they were bound by nothing more than a voluntary agreement, and which could summon no physical force to their assistance.' Much ill-feeling was unfortunately created by a perfectly needless proclamation of Governor Hobson, declaring that the measures necessarily adopted by the colonists for self-protection until a regular government could be established 'amounted to high treason,' and styling the magistrates provisionally appointed 'an usurping government.' To his further definition of the Port Nicholson settlers as 'adventurers' they replied with spirit. 'It is true that we are adventurers. We have ventured property and life, our own property and that of our children, in an undertaking which was rightly called by the sagacious Bacon heroic. If our adventure be successful we shall have laid the foundation of a community speaking the language and enjoying the institutions of England.' Hobson, nevertheless, meant well, and would probably have acted otherwise if he had seen Wellington for himself, but he was detained in the north by a stroke of paralysis. A great opportunity of conciliating all classes of settlers was lost when he proclaimed the seat of government at Auckland, founded by himself under the advice of Henry Williams, on a site admirably selected for a city, but so severed from the rest of the colony that correspondence with Wellington frequently went by way of Sydney. The original plan of laying out, long ago amended, had many fantastic features, and seemed better adapted to serve the purposes of speculators in land than those of *bonâ fide* colonists. In judging Hobson's proceedings, it must be remembered that, though as a naval officer he was a captain, as a colonial governor he was but a lieutenant, and owed deference to his superior, Sir George Gipps, Governor of New South Wales, one of the most masterful rulers our Australian possessions have ever had. Gipps, to his credit, was engaged at home in a campaign for the protection of New Zealand against the ravenous land speculators of Australia, whose ideas are well illustrated by the tale, be it *vero* or *ben trovato*, of one of them who proclaimed from the summit of the highest hill available, 'I claim for myself all the land I can see, and all that I cannot see I claim for my son John.' At this system, but no less at the rights and just expectations of the settlers who had come out on the faith of the Company's promises, Gipps struck an overwhelming blow by his Act of 4th August 1840, annulling all titles to land in New Zealand 'which are not or may not be hereafter allowed by Her Majesty.' The Act was as illogical as despotic, for it extended to all transactions which had taken place before New Zealand had become a British possession; otherwise, however, the Governor's purpose of frustrating the Australian land speculators would not have been attained. All the mischief came from the Home Government's delay in proclaiming New Zealand an independent colony, and their omission to send out a governor and a council along with the Company's first expedition. New Zealand having in the meantime been declared a separate colony, the Act was temporarily disallowed at home, but was re-enacted by Hobson in June 1841, Government undertaking to send out a commissioner to investigate claims. It is only just to Sir George Gipps to state that, upon receiving a deputation from Wellington, he made a temporary compromise which was not regarded as unsatisfactory, but there could be no finality until the conclusion of the commissioner's inquiries. 'This functionary's award,' says Mr Reeves, 'was not given for years. When he did give it, he cut down the Company's purchase of twenty million acres to two hundred and eighty-three thousand. Meantime, the long and weary months dragged on, and the unfortunate settlers were either not put in possession of their land at all, or had as little security for their farms as for their lives.'

It could not be expected that the New Zealand Company at home would tolerate these aggressions on its property. It had struck deep root. 'New Zealand House,' was established in Broad Street Buildings, and Wakefield had taken up his private residence under its roof. Numbers of persons had become interested in the fortunes of the Company; and New Zealand, without the stimulus of gold and diamond mining, filled nearly the same place in the popular imagination as South Africa does now. The emigrants, as Wakefield meant they should, included representatives of every class of society; among them were Domett, the friend of Browning, and Charles Armitage Brown, the friend of Keats. When, on 27th June 1839, Mr H. G. Ward brought forward his resolutions in the House of Commons on the subject of colonial lands, he was able to state that the association had sold 666 sections, containing 67,266 acres of land, for upwards of £70,000. This was while the *Tory* was still on her voyage, before a single emigrant ship had been despatched, or a single acre bought in New Zealand on account of the Company. On 29th July a public drawing was held, to determine priority of choice in the selection of lots, by this time amounting to 100,000 acres. The ladies, it was remarked, appeared the most daring speculators. Eleven thousand acres were set apart for the natives, whose representatives were fortunate in their drawings, every instance of their success eliciting loud cheers. The drawings—lotteries without blanks—continued until the company was obliged to suspend its operations. Every means was taken to lend *éclat* to the periodical despatches of emigrants. 'How well I remember,' exclaims Mr Allom, 'the steamer trips down the river and the grand dinners at Gravesend!' The original fare of eighty guineas was soon reduced to thirty-five. In 1840 a Committee of the House of Commons, to be described more particularly in a subsequent chapter, sat to investigate New Zealand questions. The draft report of the chairman, Lord Eliot, was entirely favourable to the Company, but was rejected by the majority, who simply reported the evidence without making any recommendation. It produced, however, a considerable effect on the mind of Lord John Russell, who had succeeded Lord Normanby as Colonial Secretary, and who, if somewhat stiff and supercilious, was at all events a statesman.[1] He came (November 1840) to an arrangement with the Company, guaranteeing them as many acres as should be equal to four times the number of pounds sterling expended in the despatch of ships and other necessary expenses, a virtual admission that the Company had

---

[1] 'You once asked me how Stephen and I liked Lord John's way of doing business. Very much—very different to anything before him.'—*Henry Taylor* to *Edward Villiers*, October 1839.

done well in preserving New Zealand to England by the despatch of the *Tory*. He agreed that the price of land should be a pound an acre, and that half the proceeds of sales should be expended in promoting immigration. He erected New Zealand into an independent government, and, unfortunately too late, directed Sir George Gipps to suspend the execution of his Sydney Land Act until further instructions. Above all, in February 1841, he gave the Company a legal status by bestowing upon it a charter of incorporation. Some troublesome questions respecting the amount actually expended by the Company, and the consequent extent of its claims under the agreement, remained to be settled, but these were mere questions of detail, and all might have gone well had Lord John Russell remained at the Colonial Office. Unfortunately for the Britain of the South, though not for the Britain of the North, a change of government occurred in August 1841. The new Secretary of State, Lord Stanley, belonging to the opposite party in politics, was inaccessible to the private influences which had probably worked upon Lord John Russell, and his distinguished oratorical gifts and resolute vigour were unaccompanied by any insight into the problems of statesmanship. In the interim, the Company had lost (28th July 1840) its nominal head, Lord Durham, whose health had long disabled him from actual attention to its affairs, but who served it efficaciously after his death if, as is probable, Lord

John Russell's regard for his memory had something to do with the changed attitude of the Colonial Office. Mr Somes, the Deputy Governor, succeeded him, and Wakefield became ostensibly a, as well as virtually the, director, although his name will seldom be found appended to the official documents which he drafted or inspired :—

> So that the ram, that batters down the wall,
> For the great swing and rudeness of his poise,
> They place before his hand that made the engine;
> Or those that with the fineness of their souls
> By reason guide his execution.

'I have not time,' Wakefield writes to his father, in October 1841, 'to attend to details; almost every hour of my day, to say nothing of nights, from year's end to year's end, being engaged in taking care of the principles and main points of our New Zealand enterprise, and in what Arthur calls "the management of people," which means the persuading of all sorts of dispositions to pull together for a common object.'

In the course of 1841, Lord John Russell sent out to New Zealand two of the most distinguished men who ever went there, a pair of old Cambridge friends—George Augustus Selwyn as Bishop, and Sir William Martin as Chief Justice. Martin went out in the same vessel with Swainson, appointed Attorney-General, and ere they landed the two had prepared a legal system adapted for an infant colony, which shortly bore fruit in abundant legislation. Selwyn, not to be outdone, learned Maori from a native during the voyage, and arrived speaking it fluently.

The Bishopric incarnated an idea of the New Zealand Company's already put forward in 1837. Wakefield had written to his sister Catherine in November 1841 :—[1]

'We had a long and very satisfactory interview with the Bishop yesterday. The object of the Bishop's meeting with our committee was to come to some practical determination as to what was to be done for the Church of England and benefit of the natives in the Company's settlements; and it was resolved accordingly, subject to the approval of our Court to-day—First, that the Company would advance, on the security of the native reserves at Wellington, £5000 for the purpose of immediately establishing schools for natives, where the children may live away from their parents. Secondly, that the Bishop and the Company agree to subscribe as much respectively as the other shall subscribe for endowment of the Church of England at Wellington, Wanganui, New Plymouth, and Nelson. The Bishop undertook for the great Societies and we for the Company. So there is a race between the Church and the Company as to which shall first collect the larger sum ; and the more either shall collect, the more precisely must the other furnish. We, having the money in hand, began with

[1] Printed in Dean Jacob's *History of the Church of New Zealand.*

£5000 for Nelson, which secures £10,000, the Church being bound to double our subscription. I shall do my utmost to get a large contribution from the Company for Wellington and New Plymouth. The Company has already contributed, in land and money, £2000 towards the endowment of the New Zealand bishopric.'

From the date of Lord Stanley's accession the annals of New Zealand for several years become disagreeable and uninviting. The historians of the period, from Mr Rusden on one side to Mr E. J. Wakefield on the other, offer a continual spectacle of crimination and recrimination, and the fatigued reader may well abandon the hope of arriving at any sound conclusion if he has not a firm grasp of the idea that while all parties concerned—agents of the Company, settlers, missionaries, officials—committed many and grievous errors, the mistakes of individuals were unimportant in comparison with the fundamentally vicious situation created by the indecision of the Home Government. All was confusion and uncertainty. The Company, deprived by the Government proclamation of their purchases for an indefinite period, until a commissioner should report what proportion he would allow them, and equally frustrated by Lord Stanley's action of the compensation Lord John Russell had promised them, could convey no valid titles to their colonists, who were tempted to abandon the settlement, but whose pluck and perseverance in their trials constitute a bright chapter of British colonial history. The reluctance to assume control of the country by a direct act of imperial authority had necessitated the treaty of Waitangi, which had recognised the natives as possessors of the soil, not merely where they had settled upon it, but where they were merely rovers across it, and had bound the British to respect native customs and traditions, even where these were virtually prohibitive of colonization. There could not be a stronger instance of this than in the case of Taranaki, otherwise New Plymouth, in the Northern Island, where a colony mainly drawn from Devon and Cornwall had been planted in 1841 by the New Plymouth Company, which had bought 60,000 acres of land from the New Zealand Company. These acres had been purchased by Colonel Wakefield from a tribe who claimed by right of conquest, but who had not themselves put the land to beneficial use. When the conquered tribe, at the time in a state of bondage to the victors, regained their freedom through the influence of Christianity, they demanded payment as proprietors. Was this preposterous claim to be adjudicated by English or by Maori law? Under the latter it was possibly good; at all events the successor of Hobson (who had died, more esteemed than regretted, on 10th September 1842), Captain, afterwards Admiral, Fitzroy, thought so. 'Instead,' says an impartial authority, Mr Reeves, 'of paying them fairly for the 60,000 acres—which they did not require—he handed the bulk of it back to them, penning the unhappy white settlers up in a miserable strip of 3200 acres. The result was the temporary ruin of the Taranaki settlement and the sowing of the seeds of an intense feeling of resentment and injustice, which bore evil fruit in later days.'

Admiral Fitzroy's motive for this excessive condescension was probably fear of a native war, which his pliancy was more likely to invite than to avert. He did much worse in the Middle Island. Under the provisional administration of Lieutenant Shortland (September 1842—January 1844), the most dismal tragedy that ever occurred in New Zealand had taken place. The settlement of Nelson, on Blind Bay in the Middle Island, had been founded in October 1841 by an expedition consisting of three vessels, the *Arrow*, the *Will Watch* and the *Whitby*, which had sailed on 28th April under the direction of Captain Arthur Wakefield, R.N., with whom we have already become acquainted, 'not only an able pioneer leader,' says Mr Reeves, 'but a man of high worth, of singularly fine and winning character, and far the most popular of his family.'[1]

[1] Bishop Selwyn says in an unpublished private letter: 'I believe that a more humane and judicious man than Captain Wakefield did not exist, or one more desirous of promoting a good understanding between the two races.' In Mr Gisborne's *New Zealand Rulers and Statesmen*, pp. 20-22, is a most beautiful character of Arthur Wakefield as the ideal colonist, written by Mr Alfred Domett, afterwards Prime Minister of New Zealand.

The settlement was at first most prosperous, but by June 1843, land difficulties arose with the natives, 'tampered with,' Colonel Wakefield complained, 'by a host of missionaries, protectors, magistrates and commissioners.' Huts erected by the Company in the Wairau district were burned down by two native chiefs, Rauparaha and Rangihaiatea. What ensued is described in a letter from Colonel Wakefield to his sister Catherine, not hitherto published :—

'The magistrates of Nelson granted a warrant against Rauparaha and Rangihaiatea for the offence, and the police magistrate (Mr Thompson), Arthur, and several gentlemen volunteers left Nelson, accompanied by about forty labourers, to execute the warrant. They found the natives assembled in a strong position, where the police magistrate, very rashly and against the opinion of others, insisted upon carrying his point of arresting the chiefs. An accidental shot brought on a volley from each side, after which the white men, being country labourers, unused to arms and discipline, fled, in spite of the urgent efforts of Arthur and Mr Howard to rally them. A truce was most unadvisedly demanded by means of waving a white handkerchief, the whole party of Englishmen surrendered to savages flushed with victory and inflamed with the taste for blood. The consequence is soon told. The native chiefs, surprised at their own success, and unused to give or receive quarter on the field, slaughtered the prisoners with their tomahawks. Nineteen victims have been buried on the field of action.'

Colonel Wakefield shortly afterwards wrote: 'For myself, having been four years here and having fought an uphill game with some success, I should be glad to finish my work and see the settlement established prosperously, but the loss of poor Arthur and the disgusting opposition of the Government, which has led to it, have nearly upset me, and incline me to go home myself.' In fact, Admiral Fitzroy upon his arrival found British prestige drooping, and it is only just to admit that he had not the material force which would have enabled him to revive it. But he need not have trailed it in the dust. He sought an interview with the revolted chiefs, told them that the English were in the wrong, and that he should not endeavour to avenge their deaths, gently blamed the savages for having massacred their prisoners in cold blood, and concluded by exhorting all and sundry to live in peace for the future. Rauparaha very naturally observed next day that 'the man had been talking a great lot of nonsense to him, but it was all lies, and that, in fact, he was afraid of him.' Such was indeed the fact. Admiral Fitzroy, afterwards renowned as a meteorologist, had been a man of mettle and a famous circumnavigator, and although Lord Stanley courageously pronounced his conduct not only wise but bold also, he must have been entirely unnerved by a sense of responsibility.

The consequences were soon manifest. In the following year Heke, a powerful chief of the Northern Island, entered the town of Kororareka (newly christened Russell) and cut down the staff which displayed the British flag. Encouraged by Fitzroy's vacillation, he again invaded the settlement, and this time plundered and burned it, the inhabitants escaping on board ships in the bay. An assault upon his fortified pah failed, and British prestige disappeared for the time being. Fitzroy's finance had been as unsuccessful as his fighting. He issued £15,000 in Government promissory notes, and, finding that nobody would take them, declared them legal tender. Money could not be raised at fifteen per cent. Lord Stanley's *tracasseries* had compelled the Company to suspend its operations, to the ruin of the labourers and others dependent upon it, and the colony's condition seemed hopeless when, in November 1845, Fitzroy was replaced by Sir George Grey, the saviour of South Australia. The Home Government, now thoroughly alarmed, gave Grey more support than they had accorded to Fitzroy. Something, too, he owed to good fortune, but in the main it was his energy and wisdom which restored peace and solvency within a year.

Grey's appointment marks a new era in New Zealand history. When, after an enforced withdrawal for a season, Wakefield returned to New Zealand politics, it was to act upon another stage.

During 1842 and 1843 his attention, as we have seen, had been largely engrossed by the affairs of Canada. The Wairau massacre brought him back, and the next three years, the most laborious of his life, tried him until, he said, it made him dizzy to look at New Zealand House. In the next chapter, mainly devoted to his activity as an organiser behind the scenes, we shall have to describe his contest with the Colonial Office in the Parliamentary Committee of 1844, and in the great debate of 1845. At the end of this year Lord Stanley's retirement brought Mr Gladstone to the Colonial Secretaryship, and Wakefield saw a chance. 'Deeming Mr Gladstone perfectly able to seize, and not likely to despise, the opportunity of establishing in one instance a system of colonization and Colonial Government that might serve as a model for the reform of other colonies and for after time, I submitted to him by letter a plan for the settlement of New Zealand affairs, but too late for enabling him to come to any official decision upon it.' By so doing, as Wakefield believed, but most erroneously, if Sir Henry Taylor is justified in crediting the Minister with 'more freedom from littlenesses of feeling than I have met with before in any public man,' he gave mortal offence to Mr Gladstone's successor, Earl Grey, who had recently rendered the New Zealand Company much service, but all of a sudden 'seemed incapable of deciding officially any one of the points which, out of office, he had so lately and so completely determined in his own mind.' An interview between Wakefield and the Earl gave no satisfaction to either. Wakefield, whose health had shown signs of succumbing to excessive toil in the autumn of 1844, at the time could hardly stand or speak from illness. A few days afterwards his long-overtaxed physical and mental powers forsook him. On 18th August 1846, walking in the Strand, he was struck down by paralysis of the brain, and his life was probably saved by the presence of Charles Allom, who refused to allow him to be bled. Nursed by his faithful friend, Mrs Allom, he long lay suspended between life and death.

CHAPTER IX

THE TRANSPORTATION COMMITTEE—THE COLONIAL LANDS COMMITTEE—THE NEW ZEALAND COMMITTEES OF 1840 AND 1844—THE NEW ZEALAND COMPANY AND LORD STANLEY—DEBATES IN THE COMMONS — WAKEFIELD AND ADAM SMITH — POLITICS FOR THE PEOPLE

IT is asserted by psychologists, and the assertion admits of confirmation from the experience of every reflecting man, that the absolute stock of knowledge, thought and emotion of which we are conscious bears but a small proportion to the stores latent in the mind in a sub-conscious condition, but ready to be called into activity at any moment by the application of the proper stimulus. It is equally true of the brain of the State, that the visible is but little in comparison with the invisible energy, that conspicuous events are commonly but the outcome of long, slow, and subterranean 'processes. Especially is this the case with reforms prepared by the agency of Parliamentary Committees, whose function is frequently that of mere publication. The visible proceedings of such Committees, we may be sure, bear hardly a larger proportion to the invisible forces which have set their machinery in motion than does the limited domain of fully conscious mind to the dim infinitude of unconscious cerebration. All the labour of Edward Gibbon Wakefield of which it is possible to take cognisance would probably appear insignificant in comparison with his exertions in originating, organising, coaching, cramming, sometimes, perhaps, coaxing or mystifying the various Parliamentary Committees convened to further his projects, or whose interference with these he had to avert.

Wakefield's activity as a Parliamentary engineer followed the same development as his activity as a writer and a promoter of companies; it began with gaols and ended with colonies. The transition was effected through the then prevailing system of transportation, a subject equally important to the reformer of prisons at home and to the emigrant to distant settlements.

It is a sufficient refutation of Machiavelli's and Bentham's systems of ethics, that they cannot be applied where they are least exceptionable in point of morality, and most palpably useful to the community. No one, unless when demonstrably incorrigible offenders were in question, ever proposed to extinguish crime by extinguishing criminals, although such a measure would be far less shocking to moral feeling than the sacrifice of the innocent for reasons of State, and nothing could more effectually promote 'the greatest happiness of the greatest number.' Transportation is undoubtedly the next remedy in point of effectiveness, and the existence of antipodal regions where criminals could be isolated from the sound part of the community must have at first seemed an absolute godsend. By and by the system appeared liable to grievous objections, a large proportion of which, however, did not concern Wakefield as a Builder of Greater Britain. The foundation of a penal settlement on the island of Ascension, for example, might be deplorable on many accounts, and especially detrimental to the interests of the Corporation of London, but would blight no rising nation. It was far otherwise when England took to rearing future empires on a substratum of convictism, and rendering the fair parts of the earth which she had occupied as trustee for her own surplus population uninhabitable by decent citizens. The state of affairs which thus grew up in New South Wales, divided between a small and grasping set of tyrannical officials, a middle class of 'emancipists,' or liberated convicts, from which servants or shopkeepers were chiefly recruited, a sprinkling of honest settlers, considered, Darwin says, by the emancipists as interlopers, and a labouring class of convicts serving out their sentences, may be read in Bennett's *History of Australian Discovery and Colonization*. No healthy element could be infused into a society of pardoned felons, where the Attorney-General's own clerk was an ex-convict : it was not until 1818 that two persons found their way to the colony as free passengers paying their own passage. Here was something for a colonial reformer to protest against, and Wakefield was early in the field, here as elsewhere in advance of his time, for the free colonists themselves, looking merely to cheapness of labour, and not perceiving the rottenness which they were introducing into the social fabric, were for a long time passionate advocates of deportation. Even Darwin, while admitting that any moral reform was out of the question, thought that the system had succeeded in 'making men outwardly honest, and thus giving birth to a rich and splendid country.'[1] Yet he sums up, 'Nothing but rather sharp necessity should compel *me* to emigrate.' Wakefield discussed the subject, though not very profoundly from the point of view of colonial interests, in his *Letter from Sydney*, and from that of English prison discipline, in his essay on *The Punishment of Death*. The small band of colonial reformers with whom he was associated thought with him, and at their instance it was especially enacted that no deportation of convicts should ever take place to their

---

[1] These epithets seem discordant with Darwin's generally unfavourable impression of Australia. One remark he makes is curious ; he says that wool cannot be profitably transported for any considerable distance on account of the unfitness of the country for canals. Yet the Liverpool and Manchester Railway had been opened for more than a year before he left England.

pattern colony of South Australia. Wakefield's first appearance before any Parliamentary Committee was in 1831, when he gave evidence, repeating and emphasising some of the most remarkable passages in his *Punishment of Death*, before the Committee of the Commons on Secondary Punishments. It was not until 1837 that he was able to organise the memorable inquiry which gave transportation a mortal blow.

It may appear strange to find this Committee cited as an instance of Wakefield's beneficent activity as a colonial reformer, for although his hand may be traced in its recommendations on the sale of land and the encouragement of immigration, his name seems not to occur anywhere in its two folio volumes of report, testimony, and appendices. There can be no stronger illustration of the frequently subterranean character of the most profitable political activity, for Thornton Hunt wrote truly in his obituary notice of Wakefield in the *Daily Telegraph*:—

'He had gained the active aid of several men in Parliament, and in Sir William Molesworth the colonial reformer found a mover and a chairman for the Committee on Convict Transportation which followed up Ward's.[1] Before that tribunal, by one means or other, Wakefield managed to bring such a mass of appalling evidence that it became impossible to sustain the system, which was in a few years abolished.'

[1] On colonial lands, also engineered by Wakefield.

Sir William Molesworth had already assailed transportation in the first number of the *London and Westminster Review*. A stronger Committee than that presided over by him can seldom have met. It included both the leaders of the House, Lord John Russell and Sir Robert Peel; Lord Howick and Sir George Grey; and Messrs Ward, Hawes, and Charles Buller. Sir William Molesworth's part in colonial affairs now and long afterwards was so important that his character demands a special notice, but it is not one easy to depict. In the pages of Mrs Grote, for years his intimate friend, and, notwithstanding their ultimate estrangement, far above any suspicion of malice, he appears a wayward and indocile being. His political opponents, on the other hand, thought him heavy and slow, a mere absorber of blue-books. The fact appears to be that the vehemence of his temper was at variance with the deliberation of his intellectual processes; and that the vigour of his action, when it came, seemed the more startling from the torpidity which had preceded it. Devoid of imagination or intuition, he was compelled to rely solely upon his very considerable logical faculty, but the certainty of being right which he thus acquired rendered him more absolute and imperious than the quicker minds which have not stopped to verify every step of their course. Morally, notwithstanding the unevennesses of his temper, he was one of the noblest of men. His solid worth and serious aims, steady perseverance in investigation and thorough moral and intellectual honesty are lovingly set forth in the autobiography of his friend, H. F. Chorley, in a passage the more worthy of notice as it has escaped Mr Leslie Stephen in the *Dictionary of National Biography*. Such characteristics well qualified him for the important task which, at Wakefield's instigation, he now (1837) undertook.

The searching nature of the Committee's investigations is evinced by the fact that, although no more than twenty-three witnesses were examined, their evidence occupies four hundred and fifty pages folio. The appendices of documents comprise between seven and eight hundred pages. The witnesses included official persons like the Chief Justice of New South Wales, who had himself gone out in a convict ship for want of another; Sir George Arthur, formerly Lieutenant Governor of Van Diemen's Land; Mr Macarthur, son of the man who had created the wealth of New South Wales by the introduction of merino sheep; Major Wright, ex-police magistrate; and Peter Murdock, ex-superintendent of convicts. There was also representative colonists like Dr Lang, ministers of religion like Dr Ullathorne, afterwards Roman Catholic Bishop of Birmingham, and superintendents of emigration like Mr John Marshall. The appendices are crammed with essays, despatches, reports, petitions, complaints of the scarcity of labour, controversies respecting the charge of Mr Justice Burton, who had frankly told the community that 'the main business of them all was the commission of crime or the punishment of it,' and statistics of all kinds down to the number of lashes inflicted by 'the standard scourging-cat.' Evidence and appendices alike teem with details of ill-doing, from the atrocity of the man Pearce, who not only killed the man Cox but ate him, down to the misdemeanour of Mrs Murdock's convict servant, who 'was found lying on the bed with what she called the yard of clay in her mouth, and drinking a pot of porter, and blowing a cloud; that was her expression to Mrs Murdock.' On the whole, a more uninviting picture was probably never traced of any society: 'as the greater portion of the agricultural labourers,' Sir William Molesworth quaintly remarked in his report, 'belong to the criminal population, they constitute a peasantry unlike any other in the world.' The statistics adduced established, as he showed, that the number of convictions for highway robbery in New South Wales, in proportion to the population, exceeded the total number of convictions for all offences in England: that rapes, murders and attempted murders were proportionately as frequent there as petty larcenies here; that if the annual average of convictions in England had been 137,000 instead of 17,000, then, and not till then, the state of crime and punishment in the two countries would have been the same. How could such a condition of things be tolerated? The answer repeated the contention of Wakefield's *Letter from*

Sydney; he had pointed out that, owing to the great dispersion of working people and the facility of procuring land, no labour but convict labour was to be had; and it now appeared that such labour was so indispensable that the colonists were nearly unanimous in resisting any interference with a system which embittered their lives and contaminated their offspring. The Committee, however, were entirely unanimous in condemning it. Under the guidance of Sir William Molesworth, whose report is a model of exhaustive discussion, they resolved that Australia should no longer be polluted for the convenience of the mother country. They recommended the discontinuance of transportation except to distant depôts, and sought to cure the scarcity of labour by an immigration fund obtained by raising the price of land in accordance with Wakefield's principles, the only reward he could expect or receive for his unrecognised labour.

In estimating the credit due to Wakefield, Molesworth and their associates in the abolition of transportation, it must be remembered that they were not the mouthpieces of a popular demand, but were forcing reform upon unwilling colonists, as well as upon an unwilling Government. A meeting held at Hobart Town to protest against convict deportation 'was respectable, but not numerous;' and the material interests of the mother country appeared at first sight still more contrary to any change. Many of us can remember the consternation occasioned when 'ticket-of-leave' and 'garotter' became household words among us from the retention of the convict element at home. Obliged, however, to choose between safety within the four seas and the weal of her colonial empire, Britain has made the right choice, for which she may largely thank Wakefield, Molesworth, and an illustrious man who had taken up the subject from another point of view, Archbishop Whately.

The Transportation Committee had been preceded in the previous session (1836) by one of no less importance upon colonial lands, equally Wakefield's creation, and in whose proceedings he took a prominent instead of an inconspicuous part. The object was to obtain the sanction of the cardinal principles of the Wakefield system, that land should be sold by contract at a sufficient price, instead of being given away or leased at a nominal quit rent, and that the proceeds should be employed in promoting immigration. The former principle had indeed been established by Lord Goderich's New South Wales regulations of 1831, but the price of five shillings an acre thus imposed was, in Wakefield's opinion, as already stated, far too low. It was now proposed, in the words of the report of the Committee, drafted by its able chairman, Mr H. G. Ward, 'that the whole of the arrangements connected with the sale of land should be placed under the charge of a central Land Board, resident in London.' This was carried in Committee, but obstructed by the Government, whose representative, Sir

George Grey, Colonial Under Secretary (not to be confounded with the Governor of South Australia and New Zealand), voted steadily against all the specifically Wakefieldian clauses of the Report. <u>Land Commissioners, however, were ultimately appointed by Lord John Russell, but only as an appendage to the Colonial Office.</u> The evidence collected was of the highest value, conveying the opinions of such authorities as Wakefield, Torrens, Hanson and Poulett Scrope. The inquiry was also of great personal advantage to Wakefield, bringing him into connection with many members of the House of Commons; familiarising the public with his name, hitherto so much in the background; and exhibiting him as a powerful reasoner on his feet, no less than in his study. He was severely cross-examined by Roebuck, who was hardly capable of forming a serious opinion upon an economical question, but whose French Canadian clients dreaded the application of the Wakefield system to Lower Canada. Wakefield, however, felt that the tide was with him, and thus concluded the remarkable passage in his evidence, already referred to, upon New Zealand and other fields yet open to the colonizing energy of Britain :—

'These, I know, may be considered as something like dreams; but if they be so, I shall have the consolation of knowing that the plan of fixing a price upon all lands, and employing the purchase money as an immigration fund, which was described to the Committee the other day by the Honourable Member for Devonport as the only plan which any reasonable person would now think or adopting, was, not six years, not five years ago, I think I may say not three years ago, treated with derision and scorn by those who had the means of carrying it into full effect.'

Before passing on to the two great New Zealand Committees of 1840 and 1844 it will be convenient to deal briefly with the South Australian Committee of 1840, already mentioned. This did not immediately concern Wakefield, as the inquiry principally respected the proceedings of the South Australian Commissioners, with whom he had no official connection, and the alarming financial condition of the colony, for which he was in no way responsible. He nevertheless gave important evidence, advocating a stricter application of his system to the organisation of the colony, and the appendix of documents contains one of the most remarkable papers he ever wrote, his letter of the 2d June 1835 to the South Australian Commissioners, from which large quotations have already been made. The result of the inquiry was entirely favourable to his views, the Committee reporting :—

'Your Committee conceive that the first principle of the system of colonization originally recommended by Mr Wakefield (to realise which was the object of founding the colony of South Australia) is that of maintaining a due proportion between the extent of land which is appropriated and the population by which it is occupied, by imposing such a price upon land as shall prevent its being bought until the number of its inhabitants is sufficient to make use of to advantage. Your Committee, persuaded by the soundness of this principle, consider the fact stated by Colonel Gawler to be conclusive as to the inadequacy of the price hitherto imposed upon land in South Australia, since the appropriation of so much greater an extent of land than is required to supply the wants of the inhabitants is altogether inconsistent with the attainment of the object justly considered of paramount importance by Mr Wakefield, that, namely of rendering the industry of the colonists as productive as possible, by maintaining in a newly settled colony the same system of combination of labour and division of employments which prevails in older societies. Hence an increase in the price of land in South Australia seems to your Committee to be necessary, in order to give effect to the principle upon which the colony was established.'

The New Zealand Committee of 1840 brought out a full statement of the case between the New Zealand Company and its various opponents. Here Wakefield was the most conspicuous figure, and his evidence teems with interest as regards the state of the country before settlement, the proceedings of the company, its relations with the Government, the reserves of land for the benefit of the natives, the provisions for religion and education, the question of auction sales of land, the French expedition, and almost every point that could be raised. His assertions respecting the support originally promised to the company by Lord Howick led to a remarkable scene, thus described in his *Art of Colonization* :—

'I was examined for several days, Lord Howick not being present. When my examination was closed he attended the Committee for the first time, and complained of certain statements made by me as a witness, which he declared to be untrue. At his instance a day was fixed when I was to attend the Committee for the single purpose of being cross-examined by him, and destroyed if he made his charges good. When we met in the committee room, it contained, besides a full attendance of members of the Committee, other members of the House, who came there to witness the anticipated conflict. But hardly any conflict took place. Lord Howick, after arranging on the table a formidable mass of notes and documents, put some questions to me with a view of establishing one of his accusations. The answers established that I had spoken the exact truth, and that my accuser himself was mistaken. Instead of proceeding to another charge, he hastily gathered up his papers and left the room without a remark. The Committee's blue-book reports the words that passed: if it also described the scene you would probably, upon reading it, agree with the lookers-on that in this murderous attack upon me Lord Howick was provokingly worsted.'

The scene, in truth, can in nowise be reproduced from the Report. Blue-books do not often stir as with the sound of a trumpet, but often would if tone and manner could be reproduced as well as language. It is to Lord Howick's honour that he attended a dinner given by the New Zealand Company to Wakefield in the following year, and was friendly to the Company as long as he remained in opposition. Whether the air of Downing Street, or, as Wakefield thought, jealousy of Mr Gladstone, subsequently biased him to a different course, cannot be determined. Mr Gladstone, it should be noted, was a member of the Committee of 1840, and had it depended upon him, its proceedings would not have been abortive. He voted for the statesmanlike draft report of the chairman, Lord Eliot, which the majority shelved without putting anything into its place. Lord Eliot proposed that New Zealand should be made an independent colony, and, agreeing that all unoccupied land should be vested in the Crown, and that the Crown should have the right of pre-emption over all land actually possessed by the natives, recommended that the Company should retain land equal in value to the amount expended by it in colonization, and that until a settled revenue could be obtained, the funds necessary for State purposes should be advanced by it upon loan. Commissioners, 'wholly unconnected with New Zealand and New South Wales, and having no pecuniary interests in either colony,' were to be appointed by the Crown to regulate all questions. Crown land was to be sold by contract at a uniform price of not less than a pound an acre, and the proceeds were to be employed as an immigration fund for conveying labouring emigrants to the colony. This would have been a nearly ideal system of colonization, but the majority of the Committee elected to leave things as they were. Lord John Russell, then Colonial Secretary, was considerably influenced by Lord Eliot's abortive report, and not only approximated to the directors, as already related, but accepted a dinner from them. All seemed going well, when, to employ Carlyle's metaphor, the New Zealand minnow's little creek was perturbed by an oceanic catastrophe in the British Parliament. Lord John Russell went out, Lord Stanley came in, and war between the Government and the Company broke out anew.

It is not easy to determine why Lord Stanley should have thought it needful to undo his predecessor's work. He was the last man to be unduly deferential to missionaries. The company imputed all the 'large blue flies' of the Colonial Office to Sir James

Stephen; but Stanley was not Glenelg, nor Stephen's influence what it had been under that amiable nobleman. None ought to question Stanley's honesty of purpose: the probability is that he really discerned nothing beyond the purview of an ordinary Treasury clerk, and never suspected that this wolf of a Company was nursing an empire.

It must in justice to the Government be remembered that their patience had been severely strained by the extravagance of successive Governors of New South Wales, who had among them incurred two or three millions of liabilities with little visible return. This could not, however, justify the hostile tone towards the Company which Stanley assumed from the first, and his virtual repudiation of the engagements of his predecessor. In February 1843 he committed himself unreservedly to the Treaty of Waitangi, which was one of the leading questions for the great Parliamentary Committee of the following year. In May 1843, however, he came to an arrangement which allowed of the resumption of its suspended land sales, but they were again suspended in February 1844. On 26th April, Wakefield wrote to his sister:—

'Yesterday the New Zealand Company's proprietors learned all the truth about their affairs, which is a great relief to me. We declared war to the knife with the Colonial Office; and last night the House of Commons, on Aglionby's motion, appointed a select Committee to inquire into the whole subject.'

EDWARD GIBBON WAKEFIELD 251

This Committee engendered one of the most formidable Blue Books ever produced as regards weight and size, although its contents are frequently highly interesting and readable. 'You may guess,' says Wakefield to his sister, 'how busy I have been when I tell you that our evidence appended to the Report occupies 800 or 900 pages of print.' Between minutes of testimony and documents, the number of pages is in fact exactly a thousand. The documents include Colonel Wakefield's reports of his voyages and purchases, embodying a vast store of miscellaneous observations; Dr Dieffenbach's reports on natural history; Colonel Wakefield's correspondence with various governors, lieutenant governors, commissioners of lands, and natives' protectors; his despatches home setting forth the afflictions he underwent from these personages; the whole history of the Wairau massacre and of Captain Fitzroy's condonation of it; the accounts of the company; and the highly controversial correspondence between their chairman and Lord Stanley and his under secretary. It will be remarked that scarcely any important document on the Company's side is dated at a time when Wakefield was out of England; his name, nevertheless, occurs only twice, as the father of Edward Jerningham Wakefield and as one of the recipients of an official letter of condolence on the death of Arthur Wakefield. The evidence, less voluminous than the appendices, abounds in details respecting the purchases of the Company, the natives' notions of landed and other property, and their relations with Europeans in general. From this the Committee had to elicit, if it could, a judgment on the past transactions, a policy for the future administration of the islands, and a decision whether the Company was entitled to claim performance of the agreement entered into with Lord John Russell, and thwarted by his successor. Although ten out of fifteen members of the Committee were of Lord Stanley's political party, the result was a brilliant but barren victory for the Company, accurately described in two letters from Wakefield. The first, written on the very day (9th July 1844) of the passing of the resolutions on which the Committee's report was founded, is addressed to his brother-in-law from the House of Commons :—

'The resolutions have all passed, after a desperate fight, together with one proposed by Lord F. Egerton speaking in the handsomest terms of poor Arthur. The Report, to be based upon these resolutions, will be drawn by Lord Howick, and presented to the Committee in a fortnight. There is no doubt of its passing.'

A second letter, to his sister, is dated 4th July, but there must be some error :—

'As London secrets are very safe at Stoke, I write to tell you that we know what the Report of the Committee of the House of Commons will be, having seen a draft of it. It goes to exculpate us and condemn the Colonial Office upon almost every point of difference, and will be, I think, a complete exculpation of poor Arthur's memory, and of William's and my boy's conduct throughout. This concerns ourselves and might [should] not have been mentioned first. As to the Company, and what I care more about, the colony, measures will be recommended for putting all to rights without delay. I expect the Report will be carried by a large majority in the Committee, including the chairman (Lord Howick, who drew it), Lord Francis Egerton, Sir John Hanmer, Mr Clive and other respectable Tories. What Hope and Stanley and Stephen are to do is their affair. Fitzroy must, I think, resign; and the animals who governed in Hobson's name, and afterwards with Shortland, will be sent about their business. This is not a too sanguine account.'

Wakefield was here, as often, over sanguine; he seemed, nevertheless, to have sound reasons for his confidence. Lord Howick's report was carried as he predicted, and as proceeding from an old antagonist of the New Zealand Company, and approved by a Committee neither packed in its interest nor engineered by its managers except for the manœuvring necessary to get Lord Howick into the chair, it ought to have settled the question. It is an exceedingly able document, forcibly pointing out the mischief of the antagonism between the Crown and the Company which had existed from the first, though of course not admitting that Lord Howick himself and his colleagues were its chief authors, and even blaming the Company for the happy audacity which had preserved New Zealand to Britain. Coming, however, to the root of all actual difficulties, the indiscriminate recognition of native titles to land under the Treaty of Waitangi, Lord Howick points out that the lands held collectively, of which the possession was guaranteed to the original inhabitants of New Zealand, must have been regarded as the lands actually occupied by them, 'which would have removed from the field of discussion by far the greater part of the lands purchased by the Company. If native rights to the ownership of land had been admitted only when arising from occupation, there would have been no difficulty in giving at once to the settlers secure and quiet possession of the land they required, and they would thus have been able to begin without delay and in earnest the work of reclaiming the unoccupied soil.' Instead of this, they had been harassed by commissioners and lawsuits and a hydra growth of native claims which it was fondly deemed had been extinguished, and the majority were yet without valid titles. Practical remedies were proposed for healing this state of things, and the claim of the Company under the agreement made in November 1840 with Lord John Russell, under which the Company was to receive four acres for every pound it had expended, 'without reference to the validity, or otherwise, of its supposed purchases from the natives,' was fully upheld. That this was the view of Lord John Russell himself is clear from a letter of his in the appendix addressed to the Governor of the Company, and dated 29th June 1844 :—

'I believed the extent of land which it would be in the power of the Crown to grant to be far greater than would be enough to satisfy its engagements. I did not suppose that any claim could be set up by the natives to the millions of acres of land which are to be found in New Zealand neither occupied nor cultivated, nor in any fair sense owned by any individual. I believed, therefore, that in any case the Crown could fulfil its promise; and that when so many pounds had been proved to have been expended by the Company for purposes named in the agreement, the Crown would be able to grant to the Company four acres of land for each pound so expended.'

Lord Stanley, however, had no notion of giving in, and his despatches to New Zealand were of a nature to practically nullify the decision of the Committee. Much friction consequently arose. Wakefield tells his sister in an undated letter, which must have been written about this time :—

'The New Zealand war waxes fiercer every week. The correspondence with Lord Stanley has now got to a ludicrous pitch of Billingsgate on both sides. Cheat, liar, fool are not common words in the letters, but express ideas commonly found there. There is little to choose between the parties as to fierceness, but we have the great advantage of having truth on our side. The correspondence rolls the proud Stanley in the dirt, and how he will ever bring himself to let the public see it passes my comprehension. His part in it is a series of tricks and falsehoods which our part remorselessly exposes. Lord John Russell, who is a most important witness in the cause, agrees with us on main points. I rely on the justice of the Prime Minister, to whom we shall probably be compelled to appeal.'

It is indeed likely that if Sir Robert Peel could have had his own way a settlement would have been arrived at. He always treated the question with becoming reserve and moderation, and disapproved of the Treaty of Waitangi, which had been ratified when he was out of office. He could not openly overrule so important a colleague as Stanley, but it was probably owing to his influence, augmented by the general tone of a debate raised by Charles Buller in March 1845, that Government for awhile seemed inclined to come to terms:—

'The recent debates about New Zealand,' Wakefield writes to his sister on 23d March, 'have had the desired effect; the Government, not Lord Stanley alone, but his principal colleagues, with his consent, having made us an overture of reconciliation. We have said "Yes" on the understanding that we are not to patch up the old arrangement, which is too vague, and makes us too dependent on the goodwill

f Government, but have a new one, which, subject
) certain well-defined checks, shall render us inde-
endent. We require, in short, security for the future
; well as indemnity for the past; and the reply has
een, " Very well ; it is best to make an effective and
ısting arrangement whilst we are about it." The
egotiation is now in full swing.'

A scheme was, in fact, drawn out in private com-
ıunications between Charles Buller and Sir James
ıraham, which failed from the opposition of Lord
tanley. Wakefield writes to his sister, apparently
n 6th June :—

'The negotiation is over and has not resulted in
ny agreement. Our proposal is rejected by Stanley ;
nd we have rejected an offer from him to pay off
he shareholders of the Company. The whole must
ome out next week, and will have at least the effect
f improving our position : since the Government
ave entertained the plan of handing over to us the
overeignty of New Zealand, and have offered the
hareholders full compensation of their loss of £300,000.
am better than might have been expected, and
ıave been able to take all the part I wished in the
ıegotiation and in rejecting the offer of the Govern-
nent.'

Nothing remained for the New Zealand Company
)ut to bring their case before Parliament, though with
he certainty of being outvoted. They had already,
)n 16th April, even while the negotiations with Lord

R

Stanley were pending, presented an elaborate petition stating their grievances, and their case was now entrusted to Charles Buller. Nothing but his premature death prevented this gifted man from taking a foremost rank among the orators as well as the statesmen of his time. He had already, in 1843, delivered a great speech on colonization, not leading or intended to lead to a division, which may be found as an appendix to Wakefield's *Art of Colonization*, and his opening speech in the debate which commenced on 17th June was worthy of his best powers. The special proposal made was that the House should resolve itself into a Committee to consider the case of the Company, which the Government chose to regard as a vote of censure on the Colonial Secretary. The result under such circumstances could not be doubtful, but, considering that the Government's normal majority was ninety, its reduction to fifty-one was a signal triumph for reason and justice. Stanley's fiery eloquence could not be heard; he was safely bottled up in the House of Lords. It is easy to imagine him and Wakefield listening to the debate, each thinking how much better he himself could have conducted it, and chafing at the insuperable impediment that kept him dumb. Ellen Turner was indeed avenged! Nevertheless, Wakefield's side had little reason for complaint. Sheil's eloquence was enlisted in their cause, but they derived more really valuable support from impartial and not altogether friendly speakers like Lord John Russell and Lord Howick. On the other side the official orators, Peel, Graham, Cardwell, while speaking with dignity and effect, indicated that they did not feel altogether comfortable in the position into which they had been dragged by the unruly Stanley. Nor could they well, the question being merely whether the Company, having undeniably received a promise of four acres of land for every pound they had expended, should be forthwith endowed with them out of the waste unoccupied lands belonging to the Crown, the other party to the compact; or whether a purely imaginary native right to these lands should be set up, ruinous to Company and settlers alike, and in no way advantageous to the natives, whose interests would have been much better consulted by a strict execution of the Company's original plan of reserves in their favour. But Peel was afraid of a native war.

The Company showed their confidence in their case by publishing a full report of the debate, with no comment beyond a reprint of certain documents in an appendix. The arrival of alarming news from New Zealand gave Buller an opportunity of raising the question once again on 21st July, but he was defeated by a majority of sixty-six, a result fully anticipated by Wakefield, who had written to his sister on 23d July :—

'All my power of writing, and even thinking, is so thoroughly engaged by the New Zealand affairs that I really have been unable to write to you, nor can I say more than a few words now. We shall be beaten in the Commons by a larger majority than before, as Peel has staked his Government on the issue, and people would send New Zealand, not to mention all Polynesia, to the bottom of the sea rather than turn him out *for such a cause*. But Stanley is gradually ruining himself, and everybody says he will retire when things are quiet. We mean to fight to the last, even on our own stumps. I suffer from the excitement, and now talk of going abroad after the session for three months with Charles Buller. If I could keep out of business in England it would please me better, but of that I have no chance.'

Wakefield's predictions were so far justified that Lord Stanley resigned the Colonial Secretaryship before the end of the year, ostensibly from his opposition to the Free Trade policy of Sir Robert Peel; but Wakefield always asserted that resentment at his chief's lukewarmness in supporting his New Zealand policy had much to do with it. His successor was Mr Gladstone, no novice in colonial matters, but one who had served on many colonial committees, and had always displayed eminent fairness of mind. To him, in January 1846, Wakefield addressed an elaborate memoir, which marks the transition in his own activity from that of the advocate of a company to that of the framer of a constitution. After a vigorous sketch of the prevailing dissatisfaction through all such parts of the British Colonial Empire as had not obtained relief by rebellion, and a terse and just definition of the fount of all the special ills of New Zealand as consisting in the 'placing of colonization in one set of hands and leaving all the rest of government in another set,' aptly compared to 'a pair of legs directed by different volitions, which would inevitably try to go different ways, and thus come to a standstill,' he proposes that the Company should retire from the scene altogether after receiving compensation, and that the colony should be divided into different self-governing municipalities, the Governor's office being abolished. Native affairs within the boundaries of the municipalities were to be left to the regulation of the governments; outside these precincts, to themselves. The scheme probably grew out of the negotiations then in progress for the foundation of the Otago settlement, and foreshadows the system of provincial governments which long prevailed in New Zealand. The plan is not put forward as the best conceivable, but as a substitute for the preferable scheme of administration by a chartered company, assumed to be now impracticable. It was shrewdly devised to enable the colonists to get rid of the Colonial Office, but seems to imply a more advanced condition than the New Zealand settlements had then attained.

Few Secretaries of State have had more ability or more inclination than Mr Gladstone to deal in a statesmanlike manner with colonial affairs. Two rocks he might have struck upon; his High Church sympathies, skilfully played upon by Wakefield in this very memoir, and his tendency to unwise parsimony. Could these have been repressed he might have done great things; but Free Trade at the moment swallowed up every other question, and he probably gave but little attention to New Zealand in his brief and troubled term of office, during which he was without a seat in Parliament. Wakefield's memoir, with other interesting documents, was published in a supplement to the *Spectator* of 6th June. A few days previously the disheartened Company had passed a resolution in favour of retiring altogether from the work of colonization. Two months afterwards as related above Wakefield was withdrawn from public affairs by the sudden stroke of illness, and when, after a long interval, the paralysed brain regained capacity for business, he found himself confronted with a new Secretary, a new Governor, a new Parliament, and, most important of all, a new spirit in the Company itself.

Mention may be made here of two minor writings of Wakefield's which fall within his Committee period. One, an annotated edition of Adam Smith's *Wealth of Nations*, might have been of considerable importance if it had been completed, but only the first volume, published in 1835, contains any notes of interest. Subsequent volumes were published up to 1840 with Wakefield's name as editor, but his engagements appear to have prevented his giving any serious attention to the book. The notes exhibit him as a sagacious rather than as a regularly-trained thinker. 'His practical conclusions,' says Mill, 'appear to me just and important; but he is not equally happy in incorporating his valuable speculations with the results of previous thought.' The commentary is now perhaps chiefly important for its notices of subsequent discoveries and social mutations which may tend to affect the conclusions of Smith, whose work, nevertheless, he says, 'is not only the most valuable book in the science, but one more valuable than all the others put together.' In fact, in Mill's opinion, Wakefield's doctrines are sound corollaries from Smith, though Smith himself might not have admitted it. In addition to the objects which an editor of *The Wealth of Nations* might be expected to propose to himself, Wakefield has two others. 'To warn the student against implicit faith in the doctrines of a science which yet wants a complete alphabet; to show how imperfect that science is after all that has been done for it, and to indicate some questions of great moment concerning which next to nothing has been done. Secondly, to apply the doctrines of Adam Smith and others to some new circumstances in the economical state of our own country. Urged by the belief that economical suffering has been caused by misgovernment, we are proceeding to establish a virtual democracy. It is a grand but also a fearful experiment.'

De Tocqueville's great work on *Democracy in America* had been published in the same year as that in which these words were written, 1835. Whether Wakefield had seen it or not is uncertain; his reflections had evidently led him to the same conclusions. These are further expressed in a little volume, *Popular Politics* (1837), which may be commended to those who fancy that, because he wished the aristocracy to have their share in building up the Empire, he was therefore an aristocrat. It is on the contrary a manifesto of democratic principles, which might be termed violent and crude but for its evidently designed adaptation to untrained readers, in a style imitative of Cobbett. Most of the papers are reprints from previous publications then out of print. One of the most powerful is an account from personal observation of the horror excited by the introduction of public executions into Dunkirk. In another, a judge is represented as addressing a criminal on the good turn he is doing him by sentencing him to transportation: 'For what you have done here, depend on it, you will not be punished; if you abstain from crime in the colony, you will be richly rewarded for the crime which brought you before me, fortunate rascal that you are!'

Wakefield's Radicalism, nevertheless, was of the opportunist order; he supported political reforms less on abstract grounds than as means to the ends defined in his election address to the people of Birmingham as 'high wages and high profits, both together, with high rents at the same time, such productive industry as should yield plenty for the workmen, plenty for the master, and plenty for the landlord—not by fits occasionally interrupting the ordinary state of distress, but permanently, so as to ensure to all classes at all times the means of a happy existence.'

Such was the creed of the man who has been held up to opprobrium as the tool of the aristocrat and the capitalist. But neither was he the instrument of the classes below them. He was fully as desirous that the landlord should obtain a fair rent as that the labourer should receive fair wages. Cobden and Bright denounced the selfishness of the land-owning class, an accusation retorted with equal vehemence upon the manufacturers. In Wakefield, and almost in Wakefield alone, except for Carlyle, whom he never mentions, we find perfect fairness to every class, and equal zeal for the well-being of all: an object which he thought, and Carlyle thought with him, easy of attainment, if due advantage were taken of the opportunities provided by the expansion of our Colonial Empire. There was no feature in his programme which the Conservatives could not take up as well as the Radicals, and when after a while the Conservatives did in a measure take it up, they took up the Radical candidate for Birmingham along with it.

CHAPTER X

THE LAST DAYS OF THE NEW ZEALAND COMPANY—
JOHN ROBERT GODLEY—SIR GEORGE GREY'S AD-
MINISTRATION—DEATH OF COLONEL WAKEFIELD
—'THE ART OF COLONIZATION'—CRITICISM OF
M. LEROY-BEAULIEU—DEATH OF CHARLES BULLER

SPEAKING before the New Zealand Legislative Assembly, Wakefield condensed his views as to the decline and fall of the New Zealand Company into an epigram, 'The Company was founded by men with great souls and little pockets, and fell into the hands of men with great pockets and little souls.' Such was certainly the fact, yet it does not necessarily imply any severe censure upon the managers under whose direction the Company expired. In all great movements that comprise both an ideal and a practical side, there must of necessity be both enthusiasts and men of the world, and the influence of the former will be more potent in the early stages of the movement, because the initial impetus has come from them. As they drop off, they will usually be replaced by men of a less exalted, not necessarily a less respectable type. Never, perhaps, was any association dealing with scrip and shares launched in a spirit of purer enthusiasm than the New Zealand Company. It had not, as will be recollected, been intended by its promoters to have been a joint stock company, but this character had been forced upon it by the perversity of Government.

The condescension to joint stock enterprise was ill-omened from the first, the names of the Company's first directors manifest a declension from the board of the original association. Nothing can be said against Mr Joseph Somes, but the accession of this great shipowner to Lord Durham's chair indicated that the mercantile element was prevailing over that of abstract enthusiasm for sound principles of colonization. Nor can the solid business men into whose hands the undertaking was lapsing be censured if they took a serious view of their duties to their shareholders, and lamented, though they did not seek to evade, the necessity for relinquishing their own salaries, and cutting down those of their staff by fifty per cent. A note of dissonance may perhaps be detected in Wakefield's letter to his sister in 1845, already quoted, where he speaks of 'the Company, and, what I care more for, the colony.' Superior ability, and the fact that he was the only director able to devote his whole time to the company, kept him at the head of affairs until his breakdown in August 1846, after which date no responsibility for any of its doings can be imputed to him. From that moment a complete change in the Company's policy is observable. 'My incapacity,' Wakefield told the New Zealand Committee in 1854, 'changed the whole character of the direction, which then fell into the hands of a few persons in whose minds sound principles of colonization and colonial government were as nothing compared with pounds, shillings and pence. They sold the honour of the Company and the interests of the colony for money, to come through a parliamentary obligation upon New Zealand to recompense the Company for its losses.' Here speaks the enthusiast, to whom profits are nothing in comparison with principles, but, while we admire, we must admit that the director who thinks of the interests of the shareholder has also a case. The worst of the new *régime* was that under it the Company became wholly inoperative, it served neither God nor Mammon. The arrangement so much decried by Wakefield was concluded in May 1847, and though Wakefield always asserted that it was forced upon Charles Buller, must have in some measure commended itself to his judgment, seeing that he prepared it himself. In fact, all the correspondence on both sides, the Colonial Office's as well as the company's, was written by the ambidextrous Buller. The scheme provided for an advance of £236,000 to the Company, subject to the condition that if the loan were not repaid by 1850 the Company should resign its charter and all its lands in New Zealand, and receive £268,000 as compensation for its expenses, to be paid out of the proceeds of land sales in the colony. Wakefield, in a letter to the colonists of Wellington, dated in April 1849, truly prophesied that the Company would not survive 1850, and added that its disappearance would be the best thing for New Zealand interests, removing a sham representation of them to make room, as might be hoped, for a real one. He had resigned his directorship in the preceding January, on the ostensible ground that the Company would be prejudiced by his attacks on Lord Grey in *The Art of Colonization*, but consented that his portrait should be painted for the board room. It was a fine picture by Collins, nearly identical in attitude with the daguerreotype prefixed to this volume, and including his favourite Talbot hounds and pet King Charles. It came into his possession at the dissolution of the company, and was ultimately presented by his son to the Provincial Hall at Christchurch.

While the New Zealand Company began to totter downwards like a teetotum whose initial impulse is exhausted, Wakefield was entirely withdrawn from cognisance of its affairs. Two eminent physicians gave him up, but after a while the vigorous constitution rallied, and although unable to look at a book or paper, he regained physical strength sufficiently to seek relief by easy journeys and short removes from place to place, always carrying in his pocket a card inscribed, 'Do not bleed me.' In the autumn of 1847 he repaired to Malvern, and submitted with good results to a course of hydropathic treatment under Dr Wilson, the rival of the still more celebrated Dr Gully. Thomas Attwood, the celebrated founder of the Birmingham Political Union, whose daughter Angela had married Wakefield's brother Daniel, and whose other daughter Rosabel had been, as we have seen, the friend and correspondent of Nina Wakefield, was also staying at Malvern, 'and there it was,' says his grandson and biographer, Mr Charles Marcus Wakefield, ' that I had the privilege of seeing these extraordinary men together. Though both ranked as Radicals, or at least as extreme Liberals, they differed greatly in other respects. Attwood was utterly incapable of understanding the magnificent and far-sighted views of Wakefield on colonial subjects.' Attwood, indeed, whose foundation of the Birmingham Political Union ensures him a distinguished place in the political history of the country, had impaired his influence as a public man by too exclusive a devotion to his currency theories, and lack of interest in subjects unconnected with paper, coin, or bullion.

A more congenial spirit shared Wakefield's society at Malvern, and here it was that the foundations of the Canterbury settlement was laid. John Robert

Godley, an Irish gentleman of good estate (born 1816), had been early attracted by Wakefield's writings on colonization, and had proved his own capacity as an independent thinker in a remarkable book of American travel, published in 1844, but written in the form of letters in 1842, when Wakefield was in Canada, and the two very probably met; and still more by a bold scheme for meeting the emergency of the Irish famine by emigration on a large scale. He proposed to locate a million Irishmen in Canada, charging the expense upon Irish landed property, and providing for the interest by the extension of the income tax to Ireland. An excellent project, could Godley have guaranteed that the Irish would be contented and loyal when settled down next door to the United States, but otherwise perilous to the Empire and unfair to Canada. Doubts on this point may have had their weight in determining Ministers to reject it. Published, however, by Wakefield's interposition, in the *Spectator*, it marked Godley out as an original thinker and practical statesman, and one fitted in every way to co-operate with Wakefield in the plan for a Church of England colony which had for some time been floating in the latter's mind, and which was fully considered by the two during their stay at Malvern. This remarkable undertaking will form the principal subject of the next chapter.

While the old fruit was falling from, and the new

blossom forming upon, the New Zealand orange tree at home, the colony itself was entering upon an entirely new phase of its history, strongly demarcated from that which had preceded and that which was to ensue. It may be briefly described as the autocratic phase, during which the affairs of the settlement were mainly regulated by one man of remarkable strength of will and faculty for rule. In Sir George Grey New Zealand had for the first time a capable Governor, the very type of the man whom the Romans would have entrusted with the dictatorship at a period of national peril, but made rather to rule a Crown colony than a constitutional state. It may have been an instinctive perception of his forte and foible that induced him to retain the colony in a state of pupilage as long as he could, and to take the exceedingly bold step of suspending a constitution which had been enacted by Parliament in 1846, but which he deemed unsuitable. His recalcitrancy was justified by the event. Earl Grey, usually so imperious, meekly adopted the view of a Governor whose capacity had been so brilliantly evinced by the pacification of the Maoris, and whom he justly credited with a better understanding of New Zealand affairs than was possible to himself; and thus a colony which the British Parliament had endowed with representative institutions had to submit to seven years of personal rule. In theory this was indefensible, and the undue prolongation of Sir

George Grey's powers in the long run undermined his popularity, but no one appears to have been enthusiastic for the new constitution, and there seems at present a pretty general agreement that at the time personal rule was the best thing for the colony. The argument which chiefly weighed with Earl Grey seems to have been the discontent which the new constitution was expected to excite among the natives, whom, by insisting on a knowledge of English, it practically excluded from the franchise. It may be doubted whether there was really much weight in this consideration, but it was admirably calculated to impress Ministers at home, who dreaded a Maori war above all things; and settlers in the Northern Island, where natives were numerous, saw more in it than did settlers in the Middle Island, where natives were few. According to Sir George Grey's own statement through a third party to Wakefield, with whom his relations were at this time amicable, he would have been quite willing to have proclaimed the constitution in the Middle Island, 'but he dared not himself make such a distinction between North and South, and the Office would not take his hints to them that they should do it.' 'All the Southern settlements,' Wakefield adds, 'are discontented, and Wellington in very hot water.'[1] This feeling gathered strength as time went on, and, together with an unfortunate

---

[1] *The Founders of Canterbury*, pp. 70, 71.

and policy, accounts for the comparative unpopularity, towards the conclusion of his term of office, of a Governor who had rendered the colony such signal services. The Maoris, on the other hand, gave him the strongest demonstrations of their gratitude and esteem. His position towards them had been peculiar. He was the first Governor who had been pro-Maori without being pro-missionary. Although a religious man—the intimate friend of Bishop Selwyn and the author of the first draft of the constitution of the Church of New Zealand —Grey was by no means under missionary influence. His proceedings towards missionaries who had speculated in land went far to justify the original contention of the New Zealand Company. One great mistake he made in conjunction with Bishop Selwyn —his interference with the devoted missionary, Henry Williams. The circumstance that the biographers of the Governor and Bishop alike avoid all mention of this affair, while the biographer of the missionary and the historian of the New Zealand Church relate it at great length, is abundantly significant. This, however, was but an incident. Sir George Grey did everything for the natives that could be done in his time. The diffusion of education among their children, actively promoted by the present New Zealand Government, is the only measure which can save them from extinction by reforming their insanitary habits; but this was impossible until more of their territory, useless to themselves, should have passed into the hands of white men, and they should thus have become permeated with European influences. Sir George Grey did much by the acquisition of enormous tracts of waste land in the thinly-peopled Middle Island, under the same system of reserves for native benefit as that expounded by Wakefield to the Committee of 1840.

Sir George Grey's chief mistakes were in connection with that thorniest of colonial subjects—the land question. By endeavouring to frustrate the decision of Parliament that the New Zealand Company should receive compensation for their land out of the proceeds of land sales, he lost the confidence of the Colonial Office, his relations with which were never again quite satisfactory. A more serious error was the reduction on his own authority, and within a short time of his retirement, of the price of Crown lands from one pound to ten shillings and five shillings an acre. It is doubtful whether he had any power to make such an enactment, but all felt that the matter ought to have been left to the Colonial Parliament then about to be convoked under the new constitution. Wakefield, upon his arrival in New Zealand, tested the legality of the Governor's proceedings, and gained his case in the colonial court, but the decision was overruled at home. The cheapening of land, besides destroying the fund for emigration, excited violent discontent among those who had already purchased land at higher prices; but the most serious objection was that it played directly into the hands of speculators, and frustrated the object which Sir George Grey himself most desired to promote. The result fully vindicated Wakefield's theory of the sufficient price, if only as a barrier against 'land-sharks.' It is thus stated by Mr Gisborne, a writer in general most favourable to Sir George Grey:—

'The intention, no doubt, was to place the acquisition of freeholds within the reach of every man; but the result was directly the reverse. Rent-holders and speculators were only too successful in monopolising at nominal cost enormous territories, and those of them who were not rich enough, or who could not borrow enough to do this at once, 'picked out the eyes of the land,' to use an expressive phase, in order to render the remainder of the land of little or no value to any but themselves. The effect has been to lock up large estates in the hands of comparatively few landholders.'

It has been alleged in extenuation that Sir George Grey intended to have checked the accumulation of landed property in few hands by the imposition of a land tax, but there must be some mistake about this. To have invited purchase, and then saddled the purchaser with a tax of which he had had no warning, would have been an act of bad faith of which so just and honourable a governor as Sir George Grey would have been incapable.

Up to the time of his resistance to the satisfaction of their claims, Sir George Grey had not deserved ill of the New Zealand Company. He had been on specially friendly terms with their principal agent. Writing to his sister on March 29, 1847, Colonel Wakefield says :—

'We made a trip to New Plymouth and Nelson, and passed three weeks very agreeably in one of the most powerful and well fitted up of H.M.'s steam vessels. No two people can be on better terms personally than Captain Grey and I am.' He adds, indeed, 'Our politics are nevertheless as agitated as ever, and the Governor and I do not always agree— besides, now the Company has to economise, I get the ill-will and opposition of a considerable number of the settlers, who prefer a Government that spends a deal of money. But I came prepared for all this, and have many sincere friends.'

Grey's goodwill to the Company at this time was further evinced by the active assistance which he gave in adjusting its controversies with the settlers who had made purchases on the faith of its guarantee. The ultimate arrangement was embodied in a memorandum drawn up on September 15, 1848, on which very day William Wakefield was struck by apoplexy. He expired on September 19. 'During the last three years,' wrote Sir George Grey, 'I have been in constant communication with Colonel Wakefield upon a great variety of subjects connected with the interests of New Zealand, and have found not only that he possessed abilities of a very high order, but that his whole attention and thoughts were directed to the single subject of the advancement of the interests of this country.' No man had been more fiercely assailed, but he had lived down opposition, and New Zealand has never seen such another funeral procession as that which accompanied his body to the grave.

When William Wakefield closed his eyes in New Zealand, his brother was writing *The Art of Colonization* at the Château Mabille, Boulogne. He was at the time not quite off with the old love nor yet quite on with the new. The New Zealand Company had, in his view, been virtually destroyed by the agreement of 1847, yet he clung to the hope that it might in some measure be redeemed by an alliance with the new association which had grown out of his conferences with Godley at Malvern. This project, on the other hand, was not yet fairly launched, nor could be for some time, because, as Wakefield wrote in May, 'In consequence of Lord Grey's utter neglect of his own New Zealand polity, there is at present no land on which to plant the settlement.' The intended work on colonization, much talked of and never seen, had obtained in his own circle the appellation of 'Mrs Harris,' which explains several playful allusions in his letters. He arrived at the Château Mabille in June, and, in July, summoned Mr Albert Allom (afterwards Colonial Secretary at Tobago, son of the faithful friend who had nursed him in his illness, and brother of his former secretary in Canada) to assist him in the preparation of the book as amanuensis. Mr Allom, however, did not arrive until September, when the composition of the work was begun in earnest.

'His health,' says Mr Allom in the little pamphlet of reminiscences recently published by him in Tasmania, 'did not permit him to work more than four or five hours a day, and this only was accomplished by extreme regularity in taking morning and evening exercise. As the winter approached, we often sallied forth before daylight, regardless of the weather, our pockets filled with ripe pears, and scoured the country with his fine, well-known Talbot hounds and beautiful little beagles, whose alternate deep baying and yelping in the darkness of the morning the farmers and others have good reason to remember. When at work, he would slowly pace up and down the room, dictating to me the copy, pausing occasionally the more carefully to frame a sentence or to choose a particular word.[1] He seldom made a correction. The day's work had generally been well thought out previously. Plodding on steadily day by day, the work was

---

[1] It is remarkable that Adam Smith's *Wealth of Nations* was composed in exactly the same manner, a circumstance which must have been well known to Wakefield.

finished on Christmas Eve, 1848. I had only just enough time to pack up the manuscript and hurry with it on board the steamer leaving at midnight for London. The next morning the manuscript was delivered to Mr Rintoul.'

The book was published by John William Parker, publisher of Stuart Mill, Maurice, Kingsley, and so many more of the best thinkers of the time, on February 5, 1849. The full title was *A View of the Art of Colonization, with Present Reference to the British Empire; in Letters between a Statesman and a Colonist.* Edited by (one of the writers) Edward Gibbon Wakefield. It was dedicated in terms of warm affection to Mr John Hutt, one of Wakefield's earliest friends and supporters.

From various passages in his letters, it would appear that Wakefield anticipated tangible political results from *The Art of Colonization.* These certainly were not forthcoming, and for a reason which ought not to have escaped his sagacity. The book was ill fitted to attract novices, and those who had already attended to the subject could only say, 'We knew this before.' Like most important discoveries, the Wakefield gospel is a very simple one, admitting indeed of continual repetition, but not of republication. Once prove that the backward state of the colonies arose from the divorce of land and labour occasioned by the practice of giving away land for a nominal price, and that the land ought to be made the machine of its own cultivation, by selling it at a good price and employing the proceeds of the sale by settling it with labourers, and there remained no principle to enunciate which could impress the thinker, or influence the enthusiasm of the nation at large. Everything vital to the comprehension of Wakefield's theory had long been before the world, his views had undergone no such modification as to necessitate restatement, and the further illustration and exposition he now gave, though highly acceptable, and though some topics, such as the disadvantage of land sales by auction in comparison with sales at a uniform price, were treated at more length than heretofore, was in no way sensational. This was an epithet more applicable to the early part of the book, with its lively attacks upon Earl Grey, whom Wakefield regarded as the marplot from within, as Stanley had been the enemy from without. But although such passages might help the book to find readers, they obviously could contribute nothing to its scientific value, and, animated as they are, it might have been wished that they had been omitted, but for the glimpses they afford of Wakefield's own practical activity as an actual planner and founder of colonies.

There is no sign of failing literary power in *The Art of Colonization*, unless it be a certain diffuseness, due in part to the machinery of the book. This is an interchange of letters between a statesman and a colonist, founded, Wakefield asserts in the preface, upon actual correspondence. There seems internal evidence that such was actually the case. The method of the composition of the book, however, as described by Mr Allom, shows that but little of the original documents can be left. The statesman is represented as seeking enlightenment through the medium of oral discussion, which Wakefield would no doubt have preferred. 'E. G. W.,' writes Mr Allom, 'was a master in the art of persuading. He seldom failed if he could get his victim into conversation.' But physically, he was no longer the man he had been.

'My health, instead of improving, has got worse lately, and will probably never mend. It is a disorder of the nerves which has long hindered, and now absolutely precludes, me from engaging in the oral discussion of subjects that deeply interest me, more especially if they are subjects involving argument and continuous thought. You must have observed how I suffered towards the end of our last conversation. At length I cannot disobey the doctor's injunction to stay at home and be quiet, without effects that remind me of a bird trying to fly with a broken wing, and knocking itself to pieces in the vain exertion. As respects earnest conversation, I am a helpless cripple. But there occurs to me an alternative. With the seeming caprice of most nervous disorders, mine, which forbids talking, makes far less difficulty about letting me write. The brain suffers greatly only when it is hurried—as with old hunters, "'tis the pace that kills"—but can work somehow when allowed to take its own time.'

Such a machinery, whether growing out of an actual state of things or deliberately adopted for literary purposes, has manifest advantages and defects. It is a distinct gain in vivacity of presentation; it breaks up the subject into manageable sections, and diversifies it with an agreeable infusion of personal feeling. At the same time it is both artificial and inartificial. The statesman, whether a real entity or not, is evidently merely put forward to allow Wakefield to advance what he wishes, and whether because a man with many interests is unable to correspond on even terms with a man with one, or whether Wakefield tires of writing dummy letters to himself, the disciple almost disappears from the latter part of the correspondence. On the other hand, the machinery suits Wakefield, who, to his great merit as a master of homely, forcible English, did not add the artistic instinct which would have enabled him to group and display his subject as a whole. Desultory he must be, and desultoriness is less observable in a series of letters than in a formal treatise.

The Art of Colonization, then, could not be epoch-making, for the epoch was made; nor could it present the results of the author's speculations and experience in a symmetrical and classical form. On the other hand there is a singular fascination about the earlier part of the book—'the personalities and the egotism,' as the writer calls it in a letter to Rintoul. As a mere question of literary taste, these would perhaps have been better away, but we must be thankful for the window thus opened into the breast of a remarkable man, and pleased with what it discloses. There is nothing spiteful about the personality, nothing mean about the egotism, they are rather like lyric utterances, the indignant cry of an artist who models colonies as others model statues or poems, and whose special grievance it is that his work is not only undervalued but disfigured. It is impossible not to confess that his idea is far more to him than any concurrent influence or emolument, and that his whole soul is in his noble and disinterested definition of the *summum bonum*: 'THE UTMOST HAPPINESS WHICH GOD VOUCHSAFES TO MAN ON EARTH, THE REALISATION OF HIS OWN IDEA.'

The most original part of *The Art of Colonization*, putting aside all that had been original when Wakefield first propounded it, but had become common property by the discussion it had since undergone, is descriptive of the impediments to colonization by reason of the too frequently low standard of morals and manners in the colonies, and by the subjection of the colonists to irresponsible officialism. The latter evil has long since disappeared in self-governed colonies; when Wakefield wrote it was sufficiently real, and the extension of the principle of responsible government from Canada to the other colonies, mainly inhabited by white settlers, remained a leading object with him to the end of his political career. The treatment of the other topic shows how deep a hold the Canterbury project had taken upon him. 'I am bound to add,' he says, 'that my notions on this subject were not originally formed in my own mind, but, for the most part, suggested to me by Dr Hinds,' the author, it will be remembered, of the chapter in the original manual of New Zealand colonization which dwelt on the advantage which would accrue to the colony from getting a bishop. Wakefield thought so too, but he also thought that the obligations of church and colony would be mutual. 'The Free Church of Scotland,' he wrote to Godley, 'finds the Otago colony a most valuable topic in its intercourse with the public. It is a very interesting topic. So is the conversion of savages, as used by the Church Missionary Society. There is something in it which appeals pleasantly to the imagination and the best feelings. Whereas the sole topic of the Propagation Society is religious destitution in the colonies, which is a painful topic and one of which people soon weary.' One of the finest passages in *The Art of Colonization* is an eulogium on the special deserts of the Wesleyan body.

Nothing of Wakefield's own in *The Art of Colonization* equals in a literary point of view the quotation from Charles Buller's character of 'Mr Mothercountry' in the little book on *Responsible Government for the Colonies* previously mentioned. 'Mr Mothercountry' is a leading figure throughout the latter part of the book, and the name is assuredly well chosen to imply that any opponent of the colonial reformers must be something of an old woman. Its personal application to Sir James Stephen was most unjust. It is impossible to read Sir James Stephen's letters, to go no further, without discerning in him an admirable man of high capacity. The satire, nevertheless, is deadly in so far as it strikes the abuses of the only system of government which no one defends, and at the same time the only system of which it is impossible to get rid. Monarchs may be dethroned, aristocracies exiled, democracies enslaved, but neither monarchy, aristocracy nor democracy can ever dispense with bureaucracy; the responsible government on the spot which Wakefield and Buller invoked to supplant the distant and irresponsible bureaucrat in Downing Street must have its own civil service, and there as here the clerk versed in affairs will rule the uninformed minister. The removal, however, through the concession of responsible government, of a deadweight of unpopularity from the Colonial Office, was not the least of the good effects of the system of local government advocated by Wakefield and Buller. If they had known all that has since come to light about the inner workings of the Office, they must have thought more favourably of individuals, while at the same time they must have felt more anxiety than ever to modify a system where the best intentions of rulers were liable to be frustrated by the cross-currents of politics.

Where the 'Mr Mother-country' of *The Art of Colonization* represents the opponents of the vital principles of Wakefield's system, he is entirely in place, but where he merely personifies the general spirit of official obstructiveness he is an excrescence upon a book whose sole aim should have been to instruct in the art and mystery of planting colonies. Misled into polemics, the author left this unwritten. As, nevertheless, the book is his last, it presents an opportunity of stating the general judgment of economists upon the Wakefield system more than sixty years after its promulgation. This may be best accomplished by citing the judgment of the modern economist who has discussed it with most thoroughness, and who is at the same time a recognised authority—M. Leroy-Beaulieu, in his treatise, *De la Colonisation chez les Peuples Modernes*, 1886. M. Leroy-Beaulieu's judgment appears at first sight a mixture of praise and censure, but upon attentive examination he proves more eulogistic than he supposes himself to be. He calls the theory a mixture of wheat and tares, but when the tares are pointed out it appears that they are none of Wakefield's sowing. The chief defect of the Wakefield system, in M. Leroy-Beaulieu's eyes, seems to be the pretension which he attributes to it of a rigorously scientific and almost mathematical character. No such pretension is to be found in the writings of Wakefield, who was himself so far from attributing a strictly consistent and homogeneous character to his system as to have declared that, although he attached the greatest importance to the employment of the proceeds of land sales in bringing over emigrants, still, if only the giving away of land or its disposal at a nominal value could be checked by the establishment of a sufficient price, the main point would be gained, even though these proceeds were thrown into the sea. After this criticism, which really has no application to the system as Wakefield conceived it, M. Leroy-Beaulieu gives his entire adhesion to its two main principles—the sale of land at a substantial price and the immigration fund—merely observing that the entire proceeds of the land sales cannot be safely devoted to this object, which Wakefield himself admitted, and pointing out that Government assistance must almost always be necessary. His censure of the phrase 'self-supporting colony,' employed by some of the promoters of South Australian colonisation, merely repeats Wakefield's own statement to the South Australian Committee that he regarded this phrase as quackery. M. Leroy-Beaulieu does not advert to the chief practical difficulty—that of maintaining a steady influx of new labour after the first batch of labourers had become independent.[1] In the main his view of the system seems to differ but slightly from that of its founder; it is only to be regretted that the South Australian disasters are so presented that it might appear on a superficial view as though M. Leroy-Beaulieu regarded them as in some way consequences of the method adopted in the settlement of the colony, which it is nevertheless evident that he does not.

The practical results of the system spoke sufficiently for themselves. It had the fullest and fairest trial in Canterbury and Otago. 'Out of 11,915,303 acres,' says Mr Rusden, 'sold from the foundation of the colony till 31st of October 1876 for £8,101,859, the enormous proportion of £5,395,000 had been received by Canterbury and Otago for less than 4,500,000 acres. For about the same land as that sold by Auckland, Canterbury had received thirteen times as much money.'

It would appear, then, that land was thirteen times as dear in Canterbury as in Auckland, and that nevertheless Canterbury sold as much land as Auckland, and had thirteen times as much revenue from this source to devote to immigration and public improvements. In Victoria, by 1858, three millions of acres had been sold for £4,800,000, which, under

[1] Labour soon became scarce in most of the New Zealand Company's settlements. 'The only cuss of this colony,' wrote a woman who had emigrated with her husband, 'is the exhorburnt wagers one has to pay.' 'She liked,' comments Wakefield, 'the "exhorburnt wagers" while her husband received them.'

the old system of New South Wales, from which Victoria had been detached, would have been given away in extensive tracts to individuals and have remained uncultivated. Even in New South Wales after the regulations in 1831, although the price put upon land was no more than five shillings an acre, the revenue from land sales rose from £10,000 in 1832 to £130,000 in 1836. 'In this manner,' Mr Elliott, the Emigration Commissioner, told the Lords' Committee on New Zealand in 1838, 'assisted emigration began immediately, and, the moment that commenced, a voluntary emigration arose also.' This tendency of emigration defrayed from the land fund to generate a simultaneous and independent stream of spontaneous emigration, was a noteworthy and valuable feature. While the former movement, controlled by intelligent directors with the object of providing the new country with the pick and flower of the old, contributed the elements best calculated to build up a prosperous state in the future, any tendency towards pedantry or over-regulation was checked by the second current, affording more play to the forces of nature. The high level of the colonies founded on the Wakefield principle is notorious, and was enhanced by its further development in enlisting religious bodies as colonising agents. Nothing in the system deserves more commendation than its scientific character, its progress on regular principles, and its administration by persons, whether public commissioners or private bodies, earnestly but disinterestedly concerned for its success. In this respect it surpassed even Greek colonization; not, however, by contrivance, but from the nature of the case. The Greeks, going forth to occupy a small territory, the whole of which was to be appropriated at once, were of necessity in sufficient force for the undertaking, and hence needed no reinforcements, and were from the very beginning an independent and self-subsisting power. The English, settling in regions too extensive for anything but the merest beginnings of occupation, were long in need of the tutelage of the mother country, and she, had she rightly understood her place and mission, might have nursed them into a more intimate connection than Greece ever conceived.

The Wakefield system was of course violently attacked by those who wished to acquire extensive tracts of land at nominal prices, and the assumed interest of the poor was generally made the stalking horse of such persons. In fact, so long as the price set upon the land was sufficient to deter large purchasers, no contrivance could be better adapted to favour the multiplication of small landowners. No colony that gave it a fair trial has ever definitely rejected it, and if it is now tacitly laid aside in most of them, one chief reason is that it has mainly done its work, carrying them on to the period when the cheapness and facility of communication make regular systems for directing the tide of emigration superfluous, and when the growth of an indigenous population render emigration less vitally necessary. In Canterbury, where it had the fairest trial and produced the most striking results, many of those who bought land under its provisions suffered from the unprofitableness of farming produced by the great decline in the value of the chief colonial staples after 1872. Yet when all is said, in the opinion of the present Agent-General of New Zealand, who was brought up in Canterbury, much and solid settlement remains as its result, and little would ever have been said against it had the letting of a portion of the agricultural lands gone on, *pari passu*, with the sale of freeholds. The parting with land for cash, had it been applied to a portion instead of the whole of the public estate, might have found the funds for carrying on colonising work without becoming an instrument to effect the wild land speculation which, following on the Vogel borrowing policy between 1872 and 1879, half ruined a generation of Canterbury settlers. As to that speculation, mischievous as it was, it is obviously not to be charged against Wakefield that he did not foresee the relation to his land system of a Public Works Loan Policy conceived many years after his death. Little of the earth's surface is now available for colonization in the proper sense of the term; should Britain, however, ever again become possessed of an unoccupied tract enjoying a temperate climate and otherwise fit to be the cradle of a nation, she will hardly find a better way of peopling it with settlers representative of all that is best in herself than that devised by Edward Gibbon Wakefield.

The Art of Colonization might have been a more perfect book but for the misfortune which deprived it of the revision of Charles Buller, who died unexpectedly at the end of November 1848. He had visited Wakefield in the previous month to discuss a plan of colonization ' for the special use and benefit of the Milesian-Irish race, who never colonize, but only emigrate miserably,' which Wakefield had prepared in concert with Godley. It was then intended to have formed a section of *The Art of Colonization*, but 'it was ultimately agreed that the plan would stand a better chance of being soon adopted by Parliament if it were not published in my book.' It was consequently reserved to be used by Buller as might be deemed most expedient, but his death frustrated the project, 'and,' says Wakefield, 'the plan is still in my desk.' What became of it has not been ascertained.

No circumstance in Wakefield's life affords a more substantial guarantee of his worth than his long and, notwithstanding his disapproval of the New Zealand Company's agreement, and his complaint that ' Earl Grey had spoiled Buller for a colonial reformer,' untroubled friendship with so choice a spirit as Charles Buller. 'A sound, penetrating intellect, full of adroit resources, and loyal by nature itself to all that was methodic, manful, true,' as Carlyle wrote in the *Examiner*. Wakefield composed no set eulogium on his friend, but erected a memorial to him by reprinting as an appendix to his own book Buller's great speech on 'Systematic Colonization' in 1843, an eloquent and luminous exposition of the advantage to a great industrial country of peopling the world with her children.

The New Zealand Company survived its champion by about a year and a half. In 1850, although its existence was nominally protracted some time for the sake of winding up its affairs, it virtually came to an end through its inability to repay its borrowings from Government. Its charter was surrendered, and the compensation due to it, assessed upon the proceeds of colonial land sales, was paid with much discontent by the colony—an iniquity, if such it were, necessary to prevent a greater iniquity. With a higher level of public spirit the sum would have been paid by the nation. For, though sunk into decrepitude in the absence of its leading spirit, the Company had had a heroic past. It had laid the foundations of empire broad and deep. Four flourishing settlements owed their existence to it; to two others it had given efficacious assistance. In 1851 these settlements contained 17,000 white inhabitants—but for Government interference Wakefield thought there would have been 200,000. It had baffled potentates abroad and shaken ministries at home. It deserved the most especial praise for its careful selection of emigrants, a prepared soil from which none but good fruit could spring—'men,' said Wakefield, 'already before they left home more accustomed to deal with matters of a common concern, of a public character, and of the highest importance to themselves collectively, than are any equal number of average Englishmen who stay at home, and who generally seem fitted to be the subjects and machines, rather than the springs and managers, of government.' Yet what was done was but little in comparison with what might have been done if they who wished to enlarge the empire had not been treated as though they wished to dismember it—if the rulers of the land, leagues behind its thinkers and its poets, had not assumed the old hopeless attitude of

'Blind Authority beating with his staff
The child that would have led him.'

CHAPTER XI

CHURCH COLONIZATION—THE FREE CHURCH COLONY AT OTAGO—THE CANTERBURY SETTLEMENT—LORD LYTTELTON—GODLEY AS SUPERINTENDENT—FELIX WAKEFIELD ON THE COLONY—THE NEW ZEALAND CONSTITUTION—LIFE AT REDHILL AND REIGATE — WAKEFIELD LEAVES ENGLAND FOR NEW ZEALAND

*Via prima salutis,
Qued minime reris, Graia pandetur ab urbe.*

SURELY it was by the spirit of prophecy that the pioneer vessel of New Zealand colonization was named the *Tory*. During the turmoil of the Company's battle with Lord Stanley, Wakefield must have been far from foreseeing that his ideas would be taken up and carried out by that nobleman's political supporters, and that New Zealand would wait for a constitution until the Colonial Secretary had become Prime Minister. It had seemed an axiom to him, as to all, that reform must proceed from reformers. The attitude of stolid resistance to all change assumed by the Tory party when he entered public life would alone have constrained him to range himself with the Radicals, and he would have been found sitting and voting with Grote and Molesworth but for the disaster which destroyed his prospect of a parliamentary career. He had since 'mended his shell with pearl' to some purpose, but so had the Tories. A 'Young England' school had been growing up, influenced in no small measure by modern ideas, but whose special mission it was to take up the old mediæval principles and graft them upon the new era. Carlyle's *Past and Present* expresses the essence and quintessence of this mode of thought, which pervades the contemporary novels of Disraeli, and was especially represented by those young Tories whom a breach with their party on the question of free trade had constrained to set up for themselves as Peelites. To these Wakefield's theories presented a different aspect to that which had chiefly impressed the economists of the Mill and Molesworth type. Although the sufficient price and the immigration fund had been the corner stones of the system, still the *Letter from Sydney* had laid hardly less stress upon the necessity of systematic colonization by well-selected emigrants, observing a due proportion of the sexes; and all the arrangements for the sale of land implied the persistence of social distinctions. The young Tories naturally agreed with Wakefield in preferring an aristocracy to a plutocracy, and were powerfully attracted by the vision of a well-ordered colony in which squire and clergyman should exert a preponderating influence. Wakefield himself, as we have seen, had warned them that England could not be reproduced in the Antipodes, and that those institutions alone could bear transplantation whose fitness could bear the test of experiment. The Peelites, on their part, nothing doubted the ability of princes and prelates, churches and colleges, coronets and chasubles, all things which the spirit of the age threatened with extinction at home, to acclimatise themselves beyond the seas. Strangely enough, it was precisely the Puseyite section of the Tory party, with the highest notions and most retrograde tendencies in ecclesiastical matters, that entertained the most liberal views in secular affairs. It was they who had broken with the bulk of their party on the Corn Law question, and now presented the phenomenon of a phalanx of Liberal High Churchmen, the essential point of whose contention was that the Church was a vital institution in harmony with the deepest needs of the age; nor could Wakefield be more ready to take up the Church for the sake of colonization than they were to take up colonization for the sake of the Church.

The emigration of religious bodies had been a leading feature of seventeenth century colonization. Wakefield awards the credit of reviving it to Dr

Hinds; but the germ of it may be detected in a note to his own *England and America*, vol. II., p. 255, and his letter to his sister respecting the Bishopric of New Zealand, already cited, proves how warmly he entered into it. 'Bishop Selwyn's see,' he says, writing to Godley on 21st December 1847, 'was created by us in spite of many obstacles put in our way by the Church and the Government. Indeed, we forced the measure on the Melbourne Government; and in that measure originated all the new Colonial Bishoprics. If our views had been taken up by the Church, great results would have been obtained, both for the Church and colonization.' His own sympathies were by no means ecclesiastical; his creed appears to have been a masculine Theism; but to get his plans adopted in influential quarters, and to secure desirable emigrants for his beloved colony, he would have transplanted the Grand Lama of Tibet with all his praying wheels, and did actually nibble at the Chief Rabbi. He entertained, moreover, a statesmanlike conviction of the importance of fostering the religious element in a colony, both on its own account and for all that it implies. He says in *The Art of Colonization*, ' A colony that is not attractive to women is an unattractive colony; in order to make it attractive to both sexes, you do enough if you take care to make it attractive to women. Women are more religious than men—or, at all events, there are more religious women than religious men. You might persuade religious men to emigrate, and yet in time have a colony of which the morals and manners would be detestable; but if you persuade religious women to emigrate, the whole colony will be comparatively virtuous and polite.' Further on, following Godley in his *Letters from America*, he points out that the early American colonists did not so much resort thither to escape religious persecution as to 'find a place where their own religion would be the religion of the place,' and that this system answered. 'All that colonization was more or less a religious colonization; the parts of it that prospered the most were the most religious parts; the prosperity was chiefly occasioned by the respectability of the emigration; and the respectability of the emigration to each colony had a close relation to the force of the religious attraction. I am in hopes,' he adds, 'of being able, when the proper time shall come for that part of my task, to persuade you that it would now be easy for England to plant sectarian colonies; that is, colonies with the strong attraction for superior emigrants of a peculiar religious creed in each colony.' This was written in 1848, but the idea had been worked out in theory, and seemed on the point of execution in 1843, as shown by a letter to his sister, undated, but which the announcement of the resumption of land sales in virtue of an agreement between the New Zealand Company and Lord Stanley proves to have been written in the May of that year.

'The project of a new colony in New Zealand is

so nearly ripe that I want to talk with you and Charles about it. It will be a Church of England colony; that is, the foundation fund of the colony will contain ample endowments for religious and educational purposes in connection with our Church exclusively. A body of colonists will be formed here in conjunction with eminent clergymen and laymen of the Church of England not intending to emigrate, and this body will mature the plan and offer it to the New Zealand Company, by whom it will be accepted. The project, which is mine own, is warmly approved, and will have the zealous support of the Church and eminent laymen. Dr Hinds, who is here, will work at it. . . .

'The settlement of our differences with Lord Stanley is signed and sealed, and we begin again to-day to sell land.'

It must be supposed that the renewal of disputes between the Company and the Colonial Office prevented the further prosecution of the scheme for a Church of England colony at that time. Another ecclesiastical colony, however, came almost simultaneously to birth. In July 1842, Mr George Rennie, an enterprising Scot, who had for a while represented Ipswich in Parliament, had addressed to the New Zealand directors a scheme for colonization in the Middle Island. Wakefield was then in Canada, and the directors referred Mr Rennie to the Government. The arrangement concluded with Lord Stanley in

May 1843, referred to in Wakefield's letter to his sister, quoted above, gave them, however, more freedom of action; and on 23d May, Mr Rennie and a new associate, Captain Cargill, returned to the charge with a plan embodying the important modifications that the new colony should be a Scotch Presbyterian one, comprising provision for religious and educational purposes, and that the whole ·of the emigration fund derived from land should be devoted to bringing over Scotch labourers only. Five days previously the scheme had received a great impetus from a great event—the disruption of the Church of Scotland on 18th May 1843. Free Kirk sentiment was immediately appealed to, to such effect, indeed, that the Kirk swallowed up the entire undertaking, except the original projector, rejected as an indigestible morsel. The New Zealand Company sided with Mr Rennie's opponents, the ultra Free Kirk men; lands were acquired from the natives under the auspices of Colonel Wakefield in June 1844, and, after many vexatious delays, the *John Wickliffe* and the *Philip Laing* entered Otago Harbour and founded Dunedin, capital of Otago, the most southerly of the New Zealand provinces. They brought 343 emigrants. The progress of the settlement was considered slow; nevertheless, by 1858, there were 7000 inhabitants, and 19,000 acres were enclosed. In 1861 came the gold discovery and the rush which emptied the little settlement to fill it again. By the end of the year

20,000 Australians had supervened, swamping the original Scotch element, but affording the substantial consolation of a rise in the revenue from £97,000 to £470,000. So great was the increase of population that, by 1871, the number of pupils in the public schools was equal to the entire population in 1858.

Colonies founded in pursuance of a deliberate plan have a double history—that of the emigrants on the spot, and that of the contrivers at home. The early history of Otago is mainly that of the hardy settlers, but the sister colony of Canterbury has a still more interesting tale to tell of the struggles undergone on its behalf at the other side of the world by men whom it merely interested as representing a principle. Here, as perhaps nowhere else, we may see a colony in the making, exhibited in the correspondence of one of the two principal projectors. Mr Jerningham Wakefield's grievous neglect of his father's papers is partly redeemed by his having not only preserved, but printed Wakefield's letters to Godley and other leading persons concerned with the foundation of the settlement, of which the writer had most fortunately preserved copies. *The Founders of Canterbury*, containing this correspondence from November 1847 to October 1850, is probably the worthiest monument to Wakefield ever raised, for what his other writings left matter of inference is here matter of demonstration. It might well have been conjectured that so bold a theorist, and so sagacious a judge of human nature, would not want boldness or sagacity in action; but here he is found, not merely prescribing recipes for colony-making, but himself making the colony. What elsewhere may have seemed a dry abstraction is here clothed with flesh and blood. We see the sanguine, enthusiastic projector, fertile, inventive, creative, his head an arsenal of expedients, and every failure pregnant with a remedy; imperious or suasive, as suits his turn; terrible in wrath, and exuberant in affection; commanding, exhorting, entreating, permitting, as, like an eminent personage of old, he

> '*With head, hand, wings or feet, pursues his way,
> And swims, or sinks, or wades, or creeps, or flies.*'

And to what end? Merely to demonstrate the soundness of his ideas by founding a colony, the incarnation of his thought, and, in its way, a finished work of art.

The principal actors in this exciting drama, after Wakefield himself, are Godley and Lord Lyttelton, whose figures, though Wakefield nowhere in this correspondence attempts a regular portrait, are clearly defined, and might be almost as vivid as Wakefield's, if Mr Jerningham Wakefield had performed the obvious duty of preserving their letters. Godley's character has been ably portrayed by Mr J. E. FitzGerald, in the memoir prefixed to his *Writings and Speeches* (Christchurch, 1863). Mr FitzGerald's estimate concludes:—

'He had not the comprehensive intellect of a great philosopher, nor the fire and fancy of a great poet, but he had the mind of a practical statesman, clear foresight and wise judgment, with a resolute will, unimpeachable integrity, and a chivalrous sense of honour.'

In other words, he did not possess Wakefield's originality of genius, but was as much a born leader of men as Wakefield was a born leader of thought.

Of Lord Lyttelton, who had had considerable experience of colonial affairs as Under Secretary to Mr Gladstone, Wakefield gave a glowing character in his letter to Godley on the New Zealand constitution. The principal members of the Canterbury Association had been denounced by the *Examiner* as 'Jesuits.'

'I must say another word about two of these "Jesuits." The first is Lord Lyttelton, whose indifference to power and fame keep in obscurity his singular ability and public spirit. Ever since you left England he has made himself a slave to the business of promoting New Zealand colonization and the reform of colonial government, always ready to give his whole time, his whole attention and his money without stint to the work in hand; and this without appearing to suppose that he deserves the least credit for these sacrifices. I cannot recollect another instance of equal modesty and gentle simplicity of character combined with great talents: and, with the exception of Lord Metcalfe, who did not surpass him in this respect, I have never known a politician so unlike a Jesuit in love of truth and downrightness of conduct.'

Lord Lyttelton and Godley were distinguished from the crowd of politicians in that they were, like Wakefield, idealists, but their ideals were not quite the same as his. It is doubtful whether either would have taken up colonization except in the interest of the Church of England; having once done so, however, they became enthusiasts in the cause, still keeping the Church mainly in view. Wakefield in a measure reversed the process; he could not be as good a churchman as his friends were colonizers, yet he becomes almost episcopal as he talks of the various candidates for the bishopric. One motive he had which his colleagues could not share, to confound the renegades, as he deemed them, of the old New Zealand Company:—

Virtutem videant, intabescantque relicta.

It is evident from the letter already cited, that the idea of a Church colony was in Wakefield's mind in May 1843, and the further provision defined by Mr FitzGerald as the requirement 'that ample funds should be provided, out of the proceeds of the land sales, for the religious and educational wants of the community about to be established' seems an obvious corollary, though it need not be doubted that it was taken up with especial warmth by Godley. The scheme appears to have assumed definite shape at a conference between the two at Malvern on 29th November 1847. The part which especially devolved upon Wakefield was to induce the New Zealand Company, of which he was still nominally a director, and in which two-thirds of the waste Crown lands of New Zealand were vested, to dispose of a sufficient amount of the lands to the Church colonizers to set them going: while Godley's part, in Mr FitzGerald's words, 'was the labour of bringing to the scheme a sufficient amount of influence to secure the foundation of the new colony.' As a leading contributor to the *Morning Chronicle*, for which most of the more distinguished Peelites wrote, as a brilliant Oxonian of High Church tendencies, and a member of several leading clubs, he was intimate with most of the members of the neo-Conservative party, he found no difficulty in interesting men of influence in his project, and the indispensable qualification for a New Zealand directorship was furnished by a nominal transfer of stock from Wakefield. Wakefield, on his part, wrote on 30th November to Mr John Abel Smith, one of the most important directors left on the New Zealand Board, proposing 'the old plan of a settlement of 300,000 acres to be purchased from the company for ten shillings per acre.' It was at the time intended that the location should be the valley of the Ruamahanga, near Wellington, and it is not quite clear when the

Canterbury Plains in the Middle Island were decided upon as the site of the settlement. The company took up the idea; a 'Canterbury Association' was formed by Godley's exertions, which in due time obtained a charter. Land was to be sold on the Wakefield system at a 'sufficient price,' but here the weak point—not fatal but unquestionably troublesome — of religious colonies came in. To induce the Church to enter into the scheme, it was necessary to set aside a portion of the funds for public worship and religious education, and as this could only be got out of the proceeds of the land sales, the price of the land was necessarily raised to meet the demand, and was thus rendered excessive. It was fixed at three pounds per acre, and the proportion of this devoted to church and school buildings being no less than one-third, it followed that one pound out of three was an unreproductive investment. At the same time, the high price dismayed emigrants, as the promoters found to their cost when they appealed to the public for support. The more ecclesiastically minded among them probably rejoiced in the expectation that this regulation would keep out dissenters, who would hardly pay a pound an acre for the privilege of sending their children to High Church schools; but even bigotry and virtue lost their attractiveness in the presence of excessive price. The experiment, well worth trying, will hardly be tried again; but the colony could not have been launched without it, and, after all, proved no failure, and had the especial advantage of enriching New Zealand with emigrants of an especially high standard of character and culture—'Canterbury pilgrims,' among whom knights, squires, franklins, parsons, lawyers and physicians constituted a numerous and substantial element. 'The young men of Godley's school,' wrote Wakefield, 'resemble, both in head and heart, the nobler spirits of Elizabeth's time.'

By the middle of 1848 the affairs of the embryo settlement had progressed sufficiently to justify the despatch of Captain Thomas as agent to occupy and clear the ground: but for some time afterwards they appear to have languished, and it was not until the winter of 1849 that the state of Godley's health brought about the step to which the ultimate success of the colony is mainly to be attributed, his mission as general manager and superintendent. It had been proposed that he should spend the winter in Italy. Wakefield warmly, almost passionately, urged that the equally mild climate of New Zealand should have the preference, and Godley sailed at the beginning of December. His first act on arriving was to stop all expenditure, Captain Thomas having considerably overdrawn his means; and then, finding that the expected colonists did not arrive, he betook himself to Wellington, where he successfully opposed a scheme brought forward by Sir George Grey for the government of New Zealand. It was not until November 1850 that, after raising £5000 for the advantage of the settlement upon his own security, he returned to Canterbury upon hearing of the actual despatch of a body of emigrants in September. For nearly two years from that period, in the language of a settler, 'his word was law.' 'Not with coffers full and facilities abundant,' says Mr FitzGerald, 'but in poverty of funds, amidst great difficulties, amidst much discontent, amidst the disappointment of many sanguine expectations, and the ill-concealed hostility of a Government [Sir George Grey's] which appeared vexed at the additional trouble imposed on it by the founding of a new colony within its jurisdiction, Mr Godley guided the infant fortunes of Canterbury, in the full and entire conviction of the result which must one day come.' It only needs to be corrected in this generally just description that the motive of Sir George Grey's unquestionable hostility to the Canterbury settlement was not dislike of trouble, but his conscientious though narrow antipathy to 'class colonies.'

One of Godley's first steps was to abolish, somewhat to Wakefield's alarm, the regulation of the Canterbury Association, forbidding the granting of pasturage leases except to purchasers of land. Of all New Zealand districts, Canterbury is the best adapted for sheep breeding, and the result of the change was to bring a welcome flow of capital into the colony. 'No day passes,' wrote Wakefield, in June 1850, 'without my thinking of your being there with urgent work to do and no money. But, indeed, the whole deficiency of money must be treated as an unavoidable misfortune, unless you and I are to blame for having thought of founding, with twenty-five thousand pounds, a colony whose proper foundation on the plan adopted requires a capital of two or three hundred thousand. However, courage! It is a good plan; there is a good colony of people; an excellent prospect on this side, of the largest and best emigration we ever hoped for; and we Englishmen are not apt to faint.'

Before this letter was written the vessel of the colony had been upon the rocks, and was only floated off with great difficulty, mainly by the interposition of Lord Lyttelton, who, Mr FitzGerald says, and the statement is fully borne out by Wakefield's correspondence, 'brought his strong intellect and resolute will to rescue it from destruction.' 'He threw himself into the affair,' says Wakefield, in an unpublished letter to Godley, 'as if his own fortune or life had been at stake. You and I planned, but I should have been disappointed and you discredited, if he had not taken up the work and carried it through by dint of personal effort and risk.' He became chairman of the Managing Committee in the spring of 1850, superseding Mr John Hutt, an excellent man incapacitated by advancing years and failing health, of whom Wakefield writes most characteristically :—'It is very distressing, as was the necessity for knocking him out of the chair : but if you saw your own child boring a hole in the bottom of a ship full of passengers, and you could not stop him any other way, you would shoot him, would you not ? I would.' The land sales, owing to the extra pound an acre insisted upon for Church purposes, disappointed expectation, and a guarantee to the New Zealand Company was necessary. Lord Lyttelton, Sir John Simeon, Lord Richard Cavendish and Wakefield himself each became responsible for £3750; and hence it became possible to announce in April that the first body of colonists would positively sail for their destination in the autumn. 'Thanks,' exclaims Wakefield, 'to the heart and head combined of Lord Lyttelton and Simeon in particular !' This was by no means the last of their ventures and benefactions. The first provincial assembly relieved the founders of the settlement of £18,000 obligation. Of Wakefield's own part he modestly says : 'I have always regarded my signature to the guarantee as imposing on me no real pecuniary liability. Poor I should have to pay only when Hagley, Swainston and Mr Cavendish's estate could not.'

Not all the munificence of Lord Lyttelton and his friends, however, could render the Canterbury

Association a success, but it saved the colony. The extra pound for religious and educational purposes fatally checked land sales; not more than one-tenth of the two hundred thousand acres expected to be sold during the first year or two were actually disposed of; the Association's inability to perform its engagements led to the forfeiture of the charter granted in 1850; and as soon as the colonists got their own way through the dissolution of the Association, while firmly maintaining the principle of the sufficient price, they fixed this at forty shillings. This result seemed to demonstrate that the sectarian system of colonization is only justifiable as a *pis aller*, which in the case of Canterbury it actually was. The New Zealand Company had long abandoned systematic colonization, and but for the ideas of Wakefield and Godley, and the ecclesiastical enthusiasm of Lord Lyttelton and his circle, the fair plains of Canterbury would have been long unoccupied, or have been monopolised by squatters from Australia attracted by the prospect of cheap land. The 'sufficient price,' though in this instance overdone, and the religious fervour, though narrow and exclusive, preserved them for the occupation of one of the finest bodies of emigrants ever collected, who, the first difficulties of settlement overcome, dotted them with Lyttelton, Christchurch, Timaru and Akaroa, and many another thriving town.

A lively picture of the early days of the struggling

settlement is presented in a letter to Catherine
Torlesse from her youngest brother, Felix Wakefield, the author of a valuable treatise—to which,
however, Edward Gibbon gave literary form—on the
survey of waste lands. After many years spent in
land-surveying in Tasmania, he returned to England
with his family in 1847, and was promptly impressed
by his senior into the service. He took an active part
in the preliminary arrangements for the foundation of
the settlement, and arrived there himself in December
1851. His letter gives a vivid picture of the natural
features of the colony 'like the South Downs on a
gigantic scale, entirely free from timber but with
ragged edges, and here and there some fantastic
peaks, jagged as the volcano left them when it
forced these islands above the sea.' This scarcity
of timber—which the writer himself, an enthusiastic
acclimatiser who first brought red deer and pheasants
to New Zealand, afterwards did much to remove—
was a great hindrance to the prosperity of the settlement, but not to be compared to the mountain which
blocked communication between Lyttelton, the port,
and Christchurch, the capital, an evil afterwards
remedied by driving a tunnel. 'I bitterly regret
not having come out instead of Captain Thomas,
for I could have saved a mass of disappointment
and misery by preventing a settler landing here
until the road was passable.' The colony, Felix
Wakefield thought, was, nothwithstanding, on the

road to prosperity, but prosperity was a long way off. Pending the attainment of this goal, he anticipated considerable difficulty in supporting himself and his young family, and looked forward to a long course of potato-growing as a means to this end. The colonists were an excellent body of men, 'a colony of gentlemen; and this, my deliberate opinion, was confirmed by Bishop Selwyn a few days since, when he told me that he knew of nothing like it in that respect. The labourers are, as a body, respectable, some black sheep among them, but very few; for this we may thank the workers of the scheme in England, and the chaplain and schoolmaster on board.' 'The first body of colonists,' says Wakefield, in a letter to Godley, 'was made up by infinite painstaking. Nine out of ten of them were nursed into becoming colonists.' Owing to the slowness of the land sales, the arrangements for churches and schools were in abeyance, and the voluntary system loomed darkly in the future. Mr Wakefield himself had just rescued two most promising young men from Norfolk from 'slipping back into barbarism.' He fully agreed with Godley that there was too much government from home, and that the despatches from headquarters were unduly didactic. 'Except the sale of land, and sending ships out, everything ought to be done here by Godley and the Council of the colonists.'

This feeling on Godley's part, and, as Wakefield

thought, the interference of Godley's future biographer, the then emigration agent, Mr Fitz-Gerald, a brilliant, impulsive Irishman, meteorically conspicuous in the political history of New Zealand, who had adorned the Secretary's office at the British Museum, and whose epistles to Panizzi on the subject of registration are still preserved with reverence in the archives of the printed book department, led eventually to a lamentable estrangement between Wakefield and Godley, which would not have occurred if they had not been on opposite sides of the world. 'What a pity,' Wakefield himself observes to Godley, 'that we cannot meet, and fight it out till one should give in! I pray you to believe that I am not obstinate or conceited, but really desirous to think with you.' Not all his letters were equal models of sweet reasonableness, but personal explanation would have obliterated unfavourable impressions. 'I declare,' Wakefield wrote to Lord Lyttelton from New Zealand after Godley's departure, 'that a thorough reconciliation would be more agreeable to me than anything else I can think of.' Felix Wakefield did not after all devote himself to potatoes; he went back to England, became director of the Army Works Corps in the Crimean War, and returning after some years to Canterbury, found that his property there had beome as valuable as he had expected it to prove 'if the colony did not collapse or want of a road.' The time of trial, nevertheless, had been severe, and it is not surprising that when Wakefield himself arrived at Canterbury he wrote to his sister, 'Extreme unpopularity met me on landing,' though he adds, 'It nearly all evaporated in a month.' When Lord Lyttelton, in 1868, came to view the work to which he had so largely contributed, he found it very good, especially as regarded the high religious and educational development which had been the colony's *raison d'être*.

The letters quoted, hitherto unpublished, belong to the year 1851. The printed volume is one of the raciest of books, full of humour, designed and undesigned. Nothing gave the writer more trouble than that indispensable appurtenance to a Church colony, a bishop, and anxiously did he strain his untutored vision to discover the precise tint of churchmanship which would gratify the High Churchman without absolutely infuriating the Low. 'Surely the Church comprises many earnest Churchmen who are not members of the Puseyite or Tractarian party. I would name, for example, Gladstone and the Bishop of Oxford.' (The children of this world are not *always* wiser than the children of light.) Two most eligible prelates were thought to have been caught, but both managed to give the association the slip; a third, to whom it had actually bound itself, proved so ineligible that great relief was experienced when he himself arrived at a similar conclusion as respected his intended diocese. Bishop Selwyn got no suffragan at Canterbury until December 1856. If, however, Wakefield did not shine as a theologian, his letters do him much credit as a practical moralist. The blessing promised to the peacemakers should have rested upon the writer of this letter to an eminent servant of the New Zealand Company who had quarrelled with another of equal distinction :—

'Your quarrel is to me a subject of deep regret, both on your own account and that of the colony. Is it irreparable? Men of sense never quarrel irreparably. If I could imagine you exempt from the strange violence of colonial party feeling, I should earnestly counsel and beg of you to put an end to the quarrel. In every quarrel the man who puts an end to it is he who makes the first advance to reconciliation. To do that is only considered disgraceful by petty minds : men of sense and courage deem it magnanimous. You have made a mistake. Why not retrace the step? If you have the manly sense I give you credit for, you will be able to conquer a natural disinclination to admitting the mistake. Greater men than either of us have done this very often : very little men cannot do it. I misjudge greatly if he is not a gentleman and a man of spirit : and if he is, he will cordially accept the offer of your hand. If you have, as may be natural, a difficulty about opening the way to peace, send him this letter, and wait for what he shall do. It would be a vast satisfaction to me were I thus to be the means of bringing together two men whose co-operation and friendship I consider of great importance to the welfare of New Zealand. If you make up the quarrel you will both be gainers, as well as the colony; and you will be better friends, closer allies in the pursuit of the cause as to which you have never differed—that cause which I have at heart, and to which I make every sacrifice that it requires—than if you had never quarrelled at all.'

The following is equally admirable in a different way :—

'A new colony is a bad place for a young single man. To be single is contrary to the nature of a new colony, where the laws of society are labour, peace, domestic life, increase and multiply. The hospitality is so great that a young man who can make himself agreeable may live in idleness : and the most common lot of a single young man is to do this, till he becomes unfit for marriage by becoming wedded to his pipe and his bottle, not to mention the billiard table. Whereas, if he is nicely married, he has a sweet home to go to after his day's work, and his mind is kept tranquil enough to bear without injury the intense excitement of sharing in the creation of a new society. Marriage is the most economical : the same capital goes further with a wife than without one. It is *her* moral influence that both saves the money, and stimulates her husband's energy and prudence. Whatever may be the rank and capital of the young colonist—whether a nobleman's son worth £10,000, or a labourer—let him be married for the sake of economy as well as peace and comfort.'

Wakefield's stay at Malvern had been preceded by a residence of a few months at South Stoke, near Arundel, where he begged a cottage from Mr John Abel Smith, chiefly on account of his little friend, Amy Allom, whom it pained him to find wasted by illness upon his return from his own tour. After her recovery, he settled at Warwick Lodge, Redhill, where he gathered around him the family of his brother Felix, recent arrivals from Tasmania. Constance, the eldest daughter, now Mrs D'Arblay Burney, became his secretary, an office also sometimes discharged by his nephew George, the son of his brother Howard, and afterwards an Indian civil servant. He took his brother's family with him to Boulogne, and when he afterwards moved to a pretty little outbuilding belonging to the White Hart Hotel at Reigate, quartered them at Woodhatch, a house in the neighbourhood. Mrs Burney vividly remembers her first impression of her uncle, only confirmed by subsequent acquaintance, as of one superior to all men she had ever seen or imagined. She compares him to a lion, with massive head, magnificent brow, sanguine complexion, somewhat too full habit of body, long floating hair, the token of the enthusiast, and brilliant blue eyes, indescribably tender when in gentle mood, but frequently blazing with passion or excitement. The great charm and impressiveness of his personality, notwithstanding, were incapable of definition: they lay in that mysterious magnetic power which excited feelings of intense devotion among those who came fully under its spell, detained unwilling listeners within hearing, and often subjugated them at last, but, by the law of compensation, frequently aroused violent antipathy among the unsubdued. The same contrast pervaded his own nature; in general the kindest of men—continually performing generous actions, and affectionate and tender-hearted to a fault—he had moods of perverseness, and could be bitterly resentful and vindictive when his plans were thwarted, as by Earl Grey. He was especially attached to young people, and was always striving to educate those who came under his influence. He provided his niece with teachers in French and dancing; and she remembers, with even more gratitude, his constant admonitions on punctuality, method, good handwriting, and the other valuable habits whose importance is so often undiscerned by the young. He was continually contriving parties and picnics for the amusement of his young people; but nothing was more marked in him than his exuberant spirits and fondness for practical joking, especially by alterations of apparel. He so effectually disguised the daughter of a friend as to impose on her own parents. On the whole, the impression conveyed is that of an opulent nature, whose abounding energies must have vent, and whose love of mischief and talent for stratagem might easily involve the possessor in disagreeable adventures. These perilous endowments were, nevertheless, held in check by unrivalled sagacity and shrewdness. He seemed to read unuttered thoughts, to discern character by intuition, and to foresee the future both of individuals and societies. One theme on which he was fond of dilating was the future of the Empire under the British Crown. He looked forward to the Queen's sons ruling the chief groups of the British colonies as permanent viceroys—one in Canada, another in Australia, a third at the Cape—a vision which might have proved a prevision had the Imperial sentiment, which he did so much to create, been somewhat less tardy in asserting itself. He would sometimes calm the perturbed nerves by the anodyne of a new novel, and he read *The Vicar of Wakefield* through regularly once a year. Mrs Burney copied documents and letters for him, and wrote abundantly to his dictation. It frequently happened to her to be fetched in haste, and to find her uncle closeted with some leading public man, such as Sir William Molesworth or Mr Aglionby. She would then take down an oration or disquisition from his lips, which frequently reappeared in the proceedings of the House of Commons. She also remembers Mr Rintoul, the large-browed, gentle-mannered editor of the *Spectator*, who must never be spoken to upon a Friday. The picture of life at Reigate would be incomplete without record of the enormous Talbot hounds, the awful delight of the neighbourhood, already mentioned by Mr Allom, and of a good cat, demonstrative in her affection to her master.

Another person intimately acquainted with Wakefield at this time was Sir Frederick Young, K.C.M.G., chairman and mainstay of the Royal Colonial Institute, who has most kindly placed his recollections of his old tutor in colonial politics at the writer's service:—

'My father, the late George Frederick Young, M.P.,' says Sir Frederick, 'was an active director of the New Zealand Company, and from 1839 onwards I found myself frequently in communication with Mr Wakefield. He exercised a powerful influence over all who came within his sphere, and especially over young men. His manner was striking, and most persuasive. There was a peculiar fascination about the way in which he put everything before one, which seldom failed to inspire confidence in the views which he propounded. There was a breadth, and power, and grasp of a subject in his thoughts, and a boldness in the enunciation of these that could not fail to draw attention, and generally carry conviction. In my own case he quite captivated me.

'In the year 1848 the Canterbury Association was formed, and I was induced shortly afterwards, at Mr Wakefield's suggestion, to undertake the management of their shipping department. During 1851, and part of 1852, all the ships chartered by the Association, conveying to New Zealand nearly 2000 colonists, were despatched under my personal management. During this period I was in constant communication with the Association at its offices, 9 Adelphi Terrace, Strand, which brought me into contact with Mr Wakefield, who was daily in attendance there.

'At this time he was living in a cottage, in a garden, which belonged to, and was approached from, the White Hart Inn at Reigate. It was a comfortable and commodious little residence, with a large dining-room. Here he every now and then invited me to stay with him for a day or two. On these occasions our evenings were spent in discussing various problems connected with colonization, and with the details of the progress and prospects of the new settlement of Canterbury, and the best means to be adopted for promoting its success in England. Wakefield's brother Felix was often with him at Reigate, as well as Sewell of Oxford, an active member of the Canterbury Association. I remember one night, just after Sewell had retired, and Wakefield and I were leaving the room to do the same, Wakefield, candle in hand, turned to me and said:

"What a good fellow he is! It is a pity he is such a Puseyite!"

'In those days Wakefield possessed a breed of those rare dogs, the Talbot hounds. He had two magnificent specimens, who were his constant companions, both in and out of doors. He was very fond of them, and splendid animals they were. He also had a strong cob, on which he used to ride every morning before breakfast. When I was at Reigate, I always accompanied him on foot, as he only rode at a walking pace, listening to his sage remarks, and taking in much that he propounded on the subject of colonization. He was then between fifty and sixty, about five feet six inches in height, stout and burly in figure, with a round, smooth, fair face, looking very like a prosperous English farmer. If it had not been for his unfortunate escapade in early life he would have attained a very high place in public estimation. Still, among politicians, and especially those in any way feeling an interest in colonial questions, he was undoubtedly a great power. One day he said to me, "Young, I had thirty-six members of Parliament in this room yesterday." They had travelled down to Reigate to consult him on some important colonial subject then on the tapis.

'His personal habits, when I knew him, were of the simplest kind. He was most temperate, and never indulged in any of the pleasures of the table. He rose very early and went to bed early. He lived on the simplest food, and scarcely touched wine.* He had an especial dislike to the vulgar snobbery of the *nouveaux riches*, of whom there were many specimens around him. As he was a person with a name they desired to have him at their tables, but they never could succeed in getting him. One of them said, "If you will come I will have fish down from London and dine at six." "Thank you," was the reply, "I always dine at one, on a leg of mutton and a rice pudding."

'With all his defects, Wakefield was unquestionably a great man, and possessed remarkable intellectual qualities. He was always very kind to me, and I learned much from him. He never did me any harm, and I feel honoured and proud to have known him.'

In 1850 and 1851, Wakefield united with Mr C. B. Adderley and other colonial reformers, chiefly of the more recent school, in founding a Colonial Reform Society, which materially influenced the grant of constitutions to the Australian Colonies made shortly afterwards. In 1852, his attention was chiefly given to a matter of the deepest moment to him, the New Zealand Constitution passed by the Derby Ministry, which terminated the system of personal government dominant in the islands since Sir George Grey had set aside the con-

* 'Of all men I ever knew,' writes Mr Allom, 'he had the greatest abhorrence of any person of drunken habits.'

stitution of 1846. This state of affairs, it was admitted, could not last indefinitely; and when the Derby Ministry succeeded to power in February 1852, they found a constitution in the pigeon-holes of the Colonial Office, drafted mainly under the influence of Sir George Grey. The turn which affairs then took is circumstantially described in a letter from Wakefield to Godley, of 7th June 1852, printed in the *Lyttelton Times* of 30th October, giving a complete history of the transaction, with one remarkable omission. Wakefield nowhere says that he was himself the chief author of the new constitution, yet such is the explicit assertion of Mr C. B. Adderley, afterwards Under Secretary for the Colonies, and now Lord Norton, who says in his 'Review' of Earl Grey's work on Colonial Policy (1869), 'The measure was based on a draft I drew up under the guidance of Gibbon Wakefield.' Wakefield may have considered his part as confidential, or he may have been unwilling to assume responsibility for a measure which he himself regarded as a compromise, and which he knew would prove unacceptable in many respects. It is the one aim of his able letter to reconcile the colonists to an admittedly faulty constitution, which yet contained the germ of improvement, by representing it as the sole alternative to no constitution at all.

The wisdom of the advice was soon justified. At the end of 1852, the Conservatives having, in strict fulfilment of a remarkable prophecy made by Wakefield to Rintoul in 1849, held office just long enough to weld the Peelites and the Liberals into one party, made way for their opponents, who came into power laden with pledges and projects which would have left them no time to think of New Zealand. In 1854 the Crimean War supervened, and domestic legislation ceased to interest. After all, the chief defect of the measure was unavoidable at the time. Theoretically fault might be found with the institution of six miniature parliaments under the title of Provincial Councils; but practically the settlements were so far apart and had so little in common that a collective management of their affairs was impracticable, and all that could be done was to confide the larger concerns of the country to a General Assembly, consisting of two houses, one nominated for life, the other elected by a very wide suffrage, without distinction of race. Provincial legislation required the assent of the Governor only, though, always subject to repeal by the General Assembly; acts of the General Assembly might be disallowed by the Crown. The constitution was apparently less democratic than that proposed by Sir George Grey, in so far as all the members of the Upper House of the Legislative Council were to be nominated for life by the Crown, while by Sir George's scheme the majority would have been elected for a term by the Provincial Councils. But, as Mr Reeves points out, in this case 'New Zealand would have a powerful Senate, eclipsing altogether the Lower Chamber.' It improved upon the Grey project by empowering the colonists to regulate their land sales and civil list, and to vary their constitution—a liberty which ultimately effected the abolition of the provincial system. The great defect of the absence of any provision for the selection of the Governor's responsible advisers seems to have occurred to none, either of those who prepared the measure or of those by whom it was canvassed and criticised.

The Bill received the royal assent on 30th June 1852. It had undergone, to the great indignation of Godley, an alteration by the office of Provincial Superintendent being made elective; theoretically an improvement, but which kept all New Zealand in hot water as long as Provincial Councils existed. Hostility to Provincial Councils in any form, embodied in the persons of Sir William Molesworth and Mr Robert Lowe, almost destroyed the Bill; *le mieux est souvent l'ennemi du bien.* Its passage was materially assisted by two remarkable intellectual performances—Mr Gladstone's speech and Wakefield's petition in its favour. Before the session began, Mr Gladstone had been shown the draft of a projected Bill drawn at Hams, Mr Adderley's seat, by a committee consisting of Lord Lyttelton, Mr Adderley, Messrs Fox and Weld, afterwards New Zealand Premiers, and Wakefield. He approved, and undertook to force the subject on by moving resolutions framed by himself, should the Colonial Office hang back. That this proved unnecessary was largely due, Wakefield tells Lord Lyttelton, to the private influence of Mr Gladstone with Sir John Pakington, and the advice he gave to the deputation to him 'to be very importunate.' 'And so we were.' On 21st May, Mr Gladstone delivered a remarkable speech, a pattern of close argument and classic oratory, in which, while severely criticising some provisions of the Bill, he pleaded for its passage as a whole. It is only in the light of some of the speaker's subsequent proceedings that we discern the taint of separatism, the unexpressed conviction that a divorce between the mother country and the colonies would be best for both, which is certainly there, though in too subtle a form to have impaired the admiration of the orator's contemporaries.

'The humble petition of Edward Gibbon Wakefield,' dated 2d June, and published in the *New Zealand Journal* of 18th June, is an equally characteristic performance. It would appear surprising to find it turning almost entirely on the question of the Provincial Governments, if we did not know that Molesworth's and Lowe's opposition to these Governments was the rock which jeopardised the Bill. Wakefield certainly makes out the best possible case for them. 'Evil happens,' he says, 'when the area of the colony is so large, and its means of communication so deficient, that the seat of government is what London has been as the seat of government for many remote dependencies. In such cases the benefits of Government—the means of getting done things without number which are greatly needed and which government alone can do—are confined to the seat of government and its immediate neighbourhood. The rest of the country is neglected, and stagnates almost without government.' This was true when Wakefield wrote, and he nowhere professes to regard Provincial Councils as a necessarily permanent arrangement. On the contrary, he lays especial stress on the clause in the Act allowing of its amendment from time to time, and concludes, 'Your Petitioner humbly prays that your Honourable House may be pleased to pass the Bill in question for the sake of its merits, and without regard to its obvious defects, because there is not time for amendment by present legislation here, whilst the whole measure is open to future amendment by legislation in the colony, subject to the approval of the Crown and Parliament.'

Wakefield had always contemplated emigration when his work in England should be completed, and the establishment of a constitutional system in New Zealand now seemed to open to him the prospect of a parliamentary career. He therefore arranged for quitting England in the company of Sewell, with whom, next to Lord Lyttelton, he had been most closely associated during the latter days of the Canterbury Association; of Captain Henslow, a Windsor knight, and one of his staunchest friends; and of sundry canine favourites. We have seen him put up with a cat at Lancaster Castle, whose frowning portal probably bore the legend, 'No dogs admitted.' But innate preference now reacted in the direction of bulldogs of the purest breed; he further proposed to augment the population of Canterbury by a bull and a heifer. His last news to his sister, written within an hour of sailing from Plymouth, scene of the departute of the *Mayflower* and the *Tory* on 12th October, is, 'The bull is nearly well. This morning at six, Henslow, Sewell, Bogey, Spring, Violet and I went off to the breakwater and walked there for an hour.' Four days previously he had written a letter to Lord Lyttelton embodying some of his deepest feelings and convictions :—

'PLYMOUTH, 8*th October* 1852.

'MY DEAR LORD,—The fatigues of preparation for an eternal severance from England really made it impossible for me to write to you with a collected mind. And, indeed, I had but little to say beyond offering to you my sincere and grateful thanks for all your consideration and kindness from the moment when Canterbury colonization brought me into relation with you. And this I now do with the strongest feeling of respect and attachment.

'Somehow or other, nevertheless, I cannot bring

myself to believe that I am bidding you farewell for ever. A pleasant dream is often in my mind that circumstances may yet arise that would induce you to represent the monarchy in New Zealand; and if my life, with anything like health, shall be spared, I will work hard in helping to make these circumstances take a form of reality. They would consist mainly of plentiful evidence that the colony wishes for monarchical institutions. If it should prove so, and if such institutions could be established by the only man I know who is quite fit for the task, monarchy will be preserved in the southern world; if not, we must be content with democratic republics. I am sure of this, and that there is no time to lose.'

This may seem overstrained to some, but will not to those who remember the state of opinion between 1850 and 1860; who consider that veneration for the Sovereign could not in the nature of things be so strong an influence after a reign of fifteen years as after one of fifty; and who reflect that the improved intercommunication, which has done so much to knit the Empire together, was then in its infancy.

Two months after Wakefield's departure for New Zealand, Godley left its shores homeward bound, to die a few months before his coadjutor. Permanent residence in New Zealand would probably have prolonged his life; but his work at Canterbury was done, and important employment awaited him in England. Another impressive circumstance signalised Wakefield's departure. Among those who attended his embarkation from London (29th September) was Frances Wakefield, who had unjustly suffered through him for the Turner affair, and had ever since been estranged from him, until moved to reconciliation by good Mrs Allom, after scenes surpassed for dramatic intensity by nothing off the stage, and little upon it. He knelt down and asked and received her forgiveness.

> *The earth may open and the sea o'erwhelm ;*
> *Many the ways, the little home is one ;*
> *Thither the courser leads, thither the helm ;*
> *And at one gate we meet when all is done.*

CHAPTER XII

WAKEFIELD IN NEW ZEALAND—SIR GEORGE GREY—THE FIRST NEW ZEALAND PARLIAMENT—ILLNESS AND RETIREMENT FROM PUBLIC LIFE—THE CLOSING SCENE—ESTIMATE OF HIS WORK AND CHARACTER

THE good ship *Minerva*, after a voyage no less prosperous than that vouchsafed to her predecessor the *Tory*, cast anchor at Port Lyttelton on 2d February 1853. The unpopularity of which Wakefield acknowledged himself the temporary object did not prevent his receiving an address of thanks for his services in obtaining a constitution for New Zealand. In the course of a reply that touched on many topics, he warned the colonists against discord, and professed himself 'desirous of nothing more than to see the past entirely set aside in favour of confiding and harmonious action between the Governor and the popular party in the task of bringing the new constitution into useful and creditable operation.' The peacemaker, nevertheless, presented himself at Wellington rather in the character of a stormy petrel, arriving (9th March) in the midst of a tempest which equally prevented him from landing and Sir George Grey from putting to sea. Though beset by all the difficulties described by the author of 'To all you Ladies now on Land,' Wakefield managed to indite the following epistle to the evasive Governor, if by any means he might put salt upon his tail :—

> '*Ship Minerva,*
> '*Wednesday morning,* 9*th March.*

'MY DEAR GREY,—In hopes that you are still detained by the storm which keeps me on shipboard, I write to you, as to an old friend, for the purpose of earnestly begging that you will not go away without seeing me.

'Presently after landing at Canterbury, I discovered that there are great difficulties in the way of your establishing the new constitution with advantage to the country and credit to yourself; and I lost no time in doing the little which it was then possible for me to attempt with the view of smoothing your path. You will have seen my letter to Messrs Godley and Mathias, and you will have received from some Canterbury people one which the publication of that letter really suggested. Both were intended to assist in getting your past differences with the colonists laid aside by them, so that if you had the same desire, as I could not doubt for a moment, all parties might sincerely co-operate in giving effect to the objects of

Parliament in granting powers of self-government to the colony. In the same spirit I now tender you my further services towards the same end; and if you accept the offer, it is, of course, indispensable that we should meet in order to talk over the state of parties here and the state of opinion at home with regard to New Zealand and yourself, with which I am intimately acquainted.

'But let me not be misunderstood. There is no favour which it is possible for the Governor of New Zealand to bestow upon me in a personal sense, though he may bind me to him in eternal gratitude by giving real and full effect to the New Constitutional Act. <u>My object is single and unmistakable; it is the prosperity and greatness of New Zealand which, come when it may, will be my glory, and a personal reward surpassing in value any that the power of Government could bestow upon me;</u> which will be your glory here and at home if you establish the new constitution in peace. I wish to help you, and can help you, in this rather difficult task. <u>My experience in this sort of work—at least with regard to colonies—is greater than any other man's.</u> If you go away without seeing me, I shall be very sorry, but will still do all I can to assist in the accomplishment of my only object. That, however, depends mainly upon you.

'Begging you to understand that in writing to you thus freely I do not forget the respect which is due to you officially as the Queen's representative, I remain, my dear Grey, yours very truly,

'E. G. WAKEFIELD.'

'Will you walk into my parlour? said the spider to the fly.' Sir George answers in the spirit of a dove corresponding with a serpent. Differences with the people of the country? Difficulties? Who can have told Mr Wakefield that? Is not Sir George sincerely attached to them? and does he not find warm friends among them wherever he goes? It is true that his actions have been traduced by some persons (friends of Mr Wakefield's, Sir George is sorry to say); but Sir George bears no ill-will to those individuals, and will sincerely rejoice if he sees them doing anything for the public good, and Mr Wakefield setting them the example. As to meeting Mr Wakefield just then, prior engagements put it out of the question, but Sir George hopes to see him in about two months.

Mr Wakefield is equally astounded. No differences between Sir George and the colonists! What an extraordinary assertion! Why, there are more than Mr Wakefield could conveniently enumerate in one letter. What about Sir George's hostility to the Canterbury settlement? Why are petitions signed for his recall? When Mr Wakefield wrote the day before, he had refused to believe rumours that Sir George contemplated tampering with the sale of waste lands, 'but am now credibly informed that you have issued a proclamation having that effect, if it should be deemed a lawful measure.' It is not a lawful measure, of course. 'If there is yet time, I would again implore you to reconsider your position, and to see whether means may not be devised of enabling you to obey Parliament without being troubled by anything in the past.'

Thus do eminent statesmen occasionally condescend to piece out the lion's hide with the fox's brush. Wakefield knew perfectly well that Sir George was popular at Auckland, and Sir George was equally well aware that this popularity by no means extended to the southern districts. His adversaries, not wholly without ground, explained his good repute at Auckland by the propinquity of that city to the loaves and the fishes, the staunchest allies of all governments everywhere; his friends, with equal reason, thought that it redounded to his honour to be best liked where he was best known. In truth he inherited the disastrous legacy of Governor Hobson, who, by fixing the capital at Auckland when Auckland existed merely on paper, had engendered a soreness which existed until the association of the representatives of the various provinces in a common assembly under the new constitution, when it gradually died away. It would have been better if Sir George Grey had not prolonged this unfortunate state of things by his virtual refusal to convoke a General Assembly, although he did convene the Provincial Councils. This can only be accounted for by a determination to retain power in his own hands during the remainder of his administration. He quitted New Zealand at the end of 1853, to assume the government of the Cape, little foreseeing his second governorship and yet another important part reserved for him to perform in New Zealand politics long after his troublesome antagonist should be laid in the grave.

Wakefield, meanwhile, elated by the flattering address he received on landing at Wellington, and by the apparent recovery of his health in New Zealand air, proceeded to dig this grave for himself by the eagerness with which he rushed into politics. 'I am going to throw myself upon the people,' he wrote to Lord Lyttelton. Far better for length of days and ultimate happiness if he had stood aloof from party strife, and become, as he might have in time, the acknowledged arbiter in public questions and moderator of political dissensions. 'Greater earthly reward,' Mr W. R. Greg nobly says in his essay on Sir Robert Peel, 'God out of all the riches of his boundless treasury has not to bestow.' It must be admitted, however, that Sir George Grey's land regulations were a challenge to Wakefield which he could not well decline, nor under any circumstances was he the man to play the part of a Peel. To his sanguine, impulsive temperament political excitement had the zest of an open-air game. 'You will see,' he writes to his sister, 'what a turmoil our politics are in. Though up to my eyes in it, I feel none the worse.' On this Mr Allom comments :—

'Much of this turmoil had been carefully arranged previously. I look upon this period as the most remarkable period of E. G. W.'s connection with New Zealand; the advent of men like Godley, Sewell and FitzGerald; the presence of the wily Sir George Grey; and finally the arrival of E. G. W. himself could not fail to produce a great political eruption. The result could be foreseen. I believe E. G. W. was mainly instrumental in bringing it about, and actually gloried in it quite as much as the schoolboy enjoys the bonfire he has made.'

Wakefield certainly thought himself the man for the time and place. After telling his sister (29th April) that he has attended a public meeting and 'actually spouted for an hour and a half, as I have not done since 1843 in Canadian House of Assembly,' he adds :—

''There is an immense task for me to get through, in consequence of the rotten state of public matters. But all looks well for the future, so far as the future may be affected by my obtaining an influence in the country greater than that of anybody else. Indeed, this is coming about already, by means of straightforwardness and assiduity. I work like a horse, much aided by Jerningham, who is a faithful and diligent lieutenant. If, as seems probable, he should be able to conquer some colonial habits, he will be a leading person in this country. I mean nothing bad in the really bad sense, only habits of desultory application under inordinate excitement only, and of localism with respect to thought, as well as somewhat of a turn for wrangling. He is very sociable, and is now living entirely with me.'

Unfortunately poor Jerningham could not shake off the most pernicious of all 'colonial habits,' and what might have been a very brilliant career terminated in disappointment.

Meanwhile, the drama of New Zealand politics remained in a condition of rehearsal from the obstinate refusal of Sir George Grey to provide it with a stage. Until the General Assembly should meet, politics could be merely local. Far more interest attaches to the remarkable letter in which Wakefield communicates his impressions of the colony to his old friend Rintoul—so copious that retrenchment is necessary on the ground of space :—

'I am bursting with fulness of matter for writing to you. It must come out anyhow. In the first place, the country physically far surpasses my expectations. Not that it is different, generally, from my notions of it before touching the soil, but actual familiarity with particulars has made the old impressions more distinct. The climate is to my feelings delicious, though far from resembling what we call a delicious climate in Europe, such as that of Naples in winter. Its principal characteristic is some invigorating property which affects man and beast equally, so that both horse and rider are always in good spirits. I have not had since we entered Port Lyttelton a moment of that depression and feebleness which used to make me such a cripple at home. There is abundance of wind, and, this year, superabundance of rain, but the roughest weather causes no uneasiness, and the fine weather is glorious. Perhaps it is from having been so long ill that I value so much the constant feeling of health which this climate produces. Henslow resembles me in this, the poor, crawling, sallow invalid has become almost jolly, and is afraid to brag of his happy feelings lest it should provoke a change back to the old miseries. But fine health is general in old and young. All the Creole children are plump and ruddy when not suffering from some particular complaint. I have not seen an exception, and you know how I examine the children and dogs wherever I may be. One of my dogs—the bloodhound, Bogey—having lost his mother in childbirth, and been suckled by a poor little wet-nurse, had a bad constitution, and was always ailing at home, the voyage also disagreed with him, and on landing he was like a rake in a bag; he is now in the rudest and handsomest health. . . . I could give you plenty of facts like these, but must go on to other matters.

The scenery is peculiar, though greatly varied. Upon the whole I think it most beautiful. But there are all sorts—the grand, the beautiful, and the pleasant; not even the centre of the great Canterbury Plain —an immense dead level in appearance — is ugly, because there are always in sight fine mountains, appearing, from the singular clearness of the atmosphere, to be near at hand. This district, Wellington, has great variety, though near the town, excepting the Hutt Valley, it is hilly and mountainous. Socially (I can speak from personal observation only of Canterbury and Wellington) there is much to like, and much to dislike. The newest comers from England are the best, on the whole, more especially the picked materials with which Canterbury was founded. At Canterbury I could have fancied myself in England, except for the hard-working industry of the upper classes and the luxurious independence of the common people. The upper classes are very hospitable, and very deficient in the pride of purse or mere station, and the common people are remarkably honest. Their entire independence is not disagreeable to me, who am accustomed to America, and like it. There is absolutely no servility. I think there is no lack of either real respect for what deserves it, or real politeness, though the mere outward manner of the common people seems rudely independent to such as have been always used to the hypocritical servility of tradespeople and lacqueys at home. I get on famously with the "unwashed," and like them. Sewell, as yet incapable of understanding them, thinks them rude and disagreeable. His Oxford and Isle of Wight habits of thought are shocked by the democratic ways of a carpenter here, who speaks of him as Sewell without the Mr, and calls a brother carpenter 'Mister Smith.' There is an intense jealousy of new-comers; a state of feeling which always takes possession of young colonies, and holds possession of them till they begin to grow old. For every new-comer probably comes to be the competitor or rival of somebody. Bowler has been quite upset by the shock of meeting this strong colonial sentiment, and it gives Sewell the stomach-ache. I am happily able to laugh at it. Indeed, though some are exceedingly jealous of me— those, that is, who fancy that I may trench upon their positions as political leaders—I must say the generality of colonists, and more particularly the older ones, behave very kindly to me, and seem to think that jealousy of me would be misplaced. But my case is exceptional on account of 'Auld lang syne.' The jealousy of Sewell is too strong to be at all concealed. Just what I told him would happen has come about more suddenly than I could expect. His plunge into public affairs has made his talents known, and here those talents are perfectly unrivalled. Consequently he is already feared and respected as well as—hated. Colonial jealousy of the new-comer passes away in time, and soon in proportion as the new-comer soon takes root in the land. When he is fairly planted, he in his turn becomes jealous of other new-comers.

But the worst feature, I think, of this colonial society is a general narrow-mindedness. Everybody's ideas seem to be localised in his own part of the country. I have not met with one person who is as well acquainted as I am myself with New Zealand in general. Thought abstract from the individual seems totally absent. The interests and amusements of each person are the only subjects of his thoughts. This is partly owing to the want of intercommunication among the settlements, which are, and will be, until they get local steam navigation, as much cut off from each other as if separated by a thousand miles of ocean, so that each community is naturally as small in its ideas as in its numbers; but the evil in question has another cause, which is the cause of many more evils, namely, the total absence of popular power and responsibility. The total want of political liberty produces a stagnant frame of mind, except as regards getting money or spending it. I can't find one person who has it in his head to contemplate the prosperity and greatness of this country; not one who really sympathises with my dreams of the last fifteen years. Some say that they do, and believe what they say, but a bat could see that they do not really. It is a miserable state of things, and you will think I must be very unhappy. But I am not so at all. On the contrary, I am sure that there is a good foundation to work upon in the best set of colonists that have ever left England in modern times; that poverty and crime (crime in the old country sense) are impossible; that the country is unrivalled in climate and productiveness; and that the mind of the people will be changed by the coming responsibilities of political power. Only there is heavy work for me, if I can but keep health for doing it. At present I am not in the least down-hearted.'

Mr Allom, to whom we are indebted for a copy of this invaluable letter, comments upon it as follows:—

'This letter, written little more than two months after his arrival in the colony, is an illustration of the difference between theory and practice in matters colonial, as in all others. Here we have the views of the great thinker and theorist when confronted by actual facts. We see by the manner in which he opens his heart to Rintoul, his old friend and fellow-labourer, how delighted he is with the country and the climate. But I think there is apparent throughout the letter a slight shade of disappointment. It is characteristic of Edward Gibbon Wakefield, that sometimes his own thoughts are expressed as those of others. In this way he refers to the sentiments of Sewell and Bowler, which I believe were equally his own. He seems to have quite understood the sturdy and independent attitude of the newly-arrived labourer towards his capitalist employer, and probably he recognised the position as a foreshadowing, in some degree, of those great political changes which in more recent years have become so marked a feature of our colonial democracy. It is interesting to note his remarks about the jealousy of Sewell being too strong to be concealed, and of Sewell's unrivalled abilities which have already made him feared and respected as well as — hated. I cannot help thinking that these references to Sewell apply quite as much to himself.

'In striving, at this time, to obtain for the people greater political power under the new constitution, I cannot believe that he thought it would be for their good that the "common people" should acquire the almost unlimited political power which they have since attained.'

The convocation of provincial councils before the election of a General Assembly undoubtedly worked ill for the colony. 'Superintendents and councils,' says Mr Gisborne, 'unchecked, without experience, and revelling in political freedom, seemed at first as if too much license had made them mad. But there was this method in their madness: they strove to get into their hands as much power as they possibly could.' The infinite divisibility of the public revenue became an article of faith. For a long time the provincial institutions maintained their ground as a geographical necessity, but at length disappeared - a result which Mr Gisborne thinks need not have come to pass if they had been from the first harmoniously co-ordinated with the General Assembly. This body, to which Wakefield was returned as Member for the Hutt district, in the province of Wellington, commenced its career under Colonel Wynyard, commander of the troops, who *ex officio* occupied Sir George Grey's post in the character of Acting-Governor, under very curious conditions. There was no responsible Ministry, all posts in the administration being held by officials holding permanent appointments from the Crown. There was, consequently, no front bench, and no Opposition technically, though, practically, all the House was Opposition. The principal Member of the Government was Speaker of the Upper House, and therefore speechless. By an oversight of the draftsman, the Lower House had no power of stopping the supplies, and was thus unable to control the Government. It was impossible, however, to delay the assembling of the General Legislature any longer, and Colonel Wynyard opened it on 27th May 1854, with an address assuredly not composed by the gallant officer from whom it professedly emanated, and which seems to bear traces of Wakefield's pen. The most remarkable feature was the declaration that the Provincial Councils needed much watching, and that 'it will rest with the General Assembly of these islands whether New Zealand shall become one great nation, exercising a commanding influence in the Southern Seas, or a collection of insignificant, divided and powerless petty states.' Apart from the evidence of style, so many of the ablest men in New Zealand were interested in propelling the provinces into virtual independence, that it may be doubted whether anyone else who could have said this so well would have said it at all. The point should be remembered in connection with Wakefield's subsequent action.

It is probable that his next important step was preconcerted with the Governor, for nothing else could have given constitutional government a start. It was to move 'That amongst the objects which the House desires to see accomplished without delay, the most important is the establishment of ministerial responsibility in the conduct of legislative and executive proceedings by the Governor.' 'The subject,' says Mr Swainson, then Attorney-General, and the chief contemporary authority for these transactions, 'was discussed in a debate of three days' continuance, if debate it may be called in which no difference of opinion was expressed.' The resolution was carried with virtual unanimity, but the difficulty was how to carry it into effect, the existing officials holding patent appointments under the Crown. It was at length agreed that the Colonial Secretary, the Colonial Treasurer and the Attorney-General should remain in their offices 'until they could with propriety retire,' and that four Members of the Assembly, Messrs FitzGerald, Sewell, Weld and Bartley, should be added to the Executive Council, charged with the preparation of parliamentary business, and the carrying of it through the House. Nothing less could be done if constitutional government was not to become a farce, but subsequent events showed that the country was not really much excited upon the subject. 'The Auckland members, in their humility, acknowledged that Mr Wakefield had taught them what responsible government was.'

Wakefield's first feelings were of wild, enthusiastic exultation. With all his shrewdness, no one was more liable to be carried into extravagance under the influence of excitement :—

'AUCKLAND, 14*th June* 1854.

'MY DEAR CATHERINE,—By the newspapers which I send with this you will see that New Zealand has undergone neither more nor less than a revolution. Do not be alarmed ; the change, though enormous, has been peaceful, and will be very conservative in its results. The mutilated constitution has been healed, and brought into vigorous action by the friendly concert of pro-Governor Wynyard and the House of Representatives. Mr Sewell is a Cabinet Minister, as I might also have been had I pleased. You will open your eyes and ask what all this means. It means (confining myself to what you will most care about) that after trouble and annoyance, and disappointment and suffering without end, I am as happy as anyone can be in this world, having a full realisation of what I have hoped and longed and striven for during so many years. The only drawback is a kind of apprehension arising from the greatness and suddenness of the success. My health and strength are wonderful. The greater the danger, the louder the raging of the storm, the more important the crisis, and the larger my own share of responsibility and labour, the more I have been capable of doing whatever I wished to do. Neither effort nor the highest excitement have disturbed or fatigued me. I have been as cool as you would wish, and have slept like a pig. This is all about myself, but you will like it the better for that. I write in haste to catch a Sydney mail, and my hands are full of work. God bless you both. Kind love to all.—Ever your most affectionate 'E. G. W.'

A letter to Lord Lyttelton, written the same day, reiterates much of the above, indulges in speculations, probably visionary, as to what the provinces might have done if responsible government had not been conceded, and declares that a little child might guide the New Zealand representatives in the right way. Probably the little one did not present himself, and the legislators, needing to be led somewhere, followed other guidance, for when Parliament met again, after a short recess, things had manifestly altered for the worse. Mistrust and ill-will reigned universally, nobody could quite tell why. Mr Brittan said at Canterbury that it all arose from the new Ministers having held a conclave from which Wakefield was excluded. If this is true they were to blame for having ignored him, and he was equally to blame for having retaliated; but no intrigues of his could have produced the occurrence which actually led to the break up of the Ministry, which seems to suggest the prosaic explanation that there were not places enough for the place-hunters, and that the only acceptable programme would have been *quot homines, tot portfolios*. The new Executive Ministers demanded that the three old officials who had been associated with them under the compromise of June should resign, pleading private understandings to this effect, too private to be capable of proof. The officials declined to budge. Mr FitzGerald and his colleagues, expecting to coerce the Governor, tendered their own resignations. The Governor, to their dismay, sent for Wakefield, who advised him—to all appearance rightly—that he had no power to dismiss officials holding their posts by direct appointment from the Crown. The officials professed their readiness to give up their places whenever His Excellency should ask for them, but not till then—and Wakefield advised him not to ask. It is easy to imagine the odium he thus incurred with those whom he prevented from—

*Fulfilling the prophecies
By only just changing the holders of offices.*

'Mr Wakefield,' remarks Mr Swainson, 'was much too formidable to be lightly made into an enemy; and so long as he continued to be simply a member of the House the true feelings of a large portion of the members towards him were concealed by a cloak of reserve; but no sooner was he seen in a position of influence than all reserve was thrown aside. Courted, fawned upon, and flattered, but scarcely ever trusted at the commencement of the session, Mr Wakefield was now assailed in the House in the most violent and opprobrious language, transgressing even the license of colonial debate.' It is a common misadventure in politics to be hoist with one's own petard; and many a man besides Wakefield has found the fulfilment of his hopes the disappointment of his expectations. The legislators he had struggled so hard to bring together, lately so anxious to get rid of the permanent officials, petitioned the Governor to consult them instead of his irresponsible adviser, and was informed that they always had been consulted. A long message from the Governor came down, and was being read by the clerk, when it was discovered that a page was missing. Wakefield coolly pulled a duplicate from his pocket and offered to supply the omission, which produced a scene only to be paralleled by that which occurred a few days later when the House filled up the interval between reading a message from the Governor threatening and a second message decreeing their prorogation by passing fierce resolutions, the second message meanwhile lying unread upon the table. Left, as he thought, with a clear stage, Wakefield tried to form a new Executive, but found himself unexpectedly checkmated by Mr Swainson, the Attorney-General, a sedate, astute lawyer, no great legislator, but an excellent draftsman of acts under the inspiration of Chief Justice Martin, who virtually expressed the opinion that the permanent officials could get on very well without the aid of coadjutors from the Assembly, or any such impertinences. Wakefield's minute of his interview with Mr Swainson is printed in the latter's book on New Zealand, and is one of the most curious and entertaining productions of his pen. His Excellency taking Mr Swainson's view, Wakefield 'at once retired from the position of temporary adviser, receiving the grateful acknowledgments of the Acting-Governor for the zeal and ability with which his services had been rendered.' These were not unmerited, for during the prorogation the Opposition entirely collapsed, partly from want of support in the country, and partly from the consideration touchingly set forth in their address to the Governor, 'that a large proportion of the Members of the Legislature have been detained from home upwards of five months, and will be obliged to return by the next steamer'—minus their salaries, they might have added, unless they dutifully voted the Estimates. They did vote them, and the Parliament from which so much had been expected broke up amid universal dissatisfaction: Wakefield finding himself ostracised where he had expected to rule, Mr FitzGerald[1] and his friends having thrown away places which they might very well have kept, and even the victorious officials feeling the sword of Damocles suspended over them.

New Zealanders have naturally felt ashamed of the fiasco of their first essay in Parliamentary Government, and have generally agreed to visit their mortification upon Wakefield, who seems, however, to have been mainly the victim of circumstances. He could neither help the jealousy with which he was regarded by his fellow-legislators, nor the quarrel between the old and new officials; nor could he prevent the political suicide of the Ministry, or refuse his advice to the Governor when called upon, or honestly give any other advice than he did, or control Mr Swainson when circumstances had made that gentleman master of the situation. His chief faults were to have participated, near the end of the session, in an attempt to set up an abortive Ministry, and to have inspired it, though ostensibly keeping aloof, with a scheme for the restriction of Provincial Councils, which under the circumstances was justly considered wild and unconstitutional. Yet it was rather unseasonable than unsound. The perception of the necessity for limit-

[1] Wakefield afterwards penned an unflattering character of Mr FitzGerald, one of the most vigorous pieces of invective in the language; much better unwritten, nevertheless. It is highly to Mr FitzGerald's honour to have in after years spoken of his assailant as he does in his memoir of Godley.

ing the encroachments of these bodies runs like a thread through all his political action of this period; and his foresight was vindicated when by-and-by the question arose 'whether,' in Mr Gisborne's words 'the provincial institutions were not, under the guise of local self-government, gradually absorbing general government, and tending, sooner or later, to the division of New Zealand into federal states.' One curious result of the campaign was to make Wakefield popular in Auckland, which he had always disparaged, and unpopular in the colonies which he had founded himself.

Wakefield's great mistake, however, was to have taken any part in politics except as a writer. The buoyant health of which he speaks in his letter to his sister was the effect of an unnatural stimulus, and was to be expiated by a reaction which secluded him from the world. The mortifying incidents of the session must have preyed upon his spirit, and the scenes through which he had passed might have tried stronger constitutions than that of an invalid barely recovered from paralysis of the brain. 'What he went through at Auckland,' his brother Daniel wrote, 'Chief Justice Martin tells me, was enough to break up the constitution of a very strong man. Constant labour in planning measures in the Assembly, writing, and above all, talking against a mob of opponents was too much for one in but feeble health.' In addition to this he had taken a large share in the Committee work of the

House. The ultimate breakdown is thus described in a letter from his son to Catherine Torlesse :—

'WELLINGTON, 8*th* May 1855.

'. . . About the first week in December last he attended a meeting of his constitutents in the Hutt Valley, and spoke with great earnestness and vigour for five hours consecutively in a densely-crowded room. In order, I suppose, to get away from the noise and excitement consequent on such a political meeting, he drove home in an open chaise, nine miles in the face of a cold, south-easterly gale, at two o'clock in the morning. Although he began to feel ill, he accepted an invitation a day or two afterwards to dine with the members of an Oddfellows' Lodge in this town, and sat in a hot room with an open window at his back.[1] The next day he was attacked with rheumatic fever, and suffered acute pain. This turned, I believe, into neuralgia, every nerve in his body being affected. At first he was attended by Dr Prendergast, but fell back upon complete quiet of mind and body with an occasional "lamp." For a long time he would let no one know how ill he was, and would see no one. But he then wrote to me at Canterbury, asking me to come to him. I arrived about the first week in January. I found the pains were going off, but that he was

[1] It will be remembered that December is the height of summer in New Zealand.

dreadfully weak, very nervous, and at times desponding, with no appetite, and irregular circulation. I remonstrated against the rejection of the drug system without substituting his own panacea of "packing," in which he used to have such faith. But he always replies that he feels a presentiment that the effort would be too much for him, that he has an idea it would choke him, and so on. So that he positively does nothing but rest, opens no letters, reads no local papers, indeed, tries to think about nothing on which his thoughts can have any influence.[1] To a certain degree I think this is right. He has sadly overtasked both his bodily and his mental powers during the past two years, and complete rest for the brain as well as the body will, I have no doubt, do much to restore him in course of time. My being here, of course, saves him from attending to any business, public or private, and I pass an hour or two with him nearly every day. I hope and believe him to be out of all danger for the present, but his recovery must necessarily be slow and tedious, and perhaps never perfect. My great desire is to see him strong enough to get a change of air, such as up to Charles's sheep station at Rangiora, or perhaps to Sydney, and I also trust that he may make up his mind to give up the idea of any more active political labour. But I confess to a

[1] 'The surest mark of the intensity of suffering is the limitation of the sufferer's desires to absolute repose.'—ANTHONY TROLLOPE.

dread lest, as soon as he feels at all strong, he should again endeavour, by his own efforts in public life, to arrest the progress of what he may think evil in the colony. At present he cannot walk across his room.

'I have had great satisfaction in being able to agree with him thoroughly and unreservedly in all that he has done, and of supporting his policy by every effort in my power. Although in a minority at first, his views are daily gaining strength, and I rejoice to think that but a few years will elapse before it will be generally acknowledged that a true and far-seeing patriotism has alone dictated all his public policy.—Your affectionate nephew,

'E. JERNINGHAM WAKEFIELD.'

Wakefield could never again have appeared upon a platform, but some thought that his pen would still have been active if he could have felt more confidence in the political future of his son. This may be doubted, the intellectual faculties were not in themselves impaired, but he appeared to feel that his grasp upon them had become uncertain, and that a slight shock might dissolve it altogether. He seemed at first to take refuge in absolute silence, calling to mind, perhaps, the days in Lancaster Castle, when he had boasted what good company he could find in his own self. But this was not to be; as formerly in Newgate, sunshine stole into the shady place in the person of a little girl. His niece Alice, daughter of his brother Daniel, and afterwards, as Mrs Harold Freeman, daughter-in-law of the illustrious historian, has graced the writer's pages with her affecting reminiscences of this tender sequel to a stormy life.

'The first recollection that I have of my uncle Edward Gibbon is the night of the great earthquake at Wellington.[1] I was carried out of my bed, and found myself amongst a number of frightened people who had come from the houses round, and were all passing the night out of doors. In the middle of the group was my uncle seated in an arm-chair, and he was of much interest to me, for, though we lived in the same house, I do not recall having seen him before. My father and mother had left their home in Wellington Terrace and come to live with him at his house in the Timahori Road.[2] My father, who was always devoted to his brother, had thrown up his appointment as Attorney-General on account of disagreements between Sir George Grey and my uncle. At the earthquake my uncle's attention was drawn to me, and from that time to his death in 1862 I was a great deal with him. The

[1] This alarming convulsion is graphically described in Thomson's *Story of New Zealand*, vol. ii. pp. 231-233. 'For fourteen hours the town trembled like a shaken jelly.' The site was permanently raised from three to six feet, and an intended dock is now a pleasure garden.

[2] This house had been exported from England, and had been previously occupied by Mr Eyre, celebrated as an Australian explorer and as Governor of Jamaica, at that time Lieutenant-Governor under Sir George Grey.

feelings of love and admiration that I had for him it is impossible to describe; my greatest pleasure was to be in his company; his slightest wish was my law, at any sacrifice of my own pleasure. It is only fair to my mother to say that she encouraged this devotion to my uncle, feeling that in his solitary life, often seeing no one but his man-servant William Schmidt and myself, I was the only pleasure that was left to him. All was done for me according to my uncle's views of making a child strong. I had a cold bath in the morning, then walked with him for half an hour before breakfast, then had porridge. William Schmidt was a native of Schleswig Holstein, who liked to call himself a Dane. He had been a sailor aboard the ship my uncle came out in, and broke his leg by a fall from the mast. My uncle visited him in the hospital at Wellington, and asked him if he would like to become his servant instead of returning to the life of a sailor. William proved most faithful; he was always at hand, and looked upon his master with the greatest affection and respect. My uncle gave him some land in Christchurch, and after his death William became quite a rich man. He was very fond of carpentering, and made very pretty boxes and frames out of the honeysuckle and other fine New Zealand woods. In his workshop I passed many hours with my uncle. We walked up and down a very small space, our companions, besides

William, being "Powder" and "Blucher," two bull dogs considered very fierce, but perfectly gentle with us.

'I feel convinced that I have never met any man with the power that E. G. Wakefield had, and I have never come across anyone who cared for young people and their improvement in the way that he did. I used to read books with my mother, and then repeat them chapter by chapter to my uncle. I read the whole of the Waverley Novels through twice over in this way, except *Castle Dangerous* and *Count Robert of Paris*, which he did not think worth my reading; his favourites were *Guy Mannering*, *Rob Roy*, *Waverley*, and *Old Mortality*. Repeating them like this, and listening to my uncle's comments was, I may say, a good education, and I can turn now with pleasure to Walter Scott when I do not care to read a modern novel. I also learned the whole of the *Lady of the Lake*, not one line was allowed to be missed, and in reading I was carefully taught never to skip or look on. I obeyed the slightest wish my uncle ever expressed, and never cared to do anything but what he approved. Two trials I remember, having to choose between some rather dry travels in Japan and *The Daisy Chain*. "Which would you like me to read?" said I, and on being told *The Travels*, gave up *The Daisy Chain*. On another occasion he told me I was too old to play with dolls, and I never played with a doll after that day. My uncle was not able to bear any noise, so that we never went on his side of the house, or used the rooms nearest to him : neither did my little play-fellows come to visit me. I went to see them and they would say, "Do you not dislike having to go back every day at four to walk with your uncle?" I know the very question astonished me, and I warmly replied there was nothing else I enjoyed so much. I do not remember my uncle seeing any visitors but a friend to whom he used to give lessons in the open air to cure his stammering, and another who lent him books on the Millennium. He saw my mother and Jerningham occasionally. I have a prayer book with his name in his own writing, and he once said that he should have gone to church, only from fear of disturbing people with his breathing from asthma. Colonel Palmer of Nazing[1] told me that he should always remember my uncle rather offending some Americans in conversation, and that when he saw this was the case he said, "All this does not matter; we speak the same language and are brothers; if we were in any trouble it is to you that we should look for help, and I know that you would give it." The Americans after this were quite content.

'There were one or two breaks in this complete seclusion. My father died when I was eight years

[1] The same gentleman whom we have seen endeavouring to raise a monument to Wakefield in South Australia.

old, and then my uncle was very kind to my mother, and gave directions about his funeral. At another time there was an election in which he was interested; our walks then were beyond our own gates, and I listened to my uncle persuading a man to vote, saying it was the duty of every man to vote; that, ill though he was, he would rather be carried to the poll in his bed than not give his vote. Another time I heard a long conversation which I am sure related to his first meeting with Lord Durham. It must have been about this time that I persuaded my uncle to come with me to feed an old white horse in a field near us, and he said, "Why, that is quiet enough for even me to ride," and for some time he had this horse to ride very slowly upon.[1] One morning he surprised us by going off very early and being photographed; this is the photograph after which the bust by Durham in the Colonial Office was executed. I think that his mind was in full vigour up to the last, but his bodily health had failed, and he could no longer struggle with the world.

'Many things that my uncle said come back into my mind with the memory of the impressive way in which he said everything. Once when my mother was very anxious about something he said, "Throw it aside, forget. I should have been in a lunatic asylum before now if I had not been able to put a subject out

---

[1] What a subject for a picture—the worn-out horse, the worn-out statesman, and the blooming little girl!

of my mind." Then he would say, "It is a blessing that women love needlework; it has the same soothing effect upon their minds that a pipe has upon men's." He told us once that years ago a doctor had told him that he ought to become a monk of La Trappe, talking was so bad for him; the last years of his life he might almost have belonged to this order. His mother was, I am sure, often in his thoughts, for he used to look at me and say, "Alice, I believe that you are growing like my mother," and when I wanted to name my favourite parrot he said, "Call it Susan; it was my mother's name." I never heard him mention his wife or Nina; I think he was too fond of them to talk about them. I remember his describing his residence in Italy when the news of the death of Princess Charlotte came to the Embassy, and the grief of the men was so great that they burst into tears.

'We moved from the Timahori Road to Wellington Terrace. Shortly afterwards the two bull dogs got out into the road and began fighting with another dog. William went out to separate them, and Blucher flew at him and bit him in the face. I carried off Powder, and shut him up in the stable. William went to my uncle and asked permission to have both the dogs shot. This was allowed, to my great grief; and my mother said she was sure he must be feeling much worse to have consented. No doubt the strong will had given in, and the end came very soon after. One night, 16th May 1862, he woke up William, who slept in his room, with the words, "William, this is death."[1] William woke up my mother and myself; we hurried to the room. My uncle held my hand with a tight clasp, and looked in my face with an expression that I shall never forget; he could not speak. When Jerningham entered the room in answer to a hasty summons, his father struggled hard to speak, but nothing more than the name Jerningham was distinguished.

'I do not recollect who came to the funeral. I know that two Maoris came to follow after the funeral had started. He was laid by the side of two brothers, who had been devotedly attached to him, Colonel Wakefield and my father, also my sister; the four graves are close together.

'On one occasion my uncle spoke before me with bitterness of the quick way in which people were forgotten after death, and I burst forth with the assurance that I should never forget him. This promise I have certainly kept, and I think that, child though I was, I felt the power of his mind, the fascination of his manners, tone and general bearing. All his precepts were good, and likely to influence youth for good. Nothing that I have been able to write does justice to his memory.'

Thus the powerful mind and persuasive tongue that had given so mighty an impulse to the practice, and

---

[1] The dying exclamation of George the Fourth.

such new life to the theory of colonization, that had perplexed Ministries with fear of change at home, and profoundly modified relations between the mother country and her children abroad,

> *That launched a thousand ships,*
> *And shook the topmost towers of Ilion,*

passed gently away in guiding and instructing a little girl. It seems profanation to add aught to so simple and touching a narrative: *Manum de tabula.* Yet something like a general view of Edward Gibbon Wakefield's character is necessary. As his niece, Mrs Burney, tried to describe him orally to the writer, one word was continually on her lips—'complex.' This suits him well, and is probably what Lord Lyttelton had in his mind when he described him as 'A man of much vicissitude of fortune and much inequality of character.' It does not mean that this character was a jumble of conflicting qualities, but that it was developed unsymmetrically on the two sides which are inseparable from the conception of a finite object. Ancient psychology expressed this quality by distinguishing between the animal and the intellectual soul, the inert groundwork of natural instincts and propensities, and the busy impressionable mind that soars above. In the first respect, Wakefield offers little to censure or regret; few have been more richly endowed with courage, perseverance, generosity, affection, or humanity. His faults, such as resentment degenerating into rancour, and playfulness into mischief-making, were such as are almost inseparable from an opulent nature, exuberant in all it brings forth. It was when reason was divorced from instinct, and action was entirely directed by the speculative intelligence that he sometimes went astray. His errors may be summed up in a word—unscrupulousness. Not unscrupulousness which aims at personal advantage, even in the great offence of his life, the motive was not love of money, but love of influence; but the unscrupulousness of a strong will intolerant of opposition either from men or morals, and of a statesmanship which, impatient of the jealousies and misunderstandings of inferior men, deems it no sin to circumvent where it cannot overthrow. If statesmen wielding powerful parliamentary majorities are not exempt from insincerity, if they introduce measures which they have no intention of passing, and make professions up to which they have no idea of acting, what excuse should not be made for a man without fortune, without station, and the object of general suspicion and disapproval, conscious, nevertheless, of magnificent aspirations, and full of projects in which he has unbounded faith, but of which he is impotent to realise the smallest particle, save by impressing, persuading, or cajoling? Add to this necessity of his position an unequalled personal fascination, a genius for managing men, and the instinct of a born educator, derived from his father and grandmother, and it will not appear so extraordinary that a warm-hearted, sanguine man of almost extravagantly high spirits should have gained the reputation of a cold-blooded schemer and manipulator of puppets for selfish ends. Mr Gisborne, the miniaturist of New Zealand statesmen, who had, however, a personal dislike to Wakefield, writes of him : 'His deceptiveness was ineradicable, and, like the fowler, he was ever spreading his nets. Always plausible, and often persuasive, he was never simple and straightforward. He was calculating and self-contained, and had no particle of generous chivalry in his nature.' The injustice of this character is manifest from its inconsistency with the traits most distinct in Wakefield's life and writings : yet there is this much truth that ' the skilfulness in handling puppets in high places,' which Mr Gisborne justly attributes to him, was a snare to him. Though the handling was not for private but for public ends, the puppets no less resented it when it was found out, as it could not fail to be. It is undeniable that he wore out the goodwill of several successive sets of supporters; on the other hand, the persons thus alienated were for the most part, comparatively speaking, inferior men, and the highest minds evinced the most constancy of attachment. Lord Durham and Lord Metcalfe might or might not have been estranged from him if their lives had been prolonged, but certainly gave no sign of estrangement while they lived.

Rintoul never once failed him during an intimacy of twenty-two years, and Rintoul was a shrewd Scotchman, by no means addicted to excess of sentiment. Wakefield's anonymous contributions to his *Spectator* would make a very thick volume. Charles Buller's regard survived even his official connection with Wakefield's *bête noire* Earl Grey, and Lord Lyttelton's the yet more serious trial of Wakefield's break with Godley. This grievous misfortune would not have occurred if the two had not been at opposite sides of the world; but whatever blame is to be ascribed to the men falls principally upon Wakefield, one of whose most unfortunate characteristics was an unreasonable suspiciousness. His view of human nature was anything but morbid, but in matters where he did not see his way quite clearly, his active imagination conjured up motives, intentions and proceedings which had no existence elsewhere. 'The surmises, suspicions and impressions expressed by Mr Wakefield,' drily remarks Mr Swainson, 'are to be received only as surmises, suspicions and impressions.' This defect was correlated with the vein of paradox, also the offspring of a teeming imagination, which runs through his soundest projects and best-considered writings, and the exaggerated vehemence with which he assails open adversaries and backsliding disciples. All that can be said is : no imagination, no originality; and no originality, no place among great men. ' *He is all fault who hath no fault at all.*'

If Edward Gibbon Wakefield had not possessed the imaginative genius from which some delusions and some extravagances are inseparable, it could not have been said of him, as was said with perfect truth by Thornton Hunt in his obituary notice in the *Daily Telegraph:* 'There is no part of the British Empire which does not feel in the actual circumstances of the day the effect of Edward Gibbon Wakefield's labours as a practical statesman; and perhaps the same amount of tangible result in administrative and constructive reform can scarcely be traced to the single hand of any other man during his own lifetime.' This is true, and yet the practical side of Wakefield's work seems second to the ideal, the conception of a system which methodised the previously irregular and haphazard attempts at colonization, and made it a department of statesmanship; and perhaps even this is less than the new way of regarding the relations between the mother country and the colonies, of which the system of responsible government recommended in Lord Durham's Report was the most conspicuous manifestation. Modern states, up to quite a recent period, have regarded colonies as establishments for the benefit of the mother country, and have formed new settlements as a tradesman establishes branch shops, with no notion of allowing money to accumulate in the subsidiary till. The Greeks did not thus; their colonies were entirely independent; the Roman colonies, though dependent, were never tributary; but the colonies of modern states have usually been both, and have only obtained self-government at the cost of long and cruel warfare. The idea that a colony does not exist for the mother country but for itself is an evident corollary from Wakefield's general principles; and its tacit adoption since the publication of the Durham Report has kept the British Colonial Empire intact, while others have crumbled away. 'Can one,' he asks, 'read Gibbon without seeing that the Roman Empire fell to pieces because its government was a government of mere force, which, when applied to a great and diversified empire, is necessarily weak because force cannot stretch so far, and because there is no attachment in the subjects towards the central power?'

The Colonial Office wars no longer with Edward Gibbon Wakefield; his bust adorns one of its corridors, and his spirit in a great degree animates its policy. We do not now hear eminent statesmen denouncing the idea that colonies can contribute anything to the strength of the mother country as 'a superstition as dark as any that existed in the Middle Ages'; or find veteran officials discussing in their correspondence how the parent can with least violence to her feelings turn the daughter out of doors. But while the department of State which he combated has recognised his desert, the colonies which he created have done nothing for his memory—absolutely nothing whatever. It cannot be thought that this will long continue. The storied urn will not always be lacking to Adelaide or the animated bust to Wellington; and it must be hoped that the portrait of the body will be accompanied by a portrait of the mind in the shape of an edition of his principal writings—obsolete, no doubt, as regards many of the questions discussed, but still retaining all their worth as illustrations of colonial and economical history, and capable of firing the enthusiasm of many a generation to come. When a monument does arise, whether in the South Australian capital or by the waters of Cook's Strait, it cannot—after due acknowledgment of his special achievement as founder of the colony—be more fitly inscribed than with words adapted from two distinct eulogies by Lord Lyttelton, who knew the man and had shared in his work :—

THE MAN IN THESE LATTER DAYS BEYOND COMPARISON OF THE MOST GENIUS AND THE WIDEST INFLUENCE IN THE GREAT SCIENCE OF COLONIZATION, BOTH AS A THINKER, A WRITER, AND A WORKER; WHOSE NAME IS LIKE A SPELL TO ALL INTERESTED IN THE SUBJECT.

INDEX

A

ADDERLEY, C. B. (Lord Norton), drafts New Zealand Constitution under Wakefield's guidance, 328, 330.
Adelaide, city of, founded, 104.
Allom, Albert, reminiscences of New Zealand Company, 217, 222; writes down the *Art of Colonization* from Wakefield's dictation, 280, 281; on Wakefield in New Zealand, 342, 348, 349.
Allom, Charles, Wakefield's secretary in Canada, 184; saves his life, 233.
Allom, Mrs, nurses Wakefield in his illness, 233; reconciles him with Frances Wakefield, 335.
Angas, George Fife, 96; forms a supplementary company for South Australian colonization, 103; his share in the foundation of the colony, 105-107; his misfortunes and ultimate success, 121, *note*; warns Lord Glenelg of French designs on New Zealand, 151.
Art of Colonization, 281-285.
Attwood, Rosabel, friend and correspondent of Nina Wakefield, 111.
Attwood, Thomas, M.P., 111; meets Wakefield at Malvern, 271.

Auckland, city of, founded, 219.

B

BARCLAY, Robert, of Urie, author of the *Apology for Quakerism*, an ancestor of Wakefield's, 3.
Baring, Francis, impressed by Wakefield's evidence on New Zealand, 127; chairman of New Zealand Association, 142.
Bathurst, Miss, concerned in the Turner affair, 33.
Batman, John, purchases site of Melbourne from the natives, 126, *note*.
Brougham, Henry (Lord Brougham), prosecutes Wakefield for the abduction of Ellen Turner, 31; his animosity to Lord Durham, 165, 166; humiliations inflicted by him on Lord Melbourne's Government, 171.
Buller, Charles, assists in Wakefield's South Australian project, 93; chief secretary to Lord Durham in Canada, 163; his character and abilities, 164; Chief Commissioner of Canadian Crown Lands, 169; his share in the Durham Report, 178, 179; author of *Responsible Government for the Colonies*, 180; his motion on New Zealand

affairs, 256; negotiates with Sir James Graham, 257; brings the case of the New Zealand Company forward in Parliament, 258; arranges compromise between the Company and the Government, 269; his character of 'Mr Mothercountry,' 287; his death, 294; his speech on systematic colonization reprinted by Wakefield, 295.
Burney, Mrs D'Arblay, Wakefield's niece; her impression of him, 321-324, 369.
Byron, Lord, 21, *note*.

C

CANTERBURY Settlement founded, 311.
Cargill, Captain, founder of the Otago settlement, 303.
Carlyle, Thomas, 249, 265.
Coates, Dandeson, lay secretary to the Church Missionary Society; his opposition to the New Zealand Association, 136-139.

D

DARWIN, Charles Robert, on the New Zealand missionaries, 135; on transportation to New South Wales, 237.
Davies, Rev. David, father of Frances Wakefield, 23.
Dent, Mr, historian of Canada, 185, 186.
Dilke, Sir Charles, 121, *note*.
Disraeli, B., his *Vivian Grey* compared and contrasted with Wakefield's early writings 24, 25.
Domett, Alfred, Premier of New Zealand; his character of Arthur Wakefield, 228, *note*.
Duncombe, Thomas Slingsby, M.P., his anecdotes of Wakefield in Canada, 174.
Dunedin, city of, founded, 303.
Durham, Earl of, becomes a director of the New Zealand Association, 142; his character, 143; at variance with Lord Howick, 144; communications with Colonial Office, 146; becomes chairman of the New Zealand Company, 152; Governor-General of British North America, 161; his qualifications and disqualifications, 163; his choice of advisers, 164; Lord Brougham's animosity to him, 165; letters to Melbourne and Glenelg, 168, 169; his Ordinance respecting the treatment of the rebel prisoners, 170, 171; resigns and returns home, 172; his popularity in Canada, 173; his reception in England, 174; defended by Stuart Mill, 175, 176; his Report on the affairs of Canada, 177-181; tutors his successor, 182; his death and last words, 183.

E

EGERTON, H. E., historian of British colonial policy, 143, 178.
Eliot, Lord, chairman of New Zealand Committee of 1840, 244.
Elliot, Mr, Emigration Commissioner, 291.
Elliotson, Dr, 174, *note*.
Ellis, William, writer on colonization, 62, *note*.
England and America, 75-78.
Evans, Dr G. S., 138, 139, 150.

INDEX

F

FITZGERALD, J. E., New Zealand statesman; his character of Godley, 306; his character, 317; forms the first New Zealand responsible ministry, 351; resigns, 354; his generosity towards Wakefield's memory, 357, *note*.

Fitzroy, Admiral, appointed Governor of New Zealand, 227; condones massacre of Wairau, 230; failure and recall, 231.

Flatt, Mr, catechist of the Church Missionary Society, 140.

Foster, Anthony, on the Wakefield system in South Australia, 122.

Freeman, Mrs Harold, Wakefield's niece; her reminiscences of his last days, 362-368.

Fry, Elizabeth, cousin to Wakefield, 12; visits him in prison, 40.

G

GARRAN'S *Australian Atlas*, 107.

Gawler, Colonel, Governor of South Australia, 120.

Gibbon, Isabella, Edward Gibbon Wakefield's great-grandmother, 3.

Gipps, Sir George, Governor of New South Wales, his land policy, 219, 220.

Gisborne, William, New Zealand historian, on Colonel Wakefield, 198; on Sir George Grey's land policy, 277; on E. G. Wakefield, 371.

Gladstone, Right Hon. W. E., Wakefield's appeal to on New Zealand affairs, 232; on New Zealand Committee of 1840, 248; assists passing of New Zealand Constitution Act, 330; his speech on the subject, 331.

Glenelg, Lord, his weakness as Colonial Secretary, 134; his opposition to the New Zealand Company, 148; removed from office, 152; prevents Wakefield's receiving an appointment in Canada, 167, 169.

Godley, John Robert, his antecedents, 272; joins Wakefield in founding the Canterbury Settlement, 305; his character, 306; organises the Canterbury Association, 308; proceeds to New Zealand, 310; Superintendent of the Canterbury Settlement, 311; misunderstanding with Wakefield, 317; returns to England, 334.

Gouger, Robert, Wakefield's *Letter from Sydney* published under his name, 60; assists in the foundation of South Australia, 94, 107.

Grey, Earl (Lord Howick), Under Secretary for the Colonies, 96, 97; his character, 144; misunderstandings with Lord Durham and Wakefield, 145; opposition to New Zealand Association, 149, 150; unsatisfactory interview with Wakefield, 233; scene between him and Wakefield before New Zealand Committee of 1840, 247, 248; drafts report of Committee of 1845, 253, 254; adopts Sir George Grey's views on New Zealand, 273.

Grey, Sir George, first Governor of South Australia, 121; Governor of New Zealand, 231; prevents the Constitution of 1846 from going into effect, 273; reasons for this step, 274; a benefactor to the native race, 275; his land policy, 276-277; befriends the New Zealand Company, 278; his opinion of Colonel Wakefield, 279; his hostility to the Canterbury Settlement, 313; drafts a constitution for New Zealand, 328; his correspondence with Wakefield, 337-340; appointed Governor of Cape Colony, 341.

H

HANSON, Sir Richard, Chief Justice of South Australia, on the publication of the Durham Report, 177; on its authorship, 178.

Head, John, Wakefield's cousin at Ipswich, comforts Wakefield in his imprisonment, and takes him home, 83.

Heke, New Zealand chief, 231.

Henslow, Captain, 333.

Hill, Sir Rowland, secretary to the South Australian Commissioners, 103.

Hill, William, afterwards Lord Berwick, envoy at Turin, employs Wakefield, 17; his advice to him, 19; his opinion of Mrs Wakefield, 21.

Hinds, Samuel, Bishop of Norwich, supports the New Zealand Association, 138; advocates the proposal of a bishop for New Zealand, 145; revives the idea of colonization by religious bodies, 299.

Hobson, Captain, appointed Lieutenant - Governor of New Zealand, 156; arrives in New Zealand, 201; his instructions from Sir George Gipps, 211; concludes Treaty of Waitangi, 212; frustrates French expedition to Akaroa, 214; his injudicious proclamation, 218; founds Auckland, 219; his death, 227.

Hodder, Edwin, 98, 106.

Hutt, John, *Art of Colonization* dedicated to; resigns chairmanship of Canterbury Association, 312.

K

KORORAREKA (Russell), town at the Bay of Islands; vigilance committee at, 133; burned by the natives, 231.

L

LANCASTER, Joseph, Edward Wakefield's opinion of, 7, *note*.

Leroy-Beaulieu, M., on the Wakefield system, 288-290.

Letter from Sydney, 58-61.

Lowe, Robert (Viscount Sherbrooke), opposes New Zealand Constitution Bill, 330.

Lyttelton, Lord, Wakefield's character of, 306; rescues the Canterbury Settlement from failure, 312; joins in a guarantee to the New Zealand Company, 313; aids in drafting the New Zealand Constitution, 330; Wakefield wishes him to become Governor of New Zealand, 334; his character of Wakefield, 369, 375.

INDEX

M

MARTIN, Sir William, appointed Chief Justice of New Zealand, 224; on Wakefield's illness, 358.

Melbourne, Lord, his character, 144; his attitude towards the New Zealand Association, 147, 148; objects to appointments of Turton and Wakefield, 168; weakness of his administration, 171; on the publication of Lord Durham's Report, 177.

Merivale, Herman, on the Wakefield system, 71.

Metcalfe, Sir Charles, Governor-General of Canada, 184; Wakefield's eulogium on him, 186.

Mill, James, introduced by Edward Wakefield to Francis Place, 7.

Mill, John Stuart, approves of the Wakefield system, 88; his defence of Lord Durham's conduct in Canada, 174-176; his opinion of Wakefield as a political economist, 263.

Molesworth, Sir William, an early colonial reformer, 88; chairman of Committee on Transportation, 238; his character, 239; his report, 242; opposes New Zealand Constitution Bill, 330.

Murray, Sir George, Colonial Secretary, 96.

N

NAYTI, alleged New Zealand chief, 140.

Nelson, city of, founded, 228.

Normanby, Marquis of, introduces the South Australian Act into the House of Lords, 100; Colonial Secretary, 152; his conduct towards the New Zealand Association, 153, 156.

O

OTAGO settlement founded, 303.

P

PAKINGTON, Sir John, Colonial Secretary, 331.

Palmer, Lieutenant-Colonel, South Australian Commissioner, proposes a monument to Wakefield, 123; his anecdote of Wakefield and the Americans, 365.

Palmerston, Lord, 202.

Panizzi, Antonio, aids Brougham at the Turner trial, 49.

Papineau, Canadian rebel leader, 173.

Peel, Sir Robert, 256, 259, 260.

Percy, Hon. Algernon, 22, 33, note.

Place, Francis, his account of Edward Wakefield, 6, 7; his opinion of Edward Gibbon Wakefield, 16-19.

Punishment of Death in the Metropolis, 53-58.

Q

QUARTERLY REVIEW on Lord Durham's mission to Canada, 162; on his Report, 181.

R

RANGIHAIATEA, New Zealand chief, 229.

Rauparaha, New Zealand chief, 229, 230.

Reeves, Hon. W. P., Agent-General for New Zealand, on the settlement of New Zealand by the Company, 200, 205; on the Treaty of Waitangi, 214; on the Taranaki settlement, 229; on the Wakefield system in the Canterbury colony, 293.
Rennie, George, projector of the Otago settlement, 302.
Rice, Right Hon. T. C. Spring (Lord Monteagle), 99.
Rintoul, Robert Stephen, editor of the *Spectator*, one of Wakefield's principal supporters, 88-90; Wakefield's letter to him from New Zealand, 343-348.
Roebuck, John Arthur, M.P., his opposition to Wakefield, 84, 173, 244.
Rusden, G. W., New Zealand historian, on New Zealand land sales, 290.
Russell, Lord John, as Colonial Secretary, 201, 202; concludes an arrangement with the New Zealand Company, 222, 223; resigns, 223; supports the claims of the Company, 255, 256.

S

SCARLETT, Sir James, defends Wakefield at Lancaster Assizes, 31.
Schmidt, William, Wakefield's servant, 353, 357.
Selwyn, George Augustus, Bishop of New Zealand, 224, 225, 228, *note*, 275, 316.
Sewell, Henry, New Zealand statesman, goes out to New Zealand with Wakefield, 332; his opinion of the colony, 346; enters the Fitzgerald ministry, 351; resigns, 354.
Shortland, Lieutenant, 218, 228.
Sidney, Samuel, on the Wakefield system in South Australia, 122.
Simeon, Sir John, 313.
Smith, Adam, Wakefield's edition of his *Wealth of Nations*, 262, 264.
Somes, Joseph, M.P., succeeds Lord Durham as chairman of the New Zealand Company, 224.
Spedding, James, reviews report of South Australian Committee in *Edinburgh Review*, 121, *note*.
Stanley, Captain Owen, anticipates the French at Akaroa, 213.
Stanley, Lord, Colonial Secretary, his hostility to the New Zealand Company, 223, 249, 250, 257; resigns, 260.
Stephen, Sir James, Under Secretary for the Colonies, 134, 249, 287.
Stow, J. P., on the Wakefield system in South Australia, 122.
Swainson, William, appointed Attorney-General of New Zealand, 224; on the first New Zealand Parliament, 355; frustrates the introduction of responsible government, 356.
Swan River Settlement, failure of, 85-88.
'Swing' incendiary fires, 80, 81.

T

TAYLOR, Sir Henry, reviews Spedding's article on South Australia Committee, 121, *note*; his opinion of Lord John Russell as Colonial

INDEX

Secretary, 222, *note*; on Earl Grey, 232.
Thierry, Baron de, his claims to land in New Zealand, 151.
Thomson, C. Poulett (Lord Sydenham), Governor-General of Canada, 182.
Thomson, Surgeon-Major, his *Story of New Zealand*, 131; on the earthquake at Wellington, 362, *note*.
Titchfield, Marquis of, Wakefield's published letter to, 24.
Torlesse, Catherine, Wakefield's sister, letters to, 42 and *passim*.
Torlesse, Rev. Charles, Wakefield's brother-in-law, 41; letters from Wakefield to, 128, 252.
Torrens, Colonel, on the Wakefield system, 90; one of the founders of South Australia, 95, 97, 107.
Turner, Ellen, her abduction, 29-32.
Turton, Sir Thomas, 164.

V

VOGEL, Sir Julius, 293.

W

WAIRAU massacre, 229, 230.
Wakefield, Arthur (brother of Edward Gibbon Wakefield), 128, *note*; on the colonization of New Zealand, 129; founds settlement of Nelson, 225; Bishop Selwyn and Mr Domett's opinion of him, 228, *note*; murdered by the natives, 229; eulogised by House of Commons, 252.
Wakefield, Daniel (brother of Edward Gibbon Wakefield), drafts South Australian Act, 105; judge in New Zealand, 109, *note*; on his brother Edward Gibbon's illness, 358; resides with him, 362; his death, 365.
Wakefield, Daniel (uncle of Edward Gibbon Wakefield), 41, *note*, 111, *note*.
Wakefield, Edward (grandfather of Edward Gibbon Wakefield), 3, 4.
Wakefield, Edward (father of Edward Gibbon Wakefield), birth, 4; marriage and early occupations, 5; his acquaintance with Francis Place, 6-8; his active philanthropy, 9; his work on Ireland, 10, 11; his relations with his son, 14-18; marriage with Frances Davies, 23; seeks a seat in Parliament, 34.
Wakefield, Edward Gibbon, birth and early education, 13; at Westminster School, 14; obtains diplomatic employment, 15; letter in the *Statesman* newspaper, 18; elopes with Eliza Susan Pattle, 19-20; marriage, 21; loses his wife, 22; diplomatic appointment at Paris, 23; early political writings, 23-27; his abduction of Ellen Turner, 29-31; sentenced to three years' imprisonment, 32; motive of the abduction, 33, 34; letters from Lancaster Castle, 36, 37; from Newgate, 39-45; his book on *The Punishment of Death*, 53-58; his *Letter from Sydney*, 58-61; his system of colonization, 62-73; his description of an Italian girl, 74-75; his *England and America*, 75-78; his tract on 'Swing,' 80-82; released from prison,

83; aids in establishing the Colonization Society, 85; his friendship with Rintoul, 89; promotes the settlement of South Australia, 92-102; the chief founder of the colony, 104-107; death of his daughter Nina, 116-119; projects the colonization of New Zealand, 126-129; his alliance with Lord Durham, 143-144; his misunderstandings with Lord Howick, 145; replies to Mr Dandeson Coates, 147; hastens the despatch of the *Tory* to New Zealand, 154; his agenda for meeting of the New Zealand Company, 155; adviser of Lord Durham in his Canadian mission, 163; arrives in Canada, 167; his appointment as Commissioner of Crown Lands frustrated by the Colonial Office, 168, 169; Lord Durham's high estimate of his advice, 170; returns to England, 172; sends Lord Durham's Report for publication by the *Times*, 177; his share in its composition, 178, 179; subsequent visits to Canada, 183; elected to the Canadian legislature, 184; his character of Sir Charles Metcalfe, 186; essay on colonial politics in *Fisher's Colonial Magazine*, 187-190; his grief at the death of his brother Arthur, 191; drafts instructions for the colonizing expedition to New Zealand, 192; on reserves of land for the benefit of the natives, 209, 210; virtual manager of the New Zealand Company, 224; scheme for Church Endowment in New Zealand, 225, 226; his overtures to Mr Gladstone, 232; quarrel with Earl Grey, and serious illness, 233; organises Committee on Transportation, 238; evidence before Colonial Lands Committee, 243-245; his system approved by South Australian Committee, 245, 246; evidence before New Zealand Committee of 1840, 247; controversies with Lord Stanley, 249-260; memoir on New Zealand affairs, 261; edits *The Wealth of Nations*, 262-264; *Popular Politics*, 264; his address to the electors of Birmingham, 265; loses, through illness, his control over the New Zealand Company, 269; resigns his directorship, 270; his portrait painted by subscription, 270; his convalescence at Malvern, 271; acquaintance with J. R. Godley, 272; writes *The Art of Colonization* at Boulogne, 279, 280; character of the book, 281-285; on colonization by religious bodies, 300, 301; scheme originally proposed by him in 1843, 301, 302; *The Founders of Canterbury*, 304, 305; his share in the establishment of the Canterbury Settlement, 308; joins in guarantee to the New Zealand Company, 313; estrangement from Godley, 317; on procuring a bishop for the colony, 318; letters to emigrants, 319, 320; his niece, Mrs Burney's, reminiscences of him, 321-324; recollections by Sir Frederick Young, 324-327; founds Colonial Reform Society, 327; aids in drafting the New Zealand Constitution, 328; petitions

INDEX

Parliament in its favour, 332, 333; sails for New Zealand, 333; his farewell letter to Lord Lyttelton, 333, 334; his reconciliation with Frances Wakefield, 335; arrives in New Zealand, 336; his correspondence with Sir George Grey, 337-340; plunges into New Zealand politics, 342; his letter to Rintoul, 343-348; elected to the first New Zealand Parliament, 350; moves a resolution in favour of responsible government, 351; the Governor's confidential adviser, 354; retirement from this position, 356; criticism of his conduct, 357, 358; serious illness, 359, 361; retires into private life, 361; his niece, Mrs Freeman's, reminiscences of his last days, 361 - 368; his death, 368; his character, 369-372; his services, 373-374; memorial due to him, 375.

Wakefield, Edward Jerningham (son of Edward Gibbon Wakefield), his birth, 22; goes out to New Zealand, 154; his *Adventures in New Zealand*, 217; his father's opinion of him, 342, 343; account of his father's illness, 359, 361.

Wakefield, Eliza Susan (wife of Edward Gibbon Wakefield), elopes with him, 19, 20; Mr Hill's character of her, 21; her death, 22.

Wakefield, Frances, marriage to Edward Wakefield, 23; tried as an accomplice in the Turner abduction, 31; Wakefield's letters to her from Lancaster Castle, 36, 37; reconciled to him, 335.

Wakefield, Felix, on the Canterbury Settlement, 315, 316.

Wakefield, Nina (Susan Priscilla) (daughter of Edward Gibbon Wakefield), her birth, 22; letters on South Australian Colonization, 108-116; illness and death, 116-119.

Wakefield, Priscilla (grand-(mother of Edward Gibbon Wakefield), marriage, 3; founder of savings banks, 4; on her grandson, Edward Gibbon, 13, 14; his letter to her from Newgate, 39-42.

Wakefield, Susan (mother of Edward Gibbon Wakefield), 5.

Wakefield, William, Colonel (brother of Edward Gibbon Wakefield), assists in the abduction of Ellen Turner, 29; tried and sentenced to three years' imprisonment, 31, 32; military service in Portugal, 129; proceeds to New Zealand as chief agent of the New Zealand Company, 153; his character, 197-199; his extensive land purchases, 203-205; founds Wellington, 217; his account of the Wairau massacre, 229, 230; arranges disputes between the Company and the settlers, 278; his sudden death, 278; Sir George Grey's opinion of him, 279.

Ward, Sir Henry George, chairman of the Committee on Colonial Lands, 125; moves resolutions on the subject, 221.

Westminster School, 14.

Wellington, city of, founded, 217.

Wellington, Duke of, procures the passage of the South Australian Act, 100; the city of Wellington named after him, 218.

Whately, Archbishop, 243.

Williams, Henry, Archdeacon, 212, 275.

Wynyard, Colonel, Acting Governor of New Zealand, 350, 352, 354, 356.

Y

Young, Sir Frederick, his reminiscences of Wakefield, 324-327.

THE END

www.ingramcontent.com/pod-product-compliance
Lightning Source LLC
Chambersburg PA
CBHW022113290426
44112CB00008B/665